'This scholarly book brings much needed clarification as well as new ideas on the notion of *omnipotence*. Its richness lies in the profound exploration of this concept by a broad spectrum of eminent psychoanalysts. The book covers many different aspects of omnipotence as it can be encountered both in normal development and in pathological states of mind such as in manic states. The editor's thoughtful selection and careful editing results in a very valuable contemporary contribution to the psychoanalytic literature.'

Professor Catalina Bronstein, MD, *Visiting Professor, Psychoanalysis Unit, University College London, and Fellow and Training Psychoanalyst, British Psychoanalytical Society*

'The ubiquitous invocation of the concept of omnipotence has come to obscure the increasing imprecision and casualness with which it is used. Assembling some of the finest psychoanalytic clinicians and theorists writing today, Jean Arundale's indispensable collection brings to light the fascinating variegation and complexity of this key psychic phenomenon.'

Professor Josh Cohen, *Psychoanalyst (BPAS) and Professor of Literary Theory, Goldsmiths University of London*

'This volume places omnipotence in its long overdue rightful place as a key concept in psychoanalytic metapsychology and clinical practice. Omnipotence of thought and feeling are ineradicable features of the human condition and emotional life. In addition to their numerous pathological guises, they appear as normal components of child development, achievement in the real world, and the development of self-esteem.'

Howard B. Levine, MD, *Editor-in-Chief, Routledge Wilfred R. Bion Studies Series*

The Omnipotent State of Mind

This book presents an examination and exploration of the concept of omnipotence, its qualities and expression as a psychic state, its origins in the psyche and its appearance in the psychoanalytic process and in society.

Linked with narcissism but underdeveloped as a concept in its own right, omnipotence is explored in this book from a range of psychoanalytic perspectives, including its positive value in normal development through to its potential as a destructive element in the personality. *The Omnipotent State of Mind* is presented in five parts, each exploring a specific theme. The contributors explore omnipotence in infants, children, adolescents and adults, consider why it is so difficult to give up, and examine how the omnipotent state of mind is expressed in culture and society. The range of attitudes towards omnipotence within different psychoanalytic traditions is represented by the international selection of contributors.

The Omnipotent State of Mind will be of great interest to psychoanalysts in practice and in training, to psychoanalytic psychotherapists and to other professionals interested in omnipotent states of mind.

Jean Arundale, PhD, is a training and supervising analyst of the British Psychoanalytic Association and author of the book *Identity, Narcissism, and the Other* (Routledge). She is also co-editor of *Transference and Countertransference* and *Interpretive Voices* (both Routledge).

The Omnipotent State of Mind

Psychoanalytic Perspectives

Edited by Jean Arundale

Routledge
Taylor & Francis Group
LONDON AND NEW YORK

Cover Image: © Eileen Agar, *Spiral Head*, 1954. Licensed by
Bridgeman Images

First published 2022
by Routledge
4 Park Square, Milton Park, Abingdon, Oxon OX14 4RN

and by Routledge
605 Third Avenue, New York, NY 10158

Routledge is an imprint of the Taylor & Francis Group, an informa business

© 2022 selection and editorial matter, Jean Arundale; individual chapters, the contributors

The right of Jean Arundale to be identified as the author of the editorial material, and of the authors for their individual chapters, has been asserted in accordance with sections 77 and 78 of the Copyright, Designs and Patents Act 1988.

All rights reserved. No part of this book may be reprinted or reproduced or utilised in any form or by any electronic, mechanical, or other means, now known or hereafter invented, including photocopying and recording, or in any information storage or retrieval system, without permission in writing from the publishers.

Trademark notice: Product or corporate names may be trademarks or registered trademarks, and are used only for identification and explanation without intent to infringe.

British Library Cataloguing-in-Publication Data
A catalogue record for this book is available from the British Library

Library of Congress Cataloging-in-Publication Data
A catalog record for this book has been requested

ISBN: 978-1-032-02793-7 (hbk)
ISBN: 978-1-032-02794-4 (pbk)
ISBN: 978-1-003-18519-2 (ebk)

DOI: 10.4324/9781003185192

Typeset in Times New Roman
by Apex CoVantage, LLC

Contents

Notes on contributors x
Acknowledgments xv

Introduction 1
JEAN ARUNDALE

In the beginning . . . 21

1 **The survival function of primitive omnipotence** 23
JOAN SYMINGTON

2 **The thumb-in-the-mouth phantasy and the capacity to love** 31
LESLEY STEYN

3 **Peter Pan, the omnipotent child** 43
KATHLEEN KELLEY-LAINÉ

In the adolescent . . . 51

4 **Omnipotence in adolescence** 53
SARA FLANDERS

5 **Customising the body: From omnipotence to autonomy** 68
ALESSANDRA LEMMA

In the adult . . . 83

6 **On three forms of thinking: Magical thinking, dream thinking, and transformative thinking** 85
THOMAS H. OGDEN

7	The appeal of omnipotence MICHAEL FELDMAN	108
8	A neuropsychoanalytic note on omnipotence MARK SOLMS	115
9	The relinquishment of omnipotence in a severely traumatised patient HEINZ WEISS	122
10	Possessed by a cruel God: The damaging effect of an omnipotent internal object CARLOS TAMM	135
11	From patients to presidents: The Grand Illusion FRANK SUMMERS	144

Why is omnipotence so difficult to give up?   157

12	Overcoming obstacles in analysis: Is it possible to relinquish omnipotence and accept receptive femininity? JOHN STEINER	159
13	Omnipotence and the difficulty in relinquishing it DAVID SIMPSON AND JEAN ARUNDALE	174

The desire for power in culture and society . . .   189

14	Omnipotence and the paradoxes of insight: A Darwinian look JORGE L. AHUMADA	191
15	Lear, Kane and the workings of omnipotence NOEL HESS	206
16	Applying my theory of psychosis to the Nazi phenomenon HERBERT ROSENFELD	217

17 **The destructiveness of omnipotence and 'perverted containing': Psychoanalytic reflections on the dynamic between Donald Trump and his supporters** 220
KARIN JOHANNA ZIENERT-EILTS

18 **Notes toward a model for omnipotence** 230
JEAN ARUNDALE

Index 233

Contributors

Jorge L. Ahumada is a Distinguished Fellow of the British Psychoanalytical Society since 1999 and a training and supervising analyst at the Argentinian Psychoanalytic Association. He received the Mary Sigourney Award in New York in 1996 and the Konex Prize in Buenos Aires in 2006. He was main speaker at the celebration of Freud's 150th birthday at Frankfurt University in 2006 and speaker at the Meet the Analyst conference at the International Psychoanalytic Association Prague Congress in 2013. His papers on the method and the epistemology of psychoanalysis, on the changes in the psychopathologies, and on autism have been published in nine languages. His books published in English are *The Logics of the Mind: A Clinical View* (Karnac 2001); *Insight: Essays on Psychoanalytic Knowing* (Routledge 2011); and, with Luisa C. Busch de Ahumada. *Contacting the Autistic Child: Five Successful Early Psychoanalytic Interventions* (Routledge 2017).

Jean Arundale is a training and supervising psychoanalyst of the British Psychoanalytic Association and one of the founders of BPA, primarily working in private practice in London but also as a consultant in the NHS. She has presented papers at conferences held by University College London, the European Psychoanalytical Federation, and the International Psychoanalytic Association and has taught, published, and edited variously in the field of psychoanalysis. Her book, *Identity, Narcissism, and the Other* was published in 2017. A former editor of the *British Journal of Psychotherapy*, she co-edited three books: *Interpretive Voices* in 2015, *Transference and Countertransference* in 2011, and *Terrorism and War: Unconscious Dynamics of Political Violence* in 2002.

Michael Feldman is a training analyst and Distinguished Fellow of the British Psychoanalytical Society. He trained in medicine at University College London and later worked as a psychiatrist and psychotherapist at the Maudsley Hospital, teaching and supervising psychiatric trainees. For a number of years now, he has been in private psychoanalytic practice and involved in teaching and supervision at the Institute in London and in several centres in Europe and North America. He studied with Hanna Segal, Herbert Rosenfeld, and Betty Joseph and he is particularly interested in the problems of psychoanalytic technique. He has written a number of papers addressing some of these issues, a selection of which have been published in his book, *Doubt, Conviction and the Analytic Process*, published by Routledge in 2009.

Sara Flanders is a supervisor and training analyst of the British Psychoanalytical Society. She has worked for many years at the Brent Adolescent Centre, seeing patients and supervising. She edited *The Dream Discourse Today*, published by the New Library of Psychoanalysis and, with Dana Birksted-Breen and Alain Gibault, edited *Reading French Psychoanalysis*. She has written many articles on adolescence and other subjects and serves on the Executive of the College of the IJPA. She is co-chair of the Forum on Adolescence of the EPF.

Noel Hess is a full member of the British Psychoanalytic Association and a psychoanalyst in private practice in London. He teaches clinical and theoretical seminars for the BPA and other London trainings and is active in the BPA organisation. He is presently a postgraduate film student at Birkbeck College. As a consultant clinical psychologist in psychotherapy, Noel worked in the NHS for 30 years prior to retirement in 2016. He has published papers on old age, chronic depression, staff groups, and schizoid states.

Kathleen Kelley-Lainé is a trilingual psychoanalyst working in private practice in Paris. Born in Hungary, her family immigrated to Canada, where she was educated before moving to Europe. She is an active member of the Société Psychanalytique de Paris, the European Psychoanalytical Federation, the International Psychoanalytical Association and the International Sandor Ferenczi Society. In 2001 she organised an International Psychoanalytical Conference at UNESCO, Une Mère, une Terre, une Langue, on the question of immigration and loss of the mother tongue. She is internationally known for her many conferences, published articles in psychoanalytical journals and books. Her most well-known book published in French, *Peter Pan ou l'Enfant Triste*, was translated into English, Hungarian and Greek and is still in circulation since 1992.

Alessandra Lemma is a fellow of the British Psychoanalytical Society and consultant clinical psychologist at the Anna Freud National Centre for Children and Families. She is a visiting professor at the Psychoanalysis Unit, University College London. For many years, she worked at the Tavistock Clinic, where she was, at different points, head of psychology and professor of psychological therapies. Until 2020, she was the editor of the *New Library of Psychoanalysis* book series (Routledge). She has published extensively on psychoanalysis, the body, and trauma.

Thomas H. Ogden is the author of 13 books on the theory and practice of psychoanalysis as well as literary criticism, most recently *Reclaiming Unlived Life, Creative Readings: Essays on Seminal Analytic Works*, and *Rediscovering Psychoanalysis*. He has published three novels: *The Parts Left Out, The Hands of Gravity and Chance*, and *This Will Do* . . . His work has been published in more than 25 languages. He has received the Sigourney Award for his contributions to psychoanalysis. He writes, practices, and teaches in San Francisco and Sonoma, California.

Herbert Rosenfeld was a distinguished training and supervising analyst in the British Psychoanalytical Society, working in private psychoanalytic practise in London for 40 years. Born in Nuremberg, Rosenfeld came to England to escape Nazi persecution in 1936. He obtained a medical degree in Glasgow and worked at the Maudsley and then the Tavistock before training in psychoanalysis, qualifying in 1945 at the Institute of Psychoanalysis. He specialised in the psychoanalytic treatment of psychosis, borderline personality, and aspects of destructive narcissism. Analysed by Melanie Klein, he became a leading pioneer of her approach to psychoanalysis, teaching her ideas in many countries and achieving a worldwide and lasting reputation for his theoretical innovation and clinical acumen. His books include *Impasse and Interpretation* (1987), *Psychotic States* (1965), *Herbert Rosenfeld at Work: The Italian Seminars* (2001), and *Rosenfeld in Retrospect* (2008, John Steiner, ed.), along with many published papers and also others held in the archive at the Institute of Psychoanalysis.

David Simpson is a training and supervising Analyst and is currently president of the British Psychoanalytic Association. He a fellow of the British Psychoanalytic Society. He trained in psychiatry at the Maudsley Hospital and was a consultant at the Tavistock Clinic, where he was the director of child and adolescent psychiatric training; he was honorary senior lecturer at University College London Medical School and led a service for patients with autism and learning disabilities. He works in private analytic practice in London and teaches in Eastern Europe. He is a published author and has presented papers at international conferences, including for the IPA and EPF.

Mark Solms is the director of neuropsychology at the Neuroscience Institute of the University of Cape Town at Groote Schuur Hospital. He is a member of the British Psychoanalytical Society and the American and South African Psychoanalytical Associations. He has received numerous honours and awards, including the Sigourney Prize. He has published 350 journal articles and book chapters, and he has authored eight books, the latest being *The Hidden Spring: A Journey to the Source of Consciousness* (2021). He is editor of the forthcoming revised standard edition of *The Complete Psychological Works of Sigmund Freud*.

John Steiner is a training and supervising analyst of the British Psychoanalytical Society, who has retired from clinical practice but continues to supervise and write. In the 60s, he was a registrar at the Maudsley Hospital, and then for 20 years, he was a consultant at the Tavistock Clinic. He is a much-published author of books and articles: *Psychic Retreats* (1993), *Seeing and Being Seen*

(2011), and *Illusion, Disillusion and Irony in Psychoanalysis* (2020). He has also edited and written introductions to *The Oedipus Complex Today* (1989), *Psychoanalysis, Literature and War*, by Hanna Segal (1997), *Rosenfeld in Retrospect* (2008), and Melanie Klein's 1936 *Lectures on Technique* (2017). Many terms that he originated are now common currency, such as 'pathological organisations of the personality', 'psychic retreats', 'emerging from psychic retreats', and 'patient-centred and analyst-centred interpretations'.

Lesley Steyn is a member of the British Psychoanalytical Society (BPAS) and a full member of the British Psychoanalytic Association (BPA). She is a training analyst for the British Psychotherapy Foundation, Association of Child Psychotherapists, Tavistock, and other trainings in London. At the BPA and BPF, she has taught clinical and theoretical seminars on the main psychoanalytic trainings and on external courses and has served on training, full membership, and scientific committees. She has also been a visiting lecturer at the Tavistock Centre and a clinical seminar leader on the BPAS foundation course. She has published papers in the *International Journal of Psychoanalysis* and is a long-standing member of its editorial board. In the IJP, she has recently been appointed the associate editor/regional editor for the UK.

Frank Summers is a training and supervising analyst at the Chicago Institute for Psychoanalysis and in private practice in Chicago. He is a professor of clinical psychiatry at the Feinberg School of Medicine, Northwestern University. His book *The Psychoanalytic Vision: The Experiencing Subject, Transcendence, and the Therapeutic Process* won the Gradiva Award for the best psychoanalytic book of 2013. Professional awards include the 2018 Leadership Award in the Society for Psychoanalysis and Psychoanalytic Psychology and the Hans Strupp Award for contributions to psychoanalysis. An associate editor of *Psychoanalytic Dialogues* and on the editorial board of *Psychoanalytic Psychology*, Dr. Summers has written numerous articles and presented at many national and international meetings; his work is mostly on object relations theories in psychoanalysis and the application of psychoanalysis to social issues.

Joan Symington is a psychoanalyst and child psychiatrist based in Sydney, Australia. After qualifying as a doctor in Melbourne, Joan trained as a psychiatrist at the Maudsley Hospital in London and became the Royal Free Hospital's inaugural consultant in child psychiatry. As a child psychotherapist, she was part of Esther Bick's influential Tavistock group on infant observation and also worked at the Holloway Child Guidance Clinic and in private practice. Having trained as an analyst at the British Psychoanalytic Society in London, she returned to Australia, where she is a training and supervising analyst of the Australian Psychoanalytical Society and a fellow of the Royal Australian College of Physicians, the Royal College of Psychiatrists, and the Institute of Psychoanalysis.

Carlos Tamm is an adult and a child and adolescent analyst and a fellow of the British Psychoanalytical Society. He also holds an MA in literary studies. He is a visiting lecturer, clinical supervisor, and training therapist at the Tavistock and Portman NHS Foundation Trust, where he has also worked with autistic children and families. He has published and lectured in the UK and abroad on autism and psychosis, the works of W. R. Bion, infant observation, child and adolescent development, and the relationship of psychoanalysis to literature and language studies. He works in private practice in London.

Heinz Weiss is head of the department of psychosomatic medicine at the Robert-Bosch-Krankenhaus, Stuttgart and managing director of the medical section, Sigmund-Freud-Institute, Frankfurt. He teaches at the University of Tübingen, and he is chair of the education section of the *International Journal of Psychoanalysis*. His most recent book, *Trauma, Guilt and Reparation: The Path from Impasse to Development*, was published by Routledge in 2020.

Karin Johanna Zienert-Eilts is a psychoanalyst in private practice in Berlin, a member of the German Psychoanalytic Society (DPG) and the International Psychoanalytic Association, and a lecturer at the Psychoanalytic Institute Berlin. She has published biographical works on important psychoanalysts such as Karl Abraham (2013) and Herbert Rosenfeld (2020) and is co-editor of the book *Herbert Rosenfeld und seine Bedeutung für die Psychoanalyse* (*Herbert Rosenfeld and his Significance for Psychoanalysis*) (2020). She has a PhD for her work on destructive group processes and focuses on socio-political issues, such as 'destructive populism', from a psychoanalytic perspective. In this context, she has developed the concept of 'perverted containing'. Her most recent paper is on psychoanalytic reflections on the development of fanatical convictions.

Acknowledgments

I am hugely grateful to the authors who have contributed chapters to this book; I am thankful for their interested response and enthusiasm for the topic, and it has been a pleasure working together on the book. I owe special thanks to Riccardo Steiner for his interest and helpful suggestions and to Edie Hargreaves and Sara Flanders for their thoughtful comments. I am immensely grateful to friends and family for their kind support.

I extend heartfelt thanks to Angela Rosenfeld for her kind permission to reprint the lecture by her father, Herbert Rosenfeld, its first appearance in an English publication.

I wish to credit Dr. Stefanie Sedlacek and Vic Sedlak for their translation of the lecture by Rosenfeld in Chapter 16 and also to thank them for their permission to reprint the piece that appeared in the German publication:

Zienert-Eilts, K. et al. (Ed.): Herbert Rosenfeld und seine Bedeutung für die Psychoanalyse. Psychosozial-Verlag 2020: 265–267.

For permission to use the cover image, I thank the estate of Eileen Agar and Bridgeman Images for the use of the image 'Spiral Head', from the painting by Eileen Agar.

Many thanks to the editors at Routledge who assisted in the production, Ellie Duncan and Susannah Frearson.

I owe thanks to the publishers who have kindly given permission to reprint the following material.

Articles:

Thomas Ogden (2010). On Three Forms of Thinking: Magical Thinking, Dream Thinking, and Transformative Thinking. *The Psychoanalytic Quarterly, Volume LXXIX, Number 2, 317–347.* Permission granted by Taylor and Francis.

John Steiner (2018) Overcoming Obstacles in Analysis: Is It Possible to Relinquish Omnipotence and Accept Receptive Femininity? *The Psychoanalytic Quarterly, Volume LXXXVIII Number 1, 1–22.* Permission granted by Taylor and Francis.

Joan Symington (1985). The Survival Function of Primitive Omnipotence. *International Journal of Psychoanalysis, 66:* 481–487. Permission granted by Dr. J. Symington.

Parts of articles:

Alessandra Lemma (2010) Under the Skin: A Psychoanalytic Study of Body Modification. London: Routledge. Permission to use one of the case studies in Chapter 7, granted by Informa UK Ltd.

Kathleen Kelley-Lainé (2015). Freedom to Grow. *American Journal of Psychoanalysis, Vol.75*(1), 57–64. Permission granted by Dr. Giselle Galdi, Editor-in-Chief, *American Journal of Psychoanalysis*, to use parts of clinical material.

Kelley-Lainé, K. (2016). The Economy of the Totalitarian Mind: The Case of the Immigrant Child. *American Journal of Psychoanalysis, 76*(4), 376–388. Permission granted by Dr. Giselle Galdi, Editor-in-Chief, *American Journal of Psychoanalysis*, to use parts of clinical material.

Jorge Ahumada (2021) Unbridled! Thoughts on Times of Self-Begetting and Violence. Forthcoming in the *American Journal of Psychoanalysis, Vol. 8*. Permission granted by Dr. Giselle Galdi, Editor-in-Chief, *American Journal of Psychoanalysis*, to use parts of the material on Darwin.

Jorge Ahumada (2011) *Insight: Essays on Psychoanalytic Knowing*, London: Routledge. Permission granted by Informa UK Ltd. to use parts of clinical material in Chapter 10, the double work on the clinical evidence, and the nature and limits of symbolization, 163–180.

Heinz Weiss (2019). *Trauma, Guilt and Reparation: The Path from Impasse to Development*. London: Routledge. Permission granted by Informa UK Ltd to use parts of the clinical material.

Introduction

Jean Arundale

This book is an examination and exploration of the concept of omnipotence, its qualities and expression as a psychic state, its origins in the psyche, its appearance in the psychoanalytic process and in society. The notion of omnipotence is worthy of serious attention as a psychoanalytic concept and state of mind in view of its ubiquity and the many misunderstandings and misuses of the term. Used loosely, as is often the case, diluted or tossed off lightly, a notion that we use automatically without deeper examination, omnipotent thinking is likely to be overlooked as an important source of neurotic or psychotic difficulty, leaving it intact and not well addressed in psychoanalytic practice, to its detriment.

Omnipotence is usually linked with narcissism but has not been given full attention in its own right; there are no psychoanalytic books and few articles in journals that feature omnipotence. Back in 1935, Joan Riviere called for a study of omnipotence:

> [O]ur knowledge and understanding of the factor of omnipotence has never yet been organised, formulated and correlated into a really useful theoretical unit. Omnipotence has been a vague concept, loosely and confusedly bandied about, hazily interchanged with narcissism or with phantasy-life, its meaning and especially its functions not clearly established and placed. We ought now to study this omnipotence and particularly its special development and application in the manic defence against depressive anxieties.
>
> (1999: 225)

This book is intended to be a study of omnipotence in answer to Riviere, an attempt to expand awareness and knowledge of the concept and perhaps fill a gap in psychoanalytic understanding.

Within the various psychoanalytic traditions, omnipotence is conceived in different ways, the range of which is represented by the variety of theories held by the prominent psychoanalysts contributing to this volume, including authors from the wider international community.

Before discussing omnipotence as a symptom or a pathological formation, it is important to point out that it is construed as a normal part of child development by

DOI: 10.4324/9781003185192-1

all traditions, having a place in every phase of psychoanalytic metapsychology: oral, anal, phallic, oedipal, and genital. As a component of development inherent in Freud's concepts of primary and secondary narcissism, it functions as a refuge and a defence when frustration or deprivation get too much to bear for the developing child. Withdrawing from experiences of discouraging reality and imagining its environment to be under its control, 'his Majesty the Baby' summons the world to its beck and call; thus, the child's omnipotent phantasies are built into the foundations, are there and helpfully available in the advent of later aspirations and their achievement. Alvarez (1992) draws attention to the positive aspects of omnipotence, the sense of power and potency that is significant in forming the child's sense of agency. In discussing these, Alvarez stressed the 'Kleinian distinction between processes which are defensive against pain and depression and those which are designed to overcome it and foster growth' (1992: 166). She brings to the foreground the need for the child first to have an experience of secure omnipotent possession of the love object before having to manage the experience of loss. Freud points out that the way in which the omnipotence feeling is either strengthened or destroyed in relation to the child's first serious love objects determines the child's development as an optimist or pessimist. Steiner (2020: 60) writes of how helpful omnipotent phantasies are when a person is paralysed by depression or despair or when tackling a new development that goes against the tide. Klein believed that a measure of omnipotence is helpful in order to possess a sense of hopefulness and confidence (1963: 304–305).

Thus, a degree of omnipotence is needed in the face of the difficult challenges in growing up and in living life: by splitting the good from the bad, and disowning the bad, the seemingly impossible can appear to be possible, giving hope for projects that appear too arduous or implausible. The feeling of helplessness is part of our historical past; arguably, without omnipotence, the polar opposite of helplessness, human achievement would be stunted. However, being in the grip of the mental state of full-blown omnipotence is known to be hugely problematic.

So how does omnipotence become pathological? This will be explored in the chapters of this volume. It would perhaps be helpful to start with a description from the psychoanalytic perspective and a brief phenomenology to preface the chapters in this book. Omnipotence is a term assigned in psychoanalysis to describe the clinical phenomenon of the presence of a phantasy of having an all-powerful aspect of self or mind, ordinarily unconscious. As a personality trait, omnipotence is linked with narcissism, the self-focused belief in the predominant importance of one's own self, the belief that one is special and untouched by the ordinary. Phenomenologically, these states of mind are recognisable as arrogance, pride, pomposity, a sense of superiority, entitlement, vanity, 'knowing it all', contempt. A deeper examination reveals lack of empathy, attacks on otherness, dismissal of anything not self, projection of one's own reality, usurpation of the goodness of others, inflation of one's self-image, and more. If these configurations, founded in unconscious phantasy, are given free rein, there is distortion and destruction in the personality. When caught up in the midst of omnipotent phantasy, without a firm grip on reality, there can be disastrous outcomes. The mental state of omnipotence has been known to be the culprit behind manic sprees, lost fortunes, dangerous activities, wrecked projects, damaged love, and spoiled relationships or, at the very least, impaired functioning in the real world, a hindrance to the perception of reality. The omnipotent narcissist lives in a system in which he believes that (because he thinks it, it is so, a universe made up of his projections.)

In the beginning . . .

In the beginning, there is the baby. In 1948 Esther Bick founded the unique and unprecedented practice of systematic infant observation from a psychoanalytic perspective in the family home (Bick, 1964). **Joan Symington** attended Mrs. Bick's highly esteemed seminars at the Tavistock Centre, in which babies were studied for insights into early infancy (Rustin, 2009). In **Chapter 1**, Symington, in an important article from the 1980s that has perhaps been forgotten or overlooked, writes of her baby observations, including comments by Mrs. Bick, showing how the baby's movements, sounds, and attention patterns were hypothesised as formations of primitive omnipotent defences used by the baby to hold himself together in the absence of the mother.

Making the world into what you want it to be regardless of factuality is a characteristic of omnipotence. **Leslie Steyn** in **Chapter 2** describes a thumb-sucking patient, Alice, an infant within the adult, whose demands were to be a protected, loved, and looked-after child in a utopian Garden of Eden phantasy world, where she never had to grow up and where all her needs were met. In the process of working with her, Steyn found Alice was hidden away in her utopic retreat due to a fear, which showed itself to be an actuality, of not being able to love. As the analysis proceeded, when the tiny seeds of affection that appeared in the analytic relationship were nurtured by the analyst, Alice was helped to grow emotionally and began to value real relationships.

As the child grows, Freud recognised that omnipotent magical thinking is characteristic of all children, a facility that is brought into play in the child's natural imaginative productions. **Kathleen Kelley-Lainé** in **Chapter 3** writes of Peter Pan, the boy who refused to grow up, believing he could retreat to an idyllic Neverland, omnipotently denying the reality of time, adulthood, ageing, and death. Magically flying through the air, but really a baby lost among his objects without the ability to invest in them, he protects his traumatised and fragile ego. Kelley-Lainé presents clinical material from a refugee from Eastern Europe who, as a child, survived the Holocaust.

The adolescent . . .

In Chapter 4, Sara Flanders articulates the ways in which development can go wrong for the struggling adolescent on the route to adulthood and how the use of omnipotent phantasy does no favours. Vividly picturing the shock and frenzy of adolescence after the long period of infantile dependence as she describes two teenage patients and their treatments, Flanders elucidates how 'good enough' parents can help with this transition and foster the remarkable urge in the adolescent to grow and to live. Flanders emphasises the significance of the paternal function of boundary setting, placing limits on too-wild omnipotent phantasy.

As the incipient adult looks to the future and its panoply of possibilities, **Alessandra Lemma** in **Chapter 5** sees adolescence as a special time of trying out different identities, experimenting omnipotently with bodies and personas without a need for permanent commitment to any one option. In her work with transgender patients, Lemma writes of their 'omnipotentiality' and the therapist's attempt to strike a balance between supporting their explorations and protecting the individual from destructive enactments. She describes the adolescent Kay's determination to modify her body as an omnipotent bid to take control. Lemma also presents material from work with a patient, Mrs. A, who wanted surgery instead of therapy to make her feel better. Body alteration through medical intervention has become widespread in the adult population, in pursuit of youth and an ideal or idealisable body, driven by unconscious phantasy of perfection.

Omnipotence in the adult . . .

The allure of omnipotence and its magical power, phantasies established in the infantile unconscious psyche, mean that it persists into adulthood alongside and despite rational intellectual development. In **Chapter 6, Thomas H. Ogden** elucidates how psychoanalysis has shifted its emphasis from the symbolic content of dreams and narratives and has moved to focus on processes and thinking. Magical thinking, dream thinking, and transformative thinking all exist together, each with its separate characteristics. In extended clinical discussions, Ogden illuminates these three modalities and how they interfere or interact with learning from experience.

The emotional appeal of phantasies of unlimited power is discussed in **Chapter 7** by **Michael Feldman**: their gratifications, purposes, and destructive aspects. Feldman understands that omnipotent phantasies are a solution, perhaps the only solution, to a desperate internal situation. He discusses the enduring attempt to identify with the gods of legend and mythology, Oedipus, Adam and Eve, Gilgamesh, Icarus, Dr. Faustus, and other figures, showing the human fascination with the seductive power of omnipotence and omniscience that promises to avoid the need to take active steps in the real world

In **Chapter 8, Mark Solms** illustrates how new perspectives on psychoanalytic concepts can be found through neuroscientific investigation. Omnipotence can be seen in a new light when it is induced artificially by administering drugs that give an exhilarating sense of limitlessness and boundarinessless. With the aid of Oliver Sacks's descriptions in his famous book *Awakenings*, Solms shows how the omnipotent state of mind can be modelled as mapping onto the 'seeking system' postulated by neuropsychoanalytic experimentation, constructing a model for the epistemophilic instinct, a fundamental concept in psychoanalytic thinking. Agency and optimism for success can be triggered experimentally as well as the opposite, showing what omnipotence actually is in biological developmental terms: unconstrained agency. Solms' argument that both disciplines, neuropsychoanalysis and psychoanalysis, can learn from each other is confirmed.

In **Chapter 9, Heinz Weiss** explores the treatment of a woman patient, devastated by a traumatic childhood, who secretly created a phantasy world of living in a tower with powerful, controlling men to protect herself from persecution and abandonment. When she could tell her analyst of her omnipotent phantasy, its grip on her loosened, and she broke down, leaving both patient and analyst in uncertainty and fear as to the outcome. As the treatment went on, struggling free of what she had come to know as a prison, she began new projects and found a new zest for life.

In **Chapter 10, Carlos Tamm** explores belief systems and dogmas that are maintained despite contradictory evidence. A male patient, seemingly healthy and prosperous, with good relationships with his family, was found to have a powerful omnipotent internal object that cruelly persecuted him. Commanded to do impossible tasks, this superego figure traumatised and crippled him in all his endeavours: he could 'only build sandcastles on the beach that soon were washed away'. Helping the patient own his positive capabilities was hard going for the analyst; like Pip in Dickens's *Great Expectations*, feelings of guilt impeded the achievement of what he felt was expected of him.

In **Chapter 11, Frank Summers** lays out the characteristics and dynamics of overt omnipotent self-aggrandisement, illustrated in the outrageous claims of his female patient to having fantastic abilities, similar to the claims of the US ex-president Trump, whose lies and outrageous claims have been exposed to all the world. In his clinical discussion from a Winnicottian orientation, Summers approaches the denial of any vulnerability by his omnipotent patient by careful 'holding', empathising with the pain and rage she experienced when others did not recognise her superiority. Describing his technique, he left alone the patient's defences and the emotions they sheltered until eventually she could face them, facilitated by having to face a painful loss.

Why is omnipotence so difficult to give up?

The descent from feelings of power into the psychic reality of what has been denied is experienced as being thrust into painful states of impotence, helplessness, falling to pieces, depression, humiliation, shame, etc. Given this, it is not difficult to understand the intransigence of omnipotence states designed to keep these painful states at bay, such as the idealisation of omnipotent autonomy, freedom of dependence on frustrating objects, and the perpetuation of an inflated self-image.

In **Chapter 12, John Steiner** explores the concepts of Freud and Klein in seeking to understand the obstructions and resistances to relinquishing omnipotence. He posits an antilife element as the problem, composed of destructiveness, envy, and the repudiation of the feminine. What is required by both patient and analyst to mitigate the phallic omnipotent identification, he finds, is the positive valuing and acceptance of femininity, allowing for receptivity, linking, learning, empathy, and the acceptance of the need for others. Specifically, this means adopting the feminine position of receptivity in both men and women, allowing the mind to be penetrated, a position that must be valued along with the masculine element and valued and protected in the analytic space.

In **Chapter 13**, **David Simpson** and **Jean Arundale** write of the theoretical formulations and clinical work pertaining to the difficulty in letting go of omnipotence, with a focus on the manic defence. Simpson writes of omnipotent phantasy as a feature of infant psychic life that develops in the matrix of the infant's physical helplessness and dependent relationship on the nurturing mother. Phantasies of the mother's breast arise to fill the gap during times when the breast is not available; when the gap is too great, the phantasies turn aggressive, leading to guilt. Simpson suggests that unconscious guilt acts as 'a lock' that prevents giving up omnipotence because doing so means losing the magical solution of omnipotent repair.

Arundale's case study of a male patient exemplifies the manic defence. Believing he was the cause of all his family's problems, his guilt drove him to desperately attempt to change and repair his family. His unconscious belief in his omnipotence was maintained through idealisation and identification with his powerful, controlling mother and narcissistic self-idealisation. Pathologically merged with his idealised object, he was terrified of losing her. Slowly, there appeared signs that he might find it possible to separate and to mourn.

The desire for power in culture and society . . .

There is no shortage of examples of omnipotent figures in the literary, political, and military histories of the world. There is perennial megalomania, what Horst-Eberhard Richter described as the 'God complex', the modern myth of man's omnipotence (1984: 15).

In **Chapter 14, Jorge L. Ahumada** traces from a Darwinian viewpoint the evolutionary development of the human mind, placing omnipotence early in phylogenetic formations. Ahumada examines omnipotence at individual and sociohistorical levels, ending with his unique views on postmodernity. He finds the essential aspects of omnipotence to be ambivalent and paradoxical, allowing for the possibility of mitigating omnipotence and its instinctual urges, making room for a mature and loving attachment and genital sexuality. He illustrates this with clinical material from a female patient who, similarly to Leslie Stein's patient, was unable to love.

Famous omnipotent characters are found everywhere in culture, past and present; amongst the newer cultural iterations of megalomania are a very short list: Superman, Wonder Woman, James Bond, Oscar Wilde's Selfish Giant, and Muhammad Ali's 'I am the greatest'. In **Chapter 15, Noel Hess** examines omnipotent characters from two great works of art, Shakespeare's King Lear and Orson Welles's Charles Foster Kane. Discussed within the context of object relations, with a particular focus on how and why omnipotence fails, Hess considers whether failure presents an opportunity for it to be relinquished. He takes the view shared by Steiner that omnipotence can be 'lessened' but not eliminated; Hess concludes that it is in our personalities, and we can help avoid its causing havoc, but tendencies towards omnipotence must be lived with and carefully watched over.

The idealisation of power is commonly found in the amassing of money, possession of land, victory in war, political dominance. Presently, populist movements around the world appear to be boosting right wing demagogues into leadership, displaying the idealisation of hyper-masculinity and phallic omnipotence that can lead to fascism and the ruthless drive for power, such as in Nazi Germany.

Chapter 16 consists of a paper by **Herbert Rosenfeld**, appearing here for the first time in an English publication. Rosenfeld's considerable theoretical contribution was to describe destructive narcissism, the idealisation of the omnipotent, destructive part of the self. Rosenfeld was in Germany in 1984, where he gave a paper about the similarity between a psychotic patient's delusional personality structure and the organisation of the Third Reich, Germany under the domination of the *Fuhrer*. This is a compelling picture of the omnipotent ruler merged with the omnipotent state, the totalitarian regime enforced by an omnipotent mafia gang who threaten murder.

As with Hitler, ex-president Donald Trump gathered followers who have a powerful narcissistic need for identification with a powerful leader. In **Chapter 17**, **Karin Johanna Zeinert-Eilts** combines Rosenfeld's theory of destructive narcissism and Bion's theory of the container/contained to describe the powerful dynamic existing between Trump and his voters in which the omnipotent appeal of the demagogue held his followers in thrall. She discusses the dynamics of populism to show how omnipotence was idealised and how the rising excitement of powerful affect between leader and the mass created a 'perverted container' whereby the containing function of a democratic society was increasingly decomposed and distorted.

Chapter Eighteen 18 consists of a brief summary by the editor **Jean Arundale** with suggestions for a contemporary model of omnipotence useful for our time. Omnipotence is present at every life stage in various ways and ranges along a spectrum harmoniously mixed up with the pleasure principle.

Citations of 'omnipotence' in the psychoanalytic literature

Psychoanalysts from different theoretical orientations have conceptualised omnipotence differently in their theoretical writing. These different conceptualisations have undoubtedly been at the root of the lack of coherence of omnipotence as a concept in psychoanalytic thinking. I have searched the citations of the term 'omnipotence' in the main texts from the various traditions, focusing more or less chronologically and necessarily very briefly, on each author's meaning and use of the term and its relationship to other concepts.

In Freud's thinking

Sigmund Freud (1856–1938) first mentioned omnipotence as a mental factor in humans and not simply as a quality of the gods in *Three Essays*, in regard to the perversions. He says the sexually perverse act is:

> the equivalent of an idealization of the instinct. The omnipotence of love is perhaps never more strongly proved than in such of its aberrations as these. The highest and the lowest are always closest to each other in the sphere of sexuality.
>
> (1905: 161–162)

Although Freud only mentioned omnipotence here in passing, he made the intriguing point that the origins of omnipotence inhere in idealised love, hate, and sexuality.

As he began to study obsessional neurosis (1909), Freud recognised the close relationship between omnipotence and obsessionality: that indeed, within the repetitiveness of the obsessional activity is compelling omnipotent power. He spoke of a patient:

> I refer to the omnipotence which he ascribed to his thoughts and feelings, and to his wishes, whether good or evil. . . . Indeed, all obsessional neurotics behave as though they shared this conviction. It will be our business to throw some light upon these patients' over-estimation of their powers.
>
> (1909: 233–234)

In this area, Freud dismissed the idea that omnipotence is a delusion and should be categorised with the psychoses; he attributed it to the 'old megalomania of infancy', the time of 'His Majesty the Baby'. Obsessional symptoms, Freud observed in his patients, arose from psychic ambivalence: when both love and hate are directed towards the same object and these emotions are felt, through idealisation, to be excessively powerful. He cited a patient who believed that the omnipotent power of his love would have been able to save a woman's life: 'that it would have been in his power to save her life by giving her his love. In this way he became convinced of the omnipotence of his love' (1909: 234).

There is no further mention of omnipotence in Freud's work until *Totem and Taboo* (1913), when he wrote of its particular origins in magical thinking, the primitive animistic state common to all children through fairy tales, superstitions, dreams, and wishful hopes and desires. Magic is central to omnipotence, he summarises: 'the principle governing magic . . . is the principle of the "omnipotence of thoughts."' Furthermore, 'Neurotics live in a world apart, where ... they are only affected by what is thought with intensity and pictured with emotion, whereas agreement with external reality is a matter of no importance'. This 'reveals his resemblance to the savages who believe they can alter the external world by mere thinking' (1913: 85–86).

Unconscious magical thinking, the individual's primitive belief that his mind and willpower have the ability to shape reality, persists into adulthood alongside and in spite of rational development. The power that drives the belief is, according to Freud, sexuality, the power of sexual love:

> It may be said that in primitive men the process of thinking is still to a great extent sexualized. This is the origin of their belief in the omnipotence of thoughts, their unshakable confidence in the possibility of controlling the world.
>
> (1913: 89)

Thus, in Freud's view, omnipotence is not only driven by idealised, omnipotent love of the self but is also charged with sexuality; sexual love burns with a feeling of confirmation of personal power. Within Freud's psychosexual stages, excessive self-love is theorised as fixation at the phallic-narcissistic level and thus pathological. There was, however, one area in which Freud believed omnipotence could be allowed free rein: that of its special position in the creative imagination as part of the creative process (1913: 90).

Oppositionally, in *Civilisation and Its Discontents*, Freud gave destructive omnipotence its due:

> [I]n the blindest fury of destructiveness, we cannot fail to recognize that the satisfaction of the [sadistic] instinct is accompanied by an extraordinarily high degree of narcissistic enjoyment, owing to its presenting the ego with a fulfilment of the latter's old wishes for omnipotence.
>
> (1930: 121)

Freud went on to link destructive omnipotence with the death instinct, the struggle between Eros and Thanatos, the pleasure found in omnipotent destructiveness for its own sake in a drive towards annihilation. This struggle and the conflict between the pleasure principle and the reality principle present barriers to giving up omnipotence, overcoming the pleasure of imagined power, and coming to terms with reality (Freud, 1930).

Freud's close colleague, **Sandor Ferenczi (1873–1933)**, suggested that the origin of omnipotence was in the experience of the intra-uterine state, saying the infant 'possesses a mental life when in the womb, although only an unconscious one. . . . [H]e must get from his existence the impression that he is in fact omnipotent.' (1913: 219, 222). Primitive omnipotence, he thought, was understandable not solely as a defence against reality, but as a memory about an earlier good experience Ferenczi defined omnipotence as 'the feeling that one has all that one wants, and that one has nothing left to wish for'. Outside the womb is the 'period of magical-hallucinatory omnipotence' in which the infant still does not accept any less than 'unconditional omnipotence'. This feeling of omnipotence only changes to awareness of reality by stages over time as the infant realises that more and more of his wishes are not fulfilled (1909).

The contributions to psychoanalysis by **Karl Abraham (1877–1925)** were distinguished by subtle and non-obvious insights exemplified by his 1919 paper on narcissistic presentations. In certain cases, the patient omnipotently controls the analytic process in a hidden way, aloof, holding back free associations, issuing instructions to the analyst, and believing himself to be superior, in an arrogant revolt against the father (Abraham, 1919).

As early as 1920, Abraham suggested that a primitive precursor to omnipotent thinking was in the urethral and anal productions of the infant, which went on to be developed by Klein and others, and he found examples of the unconscious omnipotence of defecation in adults by their use as an everyday expression for the toilet as the 'throne' (1927: 319–321, 375–376).

In the obsessional personality, he wrote of sadism being repressed producing guilt; this guilt can accelerate in the unconscious to such a degree that the person takes on the belief he is the worst person in the world and is able kill by means of thought (1927: 146).

Abraham wrote of 'omnipotence of thought' in relation to the eye and the glance, which he found in clinical examples as the belief that the glance was all-powerful in exciting an erotic response, and in more serious psychotic examples, the omnipotent glance could actually murder its enemies (1927: 199).

Controversial discussions

The debate within the British Society over the years 1941–1945 concerned the theoretical legitimacy of Melanie Klein's ideas and whether they belonged in psychoanalysis or deviated from Freudian theory (King and Steiner, 1991).

Anna Freud resolutely defended the theories of her father, asserting that omnipotence arises in various stages of life but holding that phantasies in children were not available for interpretation in treatment, while Klein argued that an ego existed from birth, and analysis needed to link with the child's phantasy life to be effective.

Omnipotence featured in the first series of discussions, when Susan Isaacs argued that Freud's 'wish-fulfilling hallucinations' were the same as unconscious phantasies and that these were, by their very nature, omnipotent: omnipotent because they are magically called into being by the baby's hunger and wish for total possession of the breast (1991: 278).

While the two sides disagreed about the concept of primary narcissism and whether there is an infant ego present from birth, they agreed on the concept of secondary narcissism: the baby's return to an internal state of self-love to repair narcissistic damage when the love object is unavailable. They agreed this retreat was the beginning of the omnipotent defence, a cathexis of the ego and a retreat into idealised self-sufficient narcissism and the pleasure principle, involving splitting and projection of unpleasure into the external world. Klein theorised that hallucinations, wish fulfilment, and omnipotence are bound up together, citing the Fort Da game as signifying the loss and omnipotent return of the symbolic mother (1991: 779).

Unable to align theoretically, both sides of the debate eventually agreed to tolerate one another, along with a third independent group which drew on both sets of theories, in a 'gentlemen's agreement'.

Omnipotence in the thinking of Klein

For **Melanie Klein (1882–1960)**, omnipotence was far more central than for Freud, intrinsically entwined in her theories; her concepts of unconscious infantile phantasy and projective identification are by their very nature omnipotent and unconsciously experienced by the projector as such. Used as defences against the feared consequences of these phantasies and projections are elements such as the manic defence, reparation, love, and gratitude: the essence of Klein's thinking.

Klein's first mention of omnipotence was in her earliest paper, 'The Development of a Child', about her clever little patient Fritz, aged four and a half, and his deep-rooted 'omnipotence feeling' (1921: 3–16); he believed he possessed the ability to do anything perfectly that was discussed by the grownups: cook, read, write, and speak French. He claimed he knew how to catch flies. Observations of Fritz's development showed his feeling of omnipotence was linked not only to his parents but also to the power of God, suggesting to Klein that a base was laid down that would be difficult to oppose.

In beginning to articulate theories of the psychic life of early infancy that reflected her clinical observations, Klein placed omnipotence at the very heart of her thinking, the feeling in the infant that makes both his loving and his hating impulses appear extremely powerful to him. Klein (1946: 5–6) elaborated thusly: in the process of internalising a good object through the interrelationship with the nurturing mother, omnipotent destructive phantasies can arise when the infant is hungry or lonely, when the breast is unavailable, situations that transform the absent breast into a bad, depriving breast, endangering the successful internalisation of the good breast. Aggression arising from frustration is projected into the mother, projections which derive from the oral-anal-urethral impulses, phantasies in the form of bodily substances, omnipotently expelled into the mother in order to register complaint, to get their own way, or as a bid for survival (p. 8–9). The good and the bad objects are kept apart and, in the most primitive of defences, the infant denies the existence of the bad object, which is associated with frustration and pain. In this way, psychic reality is denied by means of omnipotence as the child annihilates and destroys the difficult or painful states and the external situation as well.

As Klein developed her notions of guilt, gratitude, remorse, and reparation, her interest in omnipotence evolved to focus on the manic defence, in which the (infant's unconscious omnipotent attacks on the mother give way to guilt saturated with anxiety, which drives the desire to repair, which in its turn is omnipotent, the capacity to magically make the mother whole and good again)(1935: 277–278).

Mania or the manic state of mind is common enough as a pleasantly energised state but problematic or pathological when manifested in the extreme. Klein summarised the concept of manic defence (1952) as when the ego,(seeking refuge from situations it is unable to master, uses the primitive defences of denial, magic, and omnipotence)– 'the sense of omnipotence for the purpose of controlling and mastering objects' – to keep them safe; to master the bad, dangerous objects; and to rescue and restore the loved ones (1935: 277).

In the face of the overwhelming power of omnipotent thinking, Klein observed that for intellectual development to take place, it was the child's task to win out in the struggle between the pleasure principle and the reality principle, relinquishing omnipotence.

In Winnicott's view . . .

For **D.W. Winnicott (1896–1971)**, as distinct from Klein's view that omnipotence interferes with the perception of reality and needs to be reduced, omnipotence is valuable and must be kept alive, as it underpins cognition and creativity.

The references to omnipotence throughout the work of Donald Winnicott are manifold and essential to his theoretical position. Winnicott read his membership paper to the British Society in 1935, titled 'The Manic Defence'. In this paper, which was published in 1958, he showed how he had been affected by Klein and acknowledged how they mutually influenced each other. As he developed his own original theories and his unique writing style, becoming more and more influential as his ideas spread, he introduced the concept of omnipotence, the baby's magical control over its objects. By 1959 Winnicott had given omnipotence a crucial significance for the development of the baby, as a necessary sense of omnipotent control over its mother and others in its environment. The 'good-enough' mother, so named by Winnicott, actually enables, fosters, and helps establish the infant's sense of omnipotence, which Winnicott felt was vital to the development of the 'true self'. He said:

> The question will be asked: what is meant by the term 'good-enough'?(The good-enough mother meets the omnipotence of the infant and to some extent makes sense of it. She does this repeatedly. A True Self begins to have life, through the strength given to the infant's weak ego by the mother's implementation of the infant's omnipotent expressions.)The mother who is not good enough is not able to implement the infant's omnipotence, and so she repeatedly fails to meet the infant gesture; instead, she substitutes her own gesture which is to be given sense.
>
> (1960a: 145)

In Winnicott's view, it is the baby's feeling of magical control that subserves the functions of creativity and thinking in the individual. It is the baby's sense of having created the object and the world, bestowing meaning to them, together with the feeling of personal omnipotence that underlies dreams, play, the creative imagination, and even thinking. Winnicott goes so far as to say that the omnipotent state of mind is a requirement for psychic integration. (Importantly, as the child grows, the mother assists the process of gradually giving up infantile omnipotence through the inevitable failures and frustrations presented by reality.)

Omnipotence occurs naturally for Winnicott in the phase of primary narcissism: it is not linked with the process of manic repair as it is for Klein, nor is it a consolatory compensation for a failure, as suggested by Freud. Furthermore, omnipotence is freighted by Winnicott with great epistemic importance in psychic development:

1. By repeated recreation of the object, the infant creates the internal and external worlds (1988).
2. In 'the use of an object', when omnipotence fails and the object survives a destructive attack it is perceived as separate, external, and real (1969).
3. Omnipotence possesses a unique and powerful effect in the treatment of traumatic states within the psychoanalytic situation as the infantile feeling of omnipotent control is revived in the analytic relationship. In Winnicott's words, 'In psycho-analysis as we know it there is no trauma that is outside the individual's omnipotence. Everything eventually comes under ego-control, and thus becomes related to secondary processes' (1960b). Proceeding to develop his idea of omnipotence, Winnicott goes further:

It is very satisfactory to watch the patient's growing ability to gather all things into the area of personal omnipotence, even including the genuine traumata. Ego-strength results.... [T]he individual feels no longer trapped in an illness but feels free.... [W]e see growth and emotional development that had become held up in the original situation.

(1962: 168)

And

[G]radually the patient gathers the original failure of the facilitating environment into the area of his or her omnipotence.

(1963)

W.R.D. Fairbairn (1889–1964). One of the early developers of British object relations theory along with Klein and Winnicott, Ronald Fairbairn believed omnipotence was intrinsic within a particular personality type, the schizoid personality, which he depicted as a mentality preoccupied with internal reality and inner objects, with an overvaluation of intellectual processes. The schizoid person maintains (a secret superiority over external objects;) s/he has an omnipotent internal world characterised by the projection and introjection omnipotently into internal objects; he is operationally detached and isolated from other people, maintaining a sense of freedom and independence (1931).

Michael Balint (1896–1970). Describing the psychic area he named the *basic fault*, Balint designated this as the area of primary relationship in which the caregiver has failed or defaulted and a deficit is formed, an emptiness around which are anxieties and crucial needs for attention and affection (1968: 21). (Balint said of omnipotence that it arises from a 'desperate attempt to defend [one's self] against the crushing feeling of impotence' in relation to the basic fault.) Clinically well authenticated as secondary to and subsequent to frustration, he defined omnipotence as the taken-for-granted belief that all others have the same beliefs, wishes, and expectations as oneself; any contrary indication leads to aggressive or destructive behaviour (1968: 48). Further, he held that omnipotence is associated closely with oral greed, the demand for always more from the mother, creating the feeling of extreme need and object satisfaction as all important (1952: 145).

Balint warns in treatment, during the particular, precarious periods of regression to the area of basic fault, to be there for the patient as the 'primary substance' as 'water carrying the swimmer', not being or even appearing to be an omnipotent object or a 'separate, sharply-contoured object'. This will only increase the basic fault, he advises (1968: 187).

Heinz Kohut (1913–1981). Kohut's interest was in the formation and organisation of the self and its tendencies towards fragmentation or cohesion. In the situation in which the infant's primary narcissism is injured or disturbed by a lapse in care by the primary object, he proposes that the infant establishes either a compensatory image of the self – the grandiose self – or recreates the earlier perfection by positing an omnipotent idealised parental imago, what Kohut named a 'self-object'. In this, Kohut, departing from drive/defence theories, devised his own original conceptual framework of self-development: the infantile grandiose self, which is surrounded by self-objects that provide a matrix of support that, if undisturbed, will continue to expand and have ambitions, leaving it to experiences in reality to chip away any excessive self-regard. These inflated archaic formations can protect the developing child, Kohut believed, in the event of later conditions of trauma or disastrous lack of care. Kohut described how these archaic parts of the self could be activated in the adult in the face of wounds to narcissism or self-esteem, which can trigger massive narcissistic rage or can develop into defensive structures such as narcissistic personality disorder. In treatment, the analyst could become in the transference an omnipotent, idealised self-object (Kohut, 1971, 1972).

Wilfred Bion (1897–1979). Bion's oeuvre, altogether a masterful original work focusing on the mental processes of thinking, learning, and experiencing, brought into psychoanalysis an increased emphasis on examining and analysing the process of thinking and its unconscious roots.

The state of mind of omnipotence in Bion's thinking is an impediment to fruitful and creative thought and learning from experience and so must be diminished. Bion described how omnipotent thought arises: when seeking an object of need or desire, it is necessary to tolerate degrees of frustration when immediate gratification is not possible. Toleration of a certain amount of frustration is necessary to induce a capacity to think, to enquire, and to learn from experience. When frustration is too difficult to bear, omnipotent solutions are stimulated. A complete intolerance of frustration will trigger evasion or projection (psychotic processes) or quitting or, when there is some tolerance but an inability to wait for the mating of preconception and conception, the thinking tools on Bion's grid describing mentation, omnipotence arises, the belief that one already possesses the object of desire, an impatience that pre-empts knowing and claims possession of knowledge without fully linking to truth and reality. In this way, omnipotence cripples the process of thinking and takes the place of learning from experience and the process of discriminating what is true from what is false (1962: 32, 1967: 114–116). With a different perspective from Klein and Winnicott, Bion's theories of thinking put forward his model of learning that opposes omnipotence: 'If the learner is intolerant of the essential frustration of learning he indulges phantasies of omniscience and a belief in a state where things are [already] known' (1962: 65, 1967).

Bion (1976) followed Klein in her view of projective identification, adding his concept of container/contained: the infant's capacity for splitting off unwanted parts of the self (e.g. 'nameless dread') and projecting them into the containing mother for modification. Although Bion recognised projective identification as a means of communication (see Heimann, 1950), more importantly, he saw it as an omnipotent phantasy that something has been got rid of, leading to the erroneous and unrealistic belief that the individual is in control of the sources of pleasure and pain. Furthermore, evacuative projective identification permits the subject to believe the false notion that the object is in possession of his bad parts, and he himself has been divested of them. Not only is this false, but it is also likely to lead to persecutory or paranoid/schizoid anxiety or, in the case of projection of good parts, will leave him with psychic impoverishment (1976).

As Bion's influence grew, he became, in effect, the leader of the post Kleinians, his originality indisputable despite what many felt were his often inscrutable texts and his indecipherable table of thinking. He was the first to show an interest in the link between omnipotence and the severe superego, followed by Rosenfeld, Britton, O'Shaughnessy, and others. Bion conveyed how the failure of maternal love and containment could take form and become 'an object which, when installed in the patient, exercises the function of a severe and ego-destructive superego'. The ego may worship this powerful idealised part of himself or identify with it, resulting in an omnipotent structure that can't be questioned (1959: 107).

Herbert Rosenfeld (1910–1986). In the post-Kleinian era, psychoanalysts became acutely aware of and sensitive to the momentous difficulties of the period of early infancy. Herbert Rosenfeld was particularly interested in this period:

> Omnipotent phantasies may be stimulated during all phases from infancy to adulthood. None the less we have to remember that the omnipotent phantasies originated in infancy at a time when the individual felt helpless, small,

and incapable of coping with the reality of being born and all the problems related to it. From birth onwards he not only built up a phantasy of an omnipotent self but also omnipotently created objects (as first part-objects) which would always be present to fulfil his desires.

(Rosenfeld, 1987: 87)

Once narcissistic structures have been established, the individual will attempt to maintain the delusional omnipotent belief that self and object relations are under his control, seeing actual reality as a threat to the self. The omnipotence is often disguised in the form of a benevolent figure, a friend, a guru, a powerful saviour, or a sinister mafia group (1987: 274).

Rosenfeld described the infant's objects and projections:

In narcissistic object relations omnipotence plays a prominent part. The object, usually a part-object, the breast, may be omnipotently incorporated, which implies that it is treated as the infant's possession: or the mother or breast are used as containers into which are omnipotently projected the parts of the self which are felt to be undesirable as they cause pain or anxiety.

(1987: 107)

Rosenfeld discussed how the object can be omnipotently incorporated or, by projective identification, the subject made one with the object. This can show the extent to which separation is despised as it means anxiety about loss, dependence, jealousy, envy, or fear of aggressive responses. Omnipotent possession eliminates frustration or envy (p. 108). Working courageously with psychotic patients and P-S mental states, Rosenfeld developed from his clinical insights the idea of omnipotent destructive narcissism in relation to authoritarian regimes such as those of Hitler, Stalin, and Putin, involving the idealisation of destructive power and manifesting the death instinct (1987: 127).

Joseph Sandler (1927–1998). Without using the term 'omnipotent', Sandler defined the 'narcissistic character' as the person with a high degree of self-interest and self-preoccupation, together with feeling states of imagining himself as a hero, with low levels of object cathexis. This character is identified with an ideal self-image that has the purpose of defending against underlying painful ego states (1987: 181).

Writing of the ego ideal and the ideal 'shape' of the self, Sandler states that this can be at variance with the actual self, resulting in feelings of inferiority and unworthiness. Attempts to deal with this painful discrepancy can reach pathological levels of narcissistic disorder through 'overcompensation in fantasy, identification with idealised and omnipotent figures'. Sandler goes on to describe the most severe disturbance of narcissism as when defences involve a pathological regression to earlier ego states, to 'magical omnipotence, in which self, ideal self, and ideal object are fused into one' (1963: 157).

Hanna Segal (1918–2011). Clarifying and advancing the ideas of Klein, Segal believed omnipotent states of mind lie in the aetiology of all mental disorders. As she put it: 'In my view, all neurotic defences are rooted in psychotic omnipotence, particularly the omnipotent denial of psychic reality, that is, conflict, ambivalence, and the attendant depressive anxiety. These defences disturb both the growth of the ego and object relationships'. Segal was well aware of the damage caused by omnipotent phantasies in individuals and in the culture, and the difficulty in giving them up, how 'there is a particular compulsion to act on the phantasy in order to maintain the omnipotent world and destroy any reality that threatens it' (2007: 104). She held that omnipotent beliefs are a significant cause of war (1986: 216–223).

Andre Green (1927–2012). In alignment with Freud's second topographical model and in keeping with theoretical coherence and his own clinical experience, Green postulated that there exists a *negative narcissism*, distinct from masochism, aiming for non-existence, anesthesia, emptiness, and indifference: in the end this amounts to an anti-sexual drive (2001: 10).

Green speaks of this as a drive for 'oneness' – a primary oneness with the mother, which spreads to total merging with objects and ultimately with the world. This finds its origins in primary narcissism, the desire for a state in which tensions are eliminated and reduced to zero, which is even more true for negative narcissism, 'which ardently seeks a return to the quiescent state'. This is Green's interpretation of the death instinct as eminently narcissistic (2001: 169).

Green paints a picture of the narcissist as omnipotent, evolved from and merged with the archaic feelings of power when speech is initially acquired, a sense of being independent, autonomous, and aloof. Omnipotent narcissists are often chosen as leaders because of their special qualities or signs of divinity, as described by Green: 'master of the Universe, Time and Death, full of his own dialogue, without witnesses', immortal and timeless (2001: 21).

Ronald Britton (1933–) wrote of the omnipotent phantasy of projective identification when the hysteric, in phantasising the primal scene, believes that s/he can omnipotently mount the stage and take part in parental coitus, in effect becoming the parent (2003: 20–21).

In agreement with Klein and Bion, Britton stated that omnipotent projective identifications are a part of normal development, in that they exist in pre-verbal mother-baby interaction in which the baby communicates its needs to the mother. Bion and Britton agree that it is not just a phantasy, as Winnicottian theory has it, but a projection that brings about a real effect in the mother. She responds with her actions, soothing and supplying what the baby needs. This primitive mode of communication is a precursor to thinking that exists also in psychoanalysis when the analyst is made to feel the patient's anger, desire, or need without direct verbalisation (2003: 89).

Britton made the point that when omnipotence can be given up, there is movement into the depressive position whereby reality can be recognised, movement in favour of inquiry and wanting to know, aided by the ego's desire for truth (p. 96).

And finally, **John Steiner (1934–)**. In his acclaimed book, *Psychic Retreats* (1993), Steiner addressed how omnipotent defensive organisations are used to deal with fear, anxiety, chaos (p. 33); separation and loss; and mourning (p. 59). Stalemates can occur when patients are unwilling to relinquish omnipotent control over the object, taking back parts of the self that are lost through projective identification.

In his most recent book, *Illusion, Disillusion, and Irony in Psychoanalysis* (2020), Steiner wrote of the use of omnipotent phantasies to cover up and hide feelings of impotence, smallness, or inadequacy, whatever their origins. Commonly, as a defence, a heroic figure with phallic power is idealised and identified with to escape feelings of weakness (p. 92). Steiner pointed out the dangers of hubris and the omnipotent defence: the pitfalls when an excessive belief in one's own power leads to overextending and failing spectacularly, as when Icarus flew too close to the sun or when Bernie Madoff's pyramid scheme came tumbling down (p. 39).

Last word . . .

This search inevitably leaves out many pertinent thoughts and theories about omnipotence from around the world. I apologise, for its shortcomings.

References

Abraham, K. (1919). A particular form of neurotic resistance against the psychoanalytic method. In *Selected Papers on Psychoanalysis*. London: Karnac, 303–311.

Abraham, K. (1927). *Selected Papers by Karl Abraham*. London: Marefield Library. Reprinted Karnac Books, 1979.

Alvarez, A. (1992). *Live Company*. London and New York: Routledge.

Balint, M. (1952). *Primary Love and Psychoanalytic Technique*. London: Hogarth.

Balint, M. (1968). *The Basic Fault*. London: Tavistock Publications.

Bick, E. (1964). Notes on infant observation in psychoanalytic training. *International Journal of Psychoanalysis*, 45: 558–566.

Bion, W.R. (1959). Attacks on linking. *The International Journal of Psychoanalysis*, 40: 308–315.

Bion, W.R. (1962). *Learning from Experience*. London: Heinemann. Reprinted Karnac Books, 1984.

Bion, W.R. (1967). Second thoughts. In *Selected Papers on Psychoanalysis*. London: Heinemann. Reprinted Karnac Books, 1984.

Bion, W.R. (1976). *Clinical Seminars and Other Works*. Ed. F. Bion. London: Karnac Books, 1994.

Britton, R. (2003). *Sex, Death, and the Superego*. London: Karnac Books.

Fairbairn, W.R.D. (1931). *Psychoanalytic Studies of the Personality*. London: Tavistock.

Ferenczi, S. (1909). Stages in the development of the sense of reality. In *First Contribution to Psychoanalysis*. London: Karnac Books, 1993.

Ferenczi, S. (1913). Stages in the development of a sense of reality in *First Contributions to Psychoanalysis*. London: Hogarth Press, 1952. Reprinted London: Karnac Books, 1994, 213–239.
Freud, S. (1905). *Three Essays on the Theory of Sexuality. S.E. 7*. 123–246.
Freud, S. (1908). *Civilized Sexual Morality and Modern Nervous Illness. S.E. 9*. 179.
Freud, S. (1909). *Notes Upon a Case of Obsessional Neurosis. S.E. 1*. 153–320.
Freud, S. (1913). Animism, magic and the omnipotence of thoughts. In *Totem and Taboo. S.E. 13*: 1–161.
Freud, S. (1920). *Beyond the Pleasure Principle. S.E. 18*. 7–64.
Freud, S. (1930). *Civilization and its Discontents. S.E. 21*. 64–145.
Green, A. (2001). *Life Narcissism, Death Narcissism*. London: Free Association Books.
Heimann, P. (1950). On countertransference. *International Journal of Psychoanalysis*, 31: 81–84.
King, P. & Steiner, R. (Eds.). (1991). *The Freud-Klein Controversies 1941–45*. London: Tavistock/Routledge.
Klein, M. (1921). The development of a child. In *Love, Guilt and Reparation and Other Works 1921–1945*. London: Hogarth Press (1975) Reprinted London: Karnac Books, 1992, 1–53.
Klein, M. (1931). A contribution to the theory of intellectual development. *International Journal of Psychoanalysis*, 12: 206–218.
Klein, M. (1935). A contribution to the psychogenesis of manic-depressive states. In *Love, Guilt and Reparation and Other Works*. London: Hogarth Press, 1975. Reprinted London: Karnac. Books, 1992, 262–289.
Klein, M. (1937). Love, guilt and reparation. In *Love, Guilt and Reparation and Other Works*. London: Hogarth Press, 1975. Reprinted London: Karnac. Books, 1992, 306–343.
Klein, M. (1940). Mourning and its relation to manic-depressive states. In *Love, Guilt and Reparation and Other Works*. London: Karnac Books, 1940, 344–369.
Klein, M. (1946). Notes on some schizoid mechanisms. In *Envy and Gratitude and Other Works 1946–1963*. London: Vintage, 1997.
Klein, M. (1952). Some theoretical conclusions regarding the emotional life of the infant. In *Envy and Gratitude and Other Works 1946–1963*. London: Vintage, 1997, 61–93.
Klein, M. (1955). On identification. In *Envy and Gratitude and Other Works 1946–1963*. London: Vintage, 1997, 141–175.
Klein, M. (1957). Envy and gratitude. In *Envy and Gratitude and Other Works 1946–1963*. London: Vintage, 1997.
Klein, M. (1963). On the sense of loneliness. In *Envy and Gratitude and Other Works 1946–1963*. London: Hogarth.
Kohut, H. (1971). *The Analysis of the Self: A Systematic Approach to the Psychoanalytic Treatment of Narcissistic Personality Disorders*. London: Hogarth & The Institute of Psychoanalysis.
Kohut, H. (1972). Thoughts on narcissism and narcissistic rage. *Psychoanalytic Study of the Child*, 27: 360–400.
Richter, H.-E. (1984). *All Mighty. A Study of the God Complex in Western Man*. Trans. J. van Heurck. Claremont, CA: Hunter House.
Riviere, J. (1999). *Female Anxiety*. Ed. D. Bassin. London: Jason Aronson.
Rosenfeld, H. (1987). *Impasse and Interpretation*. London: Routledge.
Rustin, M. (2009). Esther Bick's legacy of infant observation at the Tavistock – Some reflections 60 years on. *The International Journal of Infant Observation and it's Applications*, 12: 29–41.

Sandler, J. (1987). *From Safety to Superego*. London: Karnac Books.

Sandler, J., Holder, H. & Meers, D. (1963). The Edo ideal and the ideal self. *Psychoanalytic Study of the Child*, 18: 139–158.

Segal, H. (1986). *The Work of Hanna Segal*. London: Free Association Books & Maresfield Library.

Steiner, J. (1993). *Psychic Retreats*. London: Karnac Books.

Steiner, J. (2020). *Illusion, Disillusion and Irony in Psychoanalysis*. London and New York: Routledge.

Winnicott, D.W. (1935). The manic defence. In *Collected Papers: Through Paediatrics to Psychoanalysis*. The Hogarth Press and the Institute of Psycho-Analysis. London and New York: Tavistock/Routledge, 129–144.

Winnicott, D.W. (1960a). Ego distortion in terms of true and false self. In *The maturational Processes and the Facilitating Environment*. London: Hogarth Press and the Institute of Psychoanalysis, 1985.

Winnicott, D.W. (1960b). The theory of the parent-infant relationship. *International Journal of Psycho-Analysis*, 41: 585–595.

Winnicott, D.W. (1962). The aims of psycho-analytical treatment. In *The Maturational Processes and the Facilitating Environment*. London: Hogarth Press and the Institute of Psychoanalysis, 1985, 166–170.

Winnicott, D.W. (1969). The use of an object. *International Journal of Psycho-Analysis*, 50: 711–716.

Winnicott, D.W. (1988). *Human Nature*. London: Free Association Books.

In the beginning . . .

Chapter 1

The survival function of primitive omnipotence

Joan Symington

Analysis is directed towards elucidating and deepening the relationship between two people, analyst and analysand. Hence, a great many interpretations are directed towards that behaviour, which is felt to be counter to deepening the analytic relationship: that is, the omnipotent, narcissistic aspects of the personality.

This chapter attempts to describe the importance of including in these sorts of interpretations the primitive basis for omnipotence, described by Bick (1968), observed in the analysis of both children and adults and *par excellence* in babies. This primitive basis for omnipotence is the struggle in which the young baby engages in order to survive when on his own without his mother.

Bick's hypothesis was that the very young baby experiences the parts of his personality as having no binding force between themselves but as being held together passively in a very precarious way by a psychic skin, equated with the physical skin. The baby feels himself to be in constant danger of suddenly spilling out in a state of unintegration should this fragile psychic skin be breached or lost. He therefore searches for a containing object which will hold his attention, in which case the parts of the personality are felt to be held together, and thus the psychic skin is felt to be intact.

The optimal containing object is the nipple in the mouth and the mother with all her containing functions. Ultimately, the containing functions of the mother are introjected, and the concept of an internal space develops. Before this happens, however, the mother, through her capacity to contain the baby's distress, is felt to strengthen the baby's psychic skin and increase its flexibility so that the baby feels its position to be less hazardous.

If the mother is absent, or present but emotionally unable to contain the baby's distress, the baby has to resort to ways of holding himself together. He is driven to this by the precariousness of the situation in which he finds himself. In other words, he is driven to act in order to survive. His catastrophic fear is of a state of unintegration and spilling out into space and of never being found and held again. An equivalent of this fear, although probably not as intense, is that experienced by an agoraphobic person when exposed to the feared situation. This state of unintegration is to be clearly distinguished from a state of fragmentation which results from a destructive attack.

DOI: 10.4324/9781003185192-3

The baby holds himself together in a variety of ways. He may focus his attention on a sensory stimulus – visual, auditory, tactile, or olfactory. When his attention is held by this stimulus, he feels held together. He may engage in constant bodily movement, which then feels like a continuous holding skin; if the movement stops, this may feel like a gap, a hole in the skin through which the self may spill out. An adult's pacing up and down to help contain anxiety is a remnant of this continuous movement. A third method consists of muscular tightening: a clenching together of particular muscle groups and maintaining them in this rigid position. This is an attempt physically to hold everything so tightly together that there can be no gap through which spilling could occur. It not only occurs with skeletal musculature but also with the smooth muscle of the internal organs so that the spasm might result, for example, in colic or constipation.

The following is a description of a baby's behaviour taken from one of a consecutive series of weekly observations. It illustrates some of these mechanisms.

The baby, aged four weeks, was asleep, lying on her front. The mother turned her over on to her back to waken her. The baby started moving her tongue in and out of her mouth; then her arms began waving and stretched towards her feet, following which her feet began to move towards each other. She started to whimper and to clench and unclench her hands until she was picked up by mother, whereupon the whimpering ceased. When the mother laid her down on the changing mat and began to undress her, the baby looked distressed and began to writhe around, arching her back and pressing her head and feet against the mat. When the mother spoke soothingly to her, she calmed briefly as though listening intently to the mother's voice. Removal of the rest of her clothes was followed by back arching again, with eyes shut tight and fists clenched. The mother lifted the baby's legs in order to remove her nappy, and the baby began to cry, urinating at the same time. This sequence of events illustrated repeated stresses for the baby being followed by attempts to hold herself together, at first by constant movement, and then by muscular tightening, in particular the arching of the back, which resulted in a much greater pressure of the head on the mat. The head was thus felt to stick to the mat, giving the baby a sense of holding to a particular point by focusing attention on this point. When the mother destroyed this holding by lifting the legs, the baby suddenly was no longer able to hold herself together, and she spilled out from both her eyes and bladder.

The next example illustrates the survival mechanism provided by holding on to a visual sensory stimulus. On arrival, the observer noticed that the mother looked tired and depressed. The mother had commented on the dark winter afternoon and on her feeling of isolation with her baby. Later in the observation, after the baby had been bathed and fed, the mother brought her into the kitchen and sat her in her baby seat on the table. At this point, the husband returned home from work and, having greeted the observer, immediately began telling his wife of some incident at work. The baby began to make demanding noises, getting louder and louder as she was ignored. The mother noticed this and went to the baby, lifting her up briefly and then putting her back in her chair. She turned back to her husband, who was also wanting her attention. The baby squirmed and wriggled in apparent distress, looked upwards, saw the light, and stared at it. Her face and body relaxed, and she smiled at the light, making a brief cooing noise. On turning back to the baby to see what had quietened her, the mother's face registered distress, even hurt. She asked why the baby was staring at the light, as though she feared that something was wrong and that she may have driven the baby into this sort of behaviour by her intolerance. This example clearly shows the relaxation in the baby when she feels held together by focusing her attention on the light. Here, too, the baby clearly relates to the light; she smiles and coos at it as though it is experienced as a substitute for mother. The mother felt alarmed in case she had damaged her child, and she also felt rejected by the baby.

A young baby experiences the loss of mother's attention as being dropped. Suddenly, he is not held; suddenly, he is falling through space, unprotected, terrified of never being caught again and rescued. At these moments, he feels he must either hold himself together or not survive. In this primitive state of mind, the baby's whole attention is devoted to holding himself together. His thought process could be described as one-dimensional, completely one-track, and utterly inflexible. This was expressed by Bick: when the light to which a baby has fixed its attention is turned off, the baby spills out; catastrophe has occurred. With more experience, the thought processes become two-dimensional, and in this case, when the light is switched off, the baby can turn quickly to find another object to stick or cling to. That is, there is some ability to fling oneself onto a new object but with minimal flexibility. Three-dimensionality develops through having a containing mother to turn to, not having to stick or cling at all, knowing safety is available. There is space for thought and choice.

Understanding the very basic nature of these survival mechanisms by which the baby attempts to hold himself together in the face of extreme stress leads one to look differently at defence mechanisms in the child and adult. It has become apparent to me that children and adults in analysis are carrying out these same sorts of survival mechanisms, over and over again, at times of crisis.

The crisis to adults, too, is an experience of an impending state of unintegration or liquefaction, no matter how transient and therefore, possibly, how insignificant from the observer's point of view. We can see that their ways of coping are the same as the infantile ways of holding the self together and that these are trusted as the first line of defence. They are readily resorted to or fallen back on because they are at least relatively effective; they are familiar and are felt to be safe and trustworthy. They can then become part of the character structure, but I am talking about this fear of unintegration as an anxiety likely to be present at some point in a majority of people.

When the patient is holding himself together with these infantile mechanisms and their more sophisticated derivatives, they are likely to be seen to be against the analytic relationship and interpreted as turning away from the analyst. Such behaviour as refusing to speak, withholding certain information, and holding back from expressing feelings can all be seen as variants of clenching the muscles tight to keep the baby self from spilling out. Similarly, the stone-walling of other defensive attitudes – for example, the triumph or contempt of the manic defence, the stubborness in the obsessional – has a primitive basis in muscular tightening.

Constant talk, flitting from one subject to another in a superficial non-stop manner, and being busy all the time can be seen as related to the primitive defence of constant movement. In a similar way, clinging to old ways of behaving and thinking, using stereotyped phrases and clichés, and producing old stale material that got a response from the analyst on a previous occasion are all ways of attempting to create a continuous unchanging psychic skin without any holes or gaps through which the self could spill. Various physical activities can also be used physically to hold the self together, by constant movement or by muscle strengthening.

The focusing on a sensory stimulus to hold the self together is seen in its most extreme and unmodified form in infantile autism, when the child focuses on a stimulus and switches off to the rest of the world. A minor degree of this can occur in watching television or in listening to music in a particular two-dimensional way. But I think that 'blinkered' vision is also an example of this – not daring to look sideways or at other possibilities in case one falls to pieces. Another example is focusing on the analyst's voice rather than on the meaning which both words and tone convey together.

It is very easy to think of patients reverting to so-called destructive behaviour on a weekend. The patient claims to have coped on his own, but because he has not mentioned missing the analysis, his behaviour has been viewed as against the analysis. For example, a patient at a Monday session said that he had felt utterly miserable at the weekend, in despair of ever getting through life. In this state, he had opened a book by Freud, and, as he read, he had started to get things in perspective again and felt less despairing. This was interpreted as a turning away from the analyst. 'I don't need you, I've got something better, Freud himself, at home'. This interpretation may well have been true, but it did not take into account the patient's desperate need to do something for himself, in order to hold himself together. Thus, the interpretation resulted in silent hurt and increased defensiveness: the hurt because parents often do praise children for coping on their own. When both the destructiveness and the feeling that he had to hold himself together were interpreted, the patient felt contained and understood.

A similar view may be taken when the patient returns on Monday apparently having forgotten the achievements of the previous week. Here, the analyst is possibly overlooking the intensity of the experience of being dropped over the weekend, especially after a fruitful week's work. If that separation was experienced as a complete lack of holding, spilling out, including from the memory, occurs, so the previous week's work may have actually gone from the mind, at least temporarily.

Another patient talked most of the time, using psychoanalytic jargon. He included interpretations of his own behaviour, often taking over the analyst's interpretations as his own. The analyst interpreted this takeover of her mind and simultaneous belittling of her, only to find it briefly acknowledged and then immediately fed back, as the patient repeated it as his own interpretive self-analytic work. There was no change in the patient's behaviour until the analyst reached out to interpret the desperate plight of the baby, clinging to the only way he knew of surviving: by talking non-stop and by doing it all himself. In other words, there was a much more primitive defence in the service of survival underlying the blocking behaviour in the sessions.

Now obviously, there are countless activities that are a deliberate turning away from the analytic relationship, but my point is that I had found myself neglecting to take into consideration the difference between those turning-away activities and activities that were in the service of the patient's survival: that is, driven by primitive fear of unintegration. It seems to me very important that this distinction is made because misunderstanding the survival mechanisms might well lead to their reinforcement as the patient feels that he does not have available to him someone who can understand and therefore hold these primitive anxieties, so he must hold on to himself.

The mother, in the example given of the baby holding on to the light, felt rejected: that is, she felt that the baby had turned away from her. She feared that she had damaged her baby in causing her to smile at the light. If the mother had understood the behaviour as the baby's vigorous attempt to master her environment, she would not have felt rejected although she may still have felt guilty.

Bick's emphasis on the struggle to live, underlying the dependency on these primitive omnipotent mechanisms, gives a deeper comprehension of the meaning of omnipotent behaviour; it isn't just innate badness, for example.

The perpetuation of these survival mechanisms forms a sort of armour-plating around the personality, a carapace or second skin, as Bick (1968) described it in her concise paper. The belief in having to do it oneself becomes so ingrained that it is difficult for anyone to get through to the fragility underneath. This sort of character structure is clearly seen in a 6-year-old boy with abdominal pain whom I used to see at a hospital. He said and did nothing that was not premeditated; he was extremely watchful and unable to relax his guard. Early in the analysis, if anything unexpected happened, he would tend to collapse physically: his legs would turn to jelly, and he would sit down doubled up, holding his stomach, looking pale and frightened. I discussed him with Mrs Bick. The following is an excerpt from a session and her comments about it.

He made a plasticine car and dropped it from a height onto the floor, saying as he did so that it was invincible. The use of a word like this was quite typical of him. In many ways, he was like a small adult, as though, as a baby, when his single mother was emotionally unavailable to him for long periods of time, he had had to learn to look after himself. He had done so by imitating adult behaviour, which he had minutely observed, in order to cope with life on his own. Hence some of his vocabulary was that of a much older person.

He then played with a metal car, saying that it was a James Bond car and could do very many different things, including turning over and righting itself and moving through deep water. He made this metal car crash into the plasticine car, damaging it. He said: 'See, it's got a numberplate now' and, after bashing it several times, said: 'It's got several numberplates'. He then rubbed his hand, which was sore because someone had banged a heavy weight on it at school.

Mrs Bick said the following:

> He has to master everything, to understand everything so that he will not collapse, because he feels that there is no one, no mother to pick him up if he does collapse. He has to rely on himself and not depend on anyone. He has to be invincible, so he says that the plasticine car is not damaged when dropped, just as he wants to deny any damage or hurt he receives. James Bond is invincible. He is assailed by so many and such terrible things and he must deal with it all by himself, and see that he is cleverer than the enemy. This boy has to be James Bond. He can't rely on anybody; nobody is there to help him, so he must do it himself. It's not the aspect of James Bond which says, 'I am the greatest, the best'. That is not the issue. The issue here is: 'I must be so clever, I must think and think in order to protect myself'. When he damages the plasticine car, he has to deny that it is not invincible, otherwise it would mean how vulnerable he is. To deny that, he says: 'See it makes a numberplate. It hasn't done any damage to me; on the contrary, it's given me something more'. If he admits defeat or damage, he is lost.

In doing this, of course, he was lying to himself and thus increasing his omnipotence, but it was not turning away from proffered help. In the transference, I was the mother whom he felt to be unavailable. He could not risk trusting me until he felt held, but he couldn't feel held through his armour of 'I must do it by myself'.

I would now like to give an example of the use of these mechanisms by a young man in analysis, the effect of misinterpretation and then of correct interpretation, and of the underlying fragmentation fears.

This youth is 16 years old, but he is mentally backward. At this time, he was using play materials – toy animals and fences – in his sessions. In this particular session, Simon was trying to get some little fences to stand up by themselves. As they repeatedly fell down, I noticed that he had started to grin in a mocking way. He had often grinned in this way before in previous sessions when I had begun to tell him what I had understood about the session. I realized that he was mocking the little child aspect of himself that was trying to become competent but couldn't yet manage to put the fences up: that is, to stand up on his own two feet, emotionally speaking. He was laughing at himself in much the way that an older sibling might laugh at his young brother's attempts to master his environment. When this sort of sequence of failure followed by mockery had occurred in previous sessions, I had tried to point out to him how he was attacking his infantile self, my baby. This had not made any difference and, if anything, had increased the mocking laughter, which was also directed at myself as the incompetent one.

In this session, I understood that he had to laugh at the incompetent little Simon rather than be identified with him. He did not want to feel weak, incompetent, full of frustration and probably rage and disappointment. It occurred to me also that

Survival function of primitive omnipotence 29

this rapid identification with the mocking one represented a way of holding himself together in the face of the threat of falling into pieces, which is what identification with the fragile baby Simon would mean. I found that when I could see the mockery as a holding together defence for his very precariously held together baby self, I could make a more effective interpretation that melted the mocking defence and left him vulnerable but held.

Simon's tough mocking side was frequently, and very adequately, illustrated in sessions by an elephant, which was described as having a rough, tough skin. For a Friday session, I was exactly two minutes late, the first time I had ever been late for him. He came in saying that I was five minutes late and that it was the last day. He made a toy calf and pig fight with each other for possession of a fence, saying that both of them wanted it. I knew that he suspected, and correctly, that I took my children to school immediately before I saw him. I said that he felt very hurt that I was late, particularly as it had occurred on the last day of the week before the weekend, especially as he was always apparently so unsure that I would return on Monday; that he felt that I had been with my child and given that child two minutes of his time, which felt much longer to him; and that he, the calf, and this greedy pig child of mine had to fight over the time spent with me.

He then said: 'Cows don't have calves'. He said this with conviction, so I was uncertain what was being expressed. I said that I thought he meant that I was such a mean cow for coming late on the last day before the weekend, that he was going to disown me, and that I didn't deserve to have him as my patient, my calf.

His next statement was: 'Babies need to be stroked'. He began to stroke the toy calf and briefly grinned to himself.

We were both well acquainted with the way he stroked away any pain and, frequently, any awareness that he felt he might be in danger of acquiring. His message to me was that through stroking, he could quickly smooth himself right out of any painful position in relation to me and into this triumphant identity, perhaps inside me. As I talked about this, he made two elephants fight each other, tearing at each other with their tusks and hitting their heads together in a brutal way.

I considered this to be a direct response to my interpretation, a comment on our interaction as a couple. He felt that our way of being with each other at that moment was a brutal battle, a battle to the death.

I therefore said to him that he did feel hurt and angry, but much more than that was the fact of my lateness, even though it was only two minutes. It had never happened before, and it felt like a devastating blow to him. It meant to him that I had suddenly dropped him and that he felt I no longer cared about him. In the face of this shock, he tried as best he could to hold himself together, initially by trying to defend his territory, then by saying: 'Cows don't have calves': in other words, that he had no mother to look after him and would therefore have to look after himself, and, finally by stroking himself into having a protective tough elephant skin through which he couldn't be hurt and from which he could hurt me, as he wanted my husband and me to hurt each other on this weekend night. I then said that he felt also that I hadn't understood how much he wanted me and how let down he felt and that my remarks to him were felt to be insensitive, rough, and cruel.

He said with relief: 'You spray cold water over the elephant, and it softens his hard skin'.

Here at last I had managed really to understand and therefore to hold together his baby self, enabling him to relinquish for the moment his holding himself together by muscular and mental toughness.

Looking back to my previous interpretation, I was aware of feeling that I had to get it through to him against some resistance. In other words, I had felt that force would be necessary to penetrate his tough skin. After he had shown me that he experienced me, for whatever reason, as brutal, and his inevitable resistance to it, I could really become aware of his fragile, unheld infantile self. Perhaps my slowness in becoming aware of it was my own tough skin, protecting me from awareness of this extremely painful, primitive emotional experience, or perhaps I had felt, because of previous experience of it, that it was very important to interpret his destructiveness, the masturbatory stroking and mockery, and so I was not sufficiently aware of the ongoing effect of the initial trauma of my being late.

To conclude, I consider that this primitive fear of the state of unintegration underlies the fear of being dependent: that to experience infantile feelings of helplessness brings back echoes of that very early unheld precariousness, and this, in turn, motivates the patient to hold himself together. At first this is done as a desperate survival measure. Gradually, these defence mechanisms become built into the character. Some will lead on to socially adaptive behaviour and special skills; others will remain as the basis on which other omnipotent defence mechanisms are superimposed, which further block emotional development.

Reference

Bick, E. (1968). The experience of the skin in early object relations. *International Journal of Psychoanalysis*, 49: 484–486.

Chapter 2

The thumb-in-the-mouth phantasy and the capacity to love

Lesley Steyn

In this chapter, I wish to explore how a lack of confidence in one's capacity to love can underlie certain phantasies of omnipotence. I will focus on a phase of five-times-weekly analysis with one patient, Alice, an intelligent, accomplished 45-year-old woman who, during these sessions, had the curious habit of putting her thumb in her mouth.[1] I found this infantile gesture striking and strange, particularly as it contrasted with her competent, adult, if somewhat brisk and prickly, aura. Gradually, as I will show, I came to understand that, in such moments, it was as though Alice was signalling that she felt unconsciously that I was, or that she wanted me to become, not a separate person but her own thumb.

It is well known that Melanie Klein thought the hallmark of narcissistic states was omnipotent identification by projection or introjection such that the internal object was identified as a part of the ego and loved as such, rather than seen as separate, and that Paula Heimann (1952) illustrated this with the imagined unconscious phantasies of the infant sucking his fingers. As he sucked, Heimann suggested, the infant could, for a moment, deny his own hunger, anxiety and dependence upon a separate mother outside his control, believing instead that he had incorporated the breast and could now independently produce his own satisfaction.

Alice's habit nudged me to be more alert to the presence of early infantile, omnipotent states of mind inside otherwise nonpsychotic patients and to think further about how to work with these states. In the transference, I found this involved firstly observing and resisting the pressure to respond in a way that made me become, in effect, some version of Alice's thumb and then trying instead to think with her about the function of such omnipotent phantasy – what she was using the phantasy to defend herself against. In this chapter, I will describe how, when the thumb-in-the-mouth phantasy pervaded the transference, I felt in the countertransference that unless I gave Alice everything she wanted, removing her suffering, I ceased to exist for her. I will show how, gradually, I came to realise that Alice made me, in phantasy, non-existent as a separate person, in part to protect me from the immediate overwhelming hatred she felt when I did not bring her peace of mind. Ultimately, I want to show how this led to recognition that the

DOI: 10.4324/9781003185192-4

thumb-in-the-mouth phantasy arose from her underlying doubts and despair about her capacity to love.

Alice sought analysis having broken off her engagement to a man who worked, as she herself did, as a business analyst. They had met at work, and he had become her first longer-term partner, but the relationship had ended within a year. Soon afterwards, Alice realised she was concerned about her capacity to commit to a relationship and afraid of growing old alone. She described a long-repeated pattern of meeting men and feeling briefly besotted until defects appeared in the men that destroyed the whole picture. The defects often involved a perceived neediness or weakness. Alice felt dismayed when someone much desired became, in her eyes, not just ordinary and human but deformed and repellent. She felt no guilt about withdrawing at this point, only a need to rid herself of an association with something felt to be defective.

Alice told me that, during her mid-teens, her father had become ill and died, and in the aftermath, her mother, distressed, had revealed that, following Alice's birth, there had been serious problems in the marriage, and her father had had an affair and left the home for a period of some months during the first year, refusing to see his wife or baby, before returning. Alice had never regarded her parents as having a close relationship, and both were described in a somewhat background way in relation to her own life. Alice mentioned that her mother, a refugee from Eastern Europe, could be moody in what she called a 'mental bi-polar' way, but Alice seemed to know little more about her past experiences and lacked curiosity about her. However, the revelation that her father had abandoned them so early on felt shattering and preoccupied Alice. She could not reconcile the kindly man who brought her up with such a betrayal. Neither, she said, could she tolerate the selfishness of her mother's behaviour in revealing this in the aftermath of his death, when Alice was a teenager trying to cope with growing up. Alice thought that she herself should have been protected from such hurtful knowledge. It must have meant, Alice thought, that underneath, both parents really put themselves first and had never really loved her enough.

In addition, Alice learned that, when her father left, her mother had been depressed and unable to continue breastfeeding Alice after a few months. Her mother clearly felt guilty, reporting about the early weaning and the perceived damage this had done and, Alice felt, rightly so since it meant that she had not received the best possible start in life. The way Alice described her mother – as well as most other people in her past and current life – suggested she tended to look down on them. She seemed to view people as either in need of her own help, which she did not want to give yet felt she alone could give properly, or as providing her with substandard care.

From the start of the analysis, I was struck by how difficult it was for Alice to recover from disappointments when people failed to fit her ideal. On a first date, she would pucker up for a kiss, and the man would not be ready at quite the right moment. Or she would plan a picnic in the sun, and her friends would want to sit in the shade. She was upset when I could not immediately offer sessions at times she had envisaged or when I did not look pleased to see her. I soon came to see that Alice felt that the main purpose of everybody was to make her feel comfortable and give her all she needed, and she found it infuriating, baffling that not everyone she met seemed to think this was their main task.

In this respect, I thought, perhaps Alice was not really so unusual. John Steiner (2018) describes as universal omnipotent phantasies of a blissful, idealised time in which the infant has every wish gratified and is protected from pain, frustration and disappointment. He says these 'Garden of Eden phantasies' are deeply imbedded in our psyche, and real-life experience, including analysis, is often found lacking by comparison. Steiner explains that Klein (1958) thought the mechanism behind these idealisations was primal splitting: bad experiences are split off in infancy so as to allow the ego to develop by establishing a good, secure, loving relationship firmly inside. Winnicott (1953) also emphasised the importance of allowing the infant this period of omnipotent illusion, internalising a good relationship even to the point of believing he possessed and controlled the breast. Following Freud (1914), Steiner suggests that the infant's family typically encourage this delusion because of their own reluctance to face reality. He underlines that, in the Oedipus myth, the King and Queen of Corinth keep from Oedipus the truth about his origins and the murderous assault by his own parents.

In Alice's case, the discovered history of her origins was certainly less traumatic than that of Oedipus, but I thought Garden of Eden phantasies could be seen to underlie her way of thinking and being in the world. The discovery of her 'flawed' origins seemed to be felt as catastrophic, and suddenly the whole world was revealed to be all bad, just as the men she fell in love with later would suddenly seem to turn all bad.

In the early sessions, when I did not understand something Alice was telling me, she felt panic and despair that everything was a terrible mess and nothing and no one existed who could help her. When I did understand her, it often felt an overwhelming experience for her: it then felt so disappointing when she could not hold on to the understanding and ensure that I always gave it to her whenever she wanted. In response, I found myself rushing to meet her needs, oversolicitous, feeling she could not bear the gaps between wanting and having but also feeling somewhat omnipotent myself, trying to be the model analyst. I made long interpretations, feeling that if I could perfect them, all would be well. If what I said failed to bring immediate relief, then Alice put her thumb in her mouth.

One afternoon, Alice told me that a man she had recently met had stayed with her the night before:

> 'He seemed a bit taken aback this morning,' she reported. 'He opened the fridge to make us breakfast and found milk days out of date. He didn't say much but then I remembered him eying the unwashed dishes in my sink when we got in last night. It made me feel a bit embarrassed that he was seeing through me, that I might not be as sophisticated as he thought, but I still didn't want to move. I've bought a new blanket and was enjoying being warm and

wrapped up in bed. After he left, I took the morning off work as a treat and went back to sleep.'

As she spoke, Alice lay curled on the couch with her thumb half in her mouth, conveying, I thought, that I would secretly be charmed and feel fondly indulgent. Then she pushed her thumb firmly in and sucked. I was not sure what I felt but knew it was not affectionate. However, I thought I was beginning to discover an unconscious phantasy that determined how she perceived and related to me. I said:

> I think you're describing the situation in the sessions. You have messy, difficult feelings that somewhere you know are very old and out of date. And you also have the idea that you shouldn't have to face those feelings now. Whatever old feelings are inside you, some grownup should deal with them because you think they're too overwhelming for you.

Alice was silent, sucking her thumb, and then said:

> Last week my washing machine broke, everything was in a mess and I immediately felt enraged with you and shouted, 'Not sufficient warning!' aloud. I realised it was mad, but I really felt you shouldn't have let this happen, should somehow have warned me to buy a new one at the right time.

I said I thought it was important that Alice realised she did believe this mad thing underneath. She did not feel it was my job to help her to grow into someone who could bear painful, messy feelings: she felt I should prevent bad things happening that caused those feelings. I said I thought she felt she would die or be defenceless against these feelings and that I would also believe this and so protect her at all costs. My job was to be the thumb in her mouth, immediately pull her in, hold her and make it better. She was silent and went on sucking her thumb.

Some months later Alice was complaining about someone at work who had not done something she thought they should. She was about to put her thumb in her mouth but then stopped herself and said:

> I feel you're going to try to help me think about my responses, how my mind works, but I don't want you to help me bear shitty situations. I shouldn't have to. I want people not to be shit in the first place. You can show me I think people should clear up my mess, protect me. I can see that's a wrong belief, but it doesn't change anything. I don't feel any different. I want to feel better.

This sounded very real, and I said, in sympathy: 'Yes, of course you want that!' Then I added, with feeling: 'Who wants the headache of thinking about their own problems?'

In the rest of that session, Alice kept starting to put her thumb in her mouth and then withdrawing it again, and I thought that, whilst she was protesting about being faced with these insights about her 'wrong belief,' Alice was nonetheless beginning to think that perhaps there was something odd about the idea that I could be her thumb.

'So long as a phantasy is omnipotent it is not a thought because it is not recognized as such,' writes Segal (1981). 'When a phantasy is recognized as a product of one's own mind, it moves into the realm of thought.' I thought what Alice might get from the analysis would be the capacity to let go of the illusion that I could change the world and smooth the way for her. But I was beginning to realise this could only happen if she felt that I was someone who could genuinely empathise with her wish for me to erase pain. That meant not talking to her as though I myself never wanted to be inside a Garden of Eden, where mess and worry were eliminated. In other words, I noticed that the more I felt myself speaking from the position of someone with my own Garden of Eden phantasies ('Yes, of course you want that!'), the less necessity she seemed to feel for me to erase all suffering.

Occasionally, from that point, I had more of a sense that Alice could see the painful reality (perhaps because she could feel I suffered too) that not everybody had been crafted to fit her purpose in the world, though mainly this did remain her position. However, what seemed to stay untouched was the underlying belief that, if she could have that forever, it would be the best thing for her. In other words, I saw and interpreted to Alice that she still believed that the ideal life would be to remain an infant eternally with a thumb in her mouth. A grownup relationship with someone separate, though she claimed to want this, seemed not to be something to aspire to, but more a second-best thing she might be forced to have if the real world did not allow her to stay wrapped up and protected. Alice agreed, saying whilst she knew she had to act like a grownup, she felt no real sense of any pleasure that could be felt in adult independence or looking after or coming to understand anyone else.

When Alice thought further about this, she agreed it was puzzling. Why would she believe that infantile satisfactions were superior? Gradually, however, I had cause to wonder, to myself and then with Alice, whether what underlay this strange preference to remain immature was a terror about something missing in her: specifically, in her capacity to love. After all, this was what she had originally consulted me about. This aspect became more apparent to me when, some way into the analysis, Alice began a potentially serious relationship with a man.

Alice met Paul when he tried to protect her from tripping over a ramp outside a train station. She had been rushing along the street, speaking on her phone, and cut a corner to walk inside. He had signalled to her to watch out, but she had swept past, ignoring him. Then the ramp rose, and she tripped up. Paul came over to help her up, and Alice had snapped, 'Not sufficient warning!' and walked off. Afterwards, she realised she had been rude and that it was not really for him to warn her, as with me and the washing machine. She turned back to apologise. Alice also told me, however, that she could not help the self-congratulatory feeling that this apology would be a nice thing for Paul to receive since he, a black man, was probably not used to white middle-class women apologising to him.

I said to Alice that I was certainly warning her now that this immediate reversing of her own dependence on others meant that, from the start, she was looking down on Paul in the same superior way that she did me. This seemed to happen at the very time when she most needed me to be concerned about her. I said this was a danger threatening all relationships, and with a part of her mind, she knew it.

As the relationship with Paul developed, I saw how Alice demanded care and affection from him but also blocked his efforts to provide it when she felt it was imperfect. I also began to notice that Alice's way of relating to Paul had a bizarre mechanical quality. In fact, the longer the relationship went on, the more bizarre she started to sound in the sessions. I felt Alice was desperate not to lose Paul and wanted him to make her feel loved, but she did not really see him as a person with thoughts and feelings or any real life of his own. She admired his achievements, but nothing about him seemed to move her; he was described only in terms of being someone who would come in and fill the hole in her life. One day she asked him to make her some tea, handing him a mug she had bought herself prior to meeting him, with the specific idea that one day someone would come along and fill it with love. She had intended this to be a charming, encouraging gesture, but Paul, she said, had looked uncomfortable, and listening to this, I did too, realising that I too felt that I only existed for Alice in terms of my capacity to fulfil some prescribed purpose for her. Now, it seemed, this purpose consisted of telling her how to get Paul to do what she wanted or making him feel towards her what she wanted him to feel.

The sessions took on a pattern in which Alice bombarded me with streams of information about things Paul had done or not done, bought or not bought for her, or said or not said. She wanted me to interpret this data in terms of whether it signalled that he liked her enough, was moving towards commitment. I felt kept at a distance, other than as a source of information as she proceeded to put facts into me so that I could produce the right answers. Alice spoke mainly through her thumb, as though to herself.

One day I tried to say what I thought, which was that she could not really cope with other people being people, but Alice did not seem to listen. She went on to describe how at work she found herself sending numerous emails asking people for input without attempting any thinking herself before handing the problems over. I said I felt that she did not believe she had a mind that could think about others or herself, and so all she could do was collect data to pass on to others to fix things for her. At the same time, in seeming contradiction to this, I said I felt she could not believe that I had any thoughts in my own head that had not come directly from what she had told me – i.e., no thoughts of my own, especially about her. So it seemed either she had no mind or I had no mind. I tried to convey these points to Alice, but my voice sounded very robotic, and she came back with more facts, distancing me further. If I could have known what I felt, I think it would have been shut out, lonely and dehumanized – but I did not feel that I existed as a person to a sufficient degree to know what I felt in these moments.

Some sessions after this, Alice recalled that she had been speaking to her mother about herself, describing what she had learned in analysis. She said:

> I told Mum you had had this interesting realisation in my analysis that I'd never really felt love for anybody, and I'd seen that was true. It was an interesting observation. When I told her, she went silent for ages, and I didn't know why she didn't seem to find the conversation interesting any more. Now I'm wondering if she felt upset that I meant I had never loved her. She might have been hurt, but I don't know; I didn't look at her. I don't tend to look at people when I'm talking to them. Interesting.

Then she continued:

> Maybe it's the same thing with you. I want insights from you but don't see you as someone I feel things for. You're like a drink machine where I pull a lever, and stuff I need comes out. It's interesting. But I think I want something different. Not just for you to tell me how to get Paul to give me what I want. . . . Now I'm realising that what I really need from you instead is something else: that you help me know how to love people, make that capacity grow in me. I see other people feeling for each other and I can copy and pretend, but I can't keep this up. I need you to do something to make this grow in me for real. That's what I want from my analysis. Otherwise, it won't work properly.

I thought this was all true. However, it was sounding very chilling again, in part because I realised Alice sounded like a parody of a robotic analyst churning out 'interesting' interpretations in a mechanical way. It alarmed me because I realised that, in the countertransference, I was often, whilst interpreting Alice's incapacity to love, feeling a wide distance from my own feelings. In truth, I was not always sure of myself as a feeling person when I spoke to Alice and sometimes had to reassure myself with the thought: I know I'm not a cold person because I do love so and so (if not Alice.) Now, however, at least I knew what I felt. I said:

> I think you're determined not to consider what I might feel about what you're doing right now because if you admit I'm a real person, then I could be feeling anything about you, even hatred.

Alice said in a cold voice:

> I'm aware you think I should be more curious and caring about you, but this is my analysis; it's surely meant to be about me, not you. Perhaps you mean that if I could feel for you as a person, it might help me do that with other people, be a useful template so I can learn to love real people.

I said: 'I am real, and you're still ignoring your fears about what I feel about you right now; it is dangerous and overwhelming.'

Alice then said quietly that she thought I hated her and probably a lot of people felt like that about her. I said I thought this was what she had to protect herself from knowing. Alice immediately put her thumb in her mouth. She then took it out and said she couldn't bear to think about the impact she had on people, that they found her hostile, mentally exhausting and might leave her. She looked very sad, and I felt moved.

The following week, she arrived and said, in a practical voice, that she was trying to re-organise her bank accounts, but everything was in a mess, and so she would not have access for some time to pay my bill, which was already some weeks late. She had considered borrowing money to pay by cash instead but feared I would find this invasive and messy. Moreover, if I refused to take the cash, she would feel I was punishing her, making her sit too long with the annoying feelings of owing and incompetence. When I didn't respond, she said it was frustrating not being told how to put it right.

I said I understood she felt disturbed and wanted to do something quickly to put right the bad feeling she felt terrified could get out of control between us, but perhaps it was important to try to think about what was happening.

Alice said nothing was happening. She wasn't doing anything different; she just couldn't get into her bank accounts. I said it might be frightening to feel that anything different was happening inside her, that new feelings were invading. Alice then remembered a dream. She had bought Paul a packet of Oxalis triangularis (love plant) seeds to grow indoors. But when they opened the packet, she couldn't find any seeds. However, Paul looked and reassured her they were there, just very tiny. When she looked again, she saw them for a moment too, but then they disappeared again.

Alice associated that this was a plant her mother liked. She then said that, in fact, she now remembered that when she had got my bill, she had had a warm, grateful feeling. She felt that she wanted to pay more and even give me a hug. She had, in fact, given Paul a hug, feeling lucky to be with him, even though he probably often found her a pain, and that this was due in part to the work I was doing with her, which was making her a bit less of a pain. Now, the feeling had gone and she just felt angry and hateful again. How dare anyone ever think she was a pain! She then spoke about a senior colleague upon whom she relied and her worry that he was leaving. Perhaps she could apply for his job, but she didn't feel she could do his job. Alice finished this chain of associations by saying: 'Overall, I'm amazed you put up with me at all. But I do also think you could be nicer to me.' She then sucked her thumb.

I said she was terrified about not being able to hold on to a good sense of me. She had the warm, grateful feeling, but she lost it and could not trust herself to re-find that good feeling when it went. This really worried her. She could feel so warm, and then suddenly, it could all be gone, and then she felt all bad, alone, with me turned completely against her and no sense there ever was any good feeling between us.

Alice was thoughtful and then said she thought the reason she had never wanted children was that she would have needed to listen out all the time to check the baby was alive. A terrible feeling kept coming to her that she drained people, could be demanding, boring, hateful. That must have been why her mother stopped breast-feeding her and her father left. She then said it was obviously different with me because I was so patient and only thought of her, not my own needs. I could never hate her, even when she deprived me by not paying me.

I said I thought Alice knew this really was not true, and it seemed she was starting to spoil some alive and growing feeling about me now by turning it into a false ideal that would kill it off. This must be because she feared that, if I were not ideal, then when she did not give me what I wanted, I could only feel hatred, and nothing else could grow out of that hatred.

Then Alice said that, okay, I probably was irritated with her but would recover. Then she said that, when she thought about her father leaving her as a child, she never thought about the fact that he actually came back. She recalled that she did know from her mother that her father had worried a great deal about money and having to move the family to a smaller house. Her father had been a proud man, she now remembered her mother emphasising to her, very worried about looking a failure. Furthermore, Alice realised now that her mother had explained this to Alice, about her father, in a sympathetic, generous way, not bitterly. Perhaps, after all, there had been more love and sympathy than hatred in the family. Alice then said she wondered whether her deepest fear was of having too much hatred or not enough love inside her.

I said perhaps it was not about quantity but what hatred did to love: she feared that hatred destroyed love because she saw love as limited, not constantly lost and recovered.

In the following sessions, Alice described coming across a picture of her parents looking happy and well off before her birth. It made her realise that she had held an underlying belief that she had been the bad, ugly baby who drained her parents' marriage. At the same time, we realised, perhaps as a defence, she had always held an equally omnipotent opposite view that she was the sunshine of her mother's life, which was why they had not needed more children. She felt her mother often idealised her as a child, not wanting to say no to her. At her seventh birthday party, another girl had arrived wearing a prettier dress than Alice's own. Alice had insisted that the other girl change dresses with her, and her parents had somehow gone along with this, even though her own dress had been carefully chosen by them.

I felt in these memories Alice was expressing her insight that neither she nor her parents were confident of their capacity to love. They could not really bear to know about their ambivalence towards one another. When people did not do what Alice wanted, she was filled with hatred that destroyed any memory or sense of love, and so she feared that this was what others, her parents and I myself, also felt towards her.

Recalling John Steiner's writing referred to earlier, I assume that the King and Queen of Corinth, in keeping the truth from Oedipus of his cruel abandonment on the mountainside, must have felt that learning about the mercy of the shepherd who saved him and the kindness of his new parents would be insufficient to mitigate against the horrifying knowledge of the hatred, cruelty and abandonment inflicted upon Oedipus. To me, this suggests, above all, that they feared that if Oedipus knew about the hatred felt towards him, he would never be able to recover a sense of feeling loved or loving. Although Alice's background was not so traumatic, she was left by her father, and her mother, it seems, withdrew from her to some extent due to their own traumatic experiences as refugees. Therefore, what I believe the omnipotent phantasy structure of the Garden of Eden defended Alice against most of all was a deep doubt about the capacity to love in herself and in others.

Priscilla Roth (1999), exploring the relationship between depression and the experience of losing one's feeling of being able to love, quotes Freud 1909 writing: 'A man who doubts his own love may, or rather must, doubt every lesser thing.' Roth emphasises that in melancholic depression, the sense of badness is absolute. When the analyst sees something bad in the patient, the patient feels that the only object there is, and has ever been, is one who hates him. Roth writes: 'The trust in his objects' love for him, and his love for them, *which is at base one and the same thing*, disappears because it was never really believed in, never really established' (p. 663). She links this with Freud's emphasis on the underlying narcissistic organisation in melancholia.

This statement of Roth's is complex and intriguing. Why is it one and the same thing, and what stops it being established? To my mind, Riviere's ideas (1936), to which Blass calls attention in a recent paper (2020), throw important light on this. Riviere argued that such patients (who have a great fear of the depressive position) are terrified of being faced with the destruction they have brought upon their objects. This is because, underneath, they have so much concern *for the object, not for themselves*, that they cannot allow themselves to get better until they can cure their objects. Therefore, paradoxically, an excess of guilt about damage done impedes the capacity to repair. I imagine this excess of guilt may happen because the original object either was, or was perceived to be, too fragile to withstand the infant's hate and destructive attacks. Thus, an apparent lack of concern as in Alice's behaviour – 'I don't tend to look at people when I'm talking to them' and her horror of weakness and neediness in the men she rejected – masks the very opposite. If this is true, then it would follow that the central task of the analyst in establishing trust in love is to show the patient that the analyst can bear the patient's hateful attacks.

Over time in this phase of analysis, Alice did come to feel that her capacity to love and care for objects was not entirely dead. As other people started to appear more real, it was frightening for Alice to feel that they had real feelings about her – saw her worst faults and, at times, hated her. She had to contend with more conscious feelings of guilt, starting to recognise that people she hurt were people with (sometimes traumatic) histories of their own. But she also had the chance to feel loved and accepted.

The analysis continued into a stormy, troubled phase. Alice became more openly envious and rivalrous with me, and her communications often had a competitive bite. But more and more, she used the analysis to help her become someone who could bear complexity and ambivalence in her own feelings and other people's, rather than avoiding them. As she struggled, I felt increasingly fonder of Alice and even when, like the Oxalis triangularis seeds, affection between us seemed hard to find, I felt more confident I could dig deeper and would find it, provided I felt freer to admit to myself when I found her hateful. At the same time, I noticed that Alice put her thumb in her mouth less, though a new habit became more frequent, in which she sucked the air between her teeth when indicating disapproval, exasperation or seething resentment when people were not doing what she wanted. I thought this showed her continued enormous frustration with many aspects of life, but it felt less denying and omnipotent than the thumb sucking.

Subsequently, I have come to recognise similar underlying patterns at times with patients, myself and perhaps all humans struggling with the problems of maturing. I, therefore, hope it has been useful to explore what stood out to me in this phase of Alice's analysis: namely that, without being able to identify herself with an ideal object who could immediately satisfy all wants and needs, she feared that any love from and for another human being would be impossible.

Note

1 I am very grateful to Priscilla Roth for her help with this patient at the time.

References

Blass, R. (2020). The role of repetition in narcissism and self-sacrifice: A Freudian Kleinian reflection on the person's foundational love of the other. *International Journal of Psycho-Analysis*, 101: 6, 1188–1202.

Freud, S. (1909). *Notes Upon a Case of Obsessional Neurosis. S.E. 10*. 153–320.

Freud, S. (1914). *On Narcissism: An Introduction. S.E. 14*. 73–102.

Heimann, P. (1952). Certain functions of introjection and projection in earliest infancy. In *Developments in Psychoanalysis*. London: Hogarth Press & Institute of Psychoanalysis.

Klein, M. (1958). On the development of mental functioning. *International Journal of Psycho-Analysis*, 39: 84–90.

Riviere, J. (1936). A contribution to the analysis of the negative therapeutic reaction. *International Journal of Psychoanalysis*, 17: 304–320.

Roth, P. (1999). Absolute zero: A man who doubts his own love. *International Journal of Psycho-Analysis*, 80: 661–670.

Segal, H. (1981). Psycho-analysis and freedom of thought. In *The Work of Hanna Segal*. New York: Jason Aronson, 221.

Steiner, J. (2018). The trauma and disillusionment of Oedipus. *International Journal of Psychoanalysis*, 99: 3, 555–568.

Winnicott, D.W. (1953). Transitional objects and transitional phenomena: A study of the first not-me possession. *International Journal of Psycho-analysis*, 34: 89–97.

Chapter 3

Peter Pan, the omnipotent child

Kathleen Kelley-Lainé

Before birth we are all 'omnipotent' in our practical functioning; one with our mother, we are completely taken care of; nothing is missing. This state is prolonged as the newborn, immature child ignores the requirements of reality and maintains this former state of omnipotent pleasure through maternal care and hallucination.

Sandor Ferenczi (1913) discusses this in his article 'Stages in the Development of the Sense of Reality'. According to Ferenczi, the 'child's megalomania' as to his own omnipotence is not a *complete* delusion. He compares the child to the obsessional patient as they both demand the impossible from reality and cannot be dissuaded from stubbornly maintaining that their wishes must be fulfilled. In fact, they are only demanding the return of a state that once existed, 'those good old days' in which they were all-powerful, during a *period of unconditional omnipotence*.

Thus, the reality of birth, the first 'catastrophe' in the maturational process, is denied. In his book *Thalassa* (1933), Ferenczi studies the biological underpinnings of genitality and links these to the psychological development in the process of growing up, surviving the never-ending transformations involved in moving from the omnipotent foetal state to becoming an adult capable of accepting the limits, frustrations and castrating experiences of reality.

Ferenczi's article 'The Problem of Acceptance of Un-pleasure' (1926) explores the maturational process more deeply. A sense of reality is in sharp contrast with flight from and the repression of pain, both very much part of psychic life. In empathy with the infantile mind, Ferenczi tries to imagine the processes at work in the omnipotent infant. At this initial stage of life, the perception of the world is 'monistic', with no discrimination between 'good' and 'bad', 'inner' or 'outer'. For Winnicott the suckling baby is sucking itself, as it has no perception of a separate mother.

What are the psychic processes involved in the developing child as it learns to accommodate complex reality? The question at hand is how the psyche comes to relinquish the boundless pleasures of 'omnipotence' to espouse the frustrations of reality. Ferenczi refers to Freud's seminal article on 'Negation':

> Freud has discovered the psychological act of negation of reality to be a transition-phase between *ignoring* and *accepting* reality; the alien and therefore hostile outer world is capable of entering consciousness, in spite of 'unpleasure', when it is supplied with the minus prefix of negation, i.e., when it is denied.

When the negative hallucinatory ignoring of the unpleasurable is no longer possible, it becomes the subject matter of perception as a negation.

Can the final obstacle to acceptance of reality be removed: i.e., the complete disappearance of the tendency to repression? For Ferenczi this is the very purpose of psychoanalysis:

> The process by which recognition or affirmation of something unpleasant is finally reached takes place before our eyes as the result of our therapeutic efforts when we cure a neurosis, and if we pay attention to the details of the curative process, we shall be able to form some idea of the process of acceptance as well.
>
> (1926: 70)

The practice of psychoanalysis brings with it both experience and ever-renewed questions about the functioning of the human psyche as an economic unit, with investments in the past, the present, its blockages, fluidity and incredible creative capacities. Perhaps the word 'totalitarian' can serve as a metaphor for the state of symbiotic oneness – a whole that functions as one unified interdependent system, often under a strict regime of 'all or nothing', black or white, kill or be killed, eat or be eaten. A kind of economy of terror that pertains to the individual as it can apply to a political system or a worldview. It refers to a survival mode – when a child is born, it is a question of 'survival': will it live or die? Political systems may become totalitarian when threatened (real or imagined) from the outside: 'them against us'. The psyche can regress to totalitarian functioning when feelings of insecurity arise. Due to its omnipotent nature, the infantile 'totalitarian' psyche is usually the most resistant to change in psychoanalytical work, often because it is well hidden from both analyst and patient.

It is rare that a patient comes to analysis with the objective to 'grow up', mature and become an adult. It is equally uncommon that someone wishes to rid themselves of their 'omnipotent' psyche. It may take years before we discover the 'young, innocent and heartless' creature, the Peter Pan on our couch.

The story of Peter Pan is a metaphor that is as relevant today as it was in the beginning of the 20th century, when it was created by its author James Matthew Barrie. It represents an omnipotent defence against an early trauma that occurred at a time when the fragile ego of the child loses itself among its objects without the ability to invest them. Object relations remain utilitarian and narcissistic, enslaved to an immature ego incapable of loving, condemned to use and lose loved ones (Kelley-Lainé, 1997, 2022).

Peter Pan was convinced that he could go back to his mother whenever he wanted, so he stayed playing with the fairies in Kensington Gardens until he said:

> 'I wish now to go back to mother for ever and always'. They had to tickle his shoulders and let him go. He went in a hurry in the end, because he had dreamt that his mother was crying and he knew what was the great thing she cried for, and that a hug from her splendid Peter would quickly make her smile. Oh! He felt sure of it, and so eager was he to be nestling in her arms that this time he flew straight to the window, which was always to be open for him.
>
> But the window was closed and there were iron bars on it and peering inside he saw his mother sleeping peacefully with her arm round another little boy.
>
> Peter called, 'Mother! Mother! But she heard him not: in vain he beat his little limbs against the iron bars. He had to fly back sobbing to the Gardens and he never saw his dear again. What a glorious boy he had meant to be to her! Ah Peter! we, who have made the great mistake, how differently we should all act at the second chance. But Solomon was right – there is no second chance, not for the most of us. When we reach the window it is Lock-out Time.
>
> The iron bars are up for life.
>
> (Barrie, 1906)

In my clinical practice, I have become aware of the effects of early childhood loss on the economy of the psyche in the process of maturation. I chose to take the long-term effects of early childhood immigration as an example. A number of my patients were torn away from their country of origin, their mother tongue and their familiar home at an early age.

Following the Second World War, many refugees from Eastern Europe who survived the Holocaust were obliged to flee the dangers of Stalinism. Today, thousands are being displaced from their homeland due to wars, massacres, earthquakes, tsunamis and other forms of chaos that are shaking up our world. Thousands of young children are losing their 'place' of origin, following the exodus of their parents, not knowing where they will land. As psychoanalysts, we are increasingly solicited by this kind of 'language of exile'. Do we have to experience this intimate loss to be able to understand the depths of its meaning for others? This early loss in childhood can be recognised by the defences, repressions and fixations deeply hidden within the adult, often displaced in the idealisation of the past. Before illustrating my thesis with a clinical vignette, I would like to mention a few of the characteristics that can alert one to the 'language of exile'.

The immigrant child cannot afford to take the time of symbolic evolution, experimenting with different identities as is wont in adolescence. It is difficult to let go of the state of childhood symbolically when it was lost in reality – lost mother tongue, lost sounds, smells, tastes of mother that are gone forever, not to be revisited. Growing up entails much fear, anxiety and narcissistic turmoil. When the homeland is firm beneath one's feet, when the parents can give their support and calm one's nightmares and when mother is there to keep the window open so that we can come and go when we want, then we can accept to lose, to win and to try again. When loss of reality does not override the symbolic, then we have a transitional space in which to grow. But when the terror of loss becomes real, we can no longer play with the metaphor of 'fort-da'; the loss of our intimate language forces us into the language of exile.

First of all, the loss of 'place' becomes the loss of 'identity' – the question of 'Where am I?' becomes confused with 'Who am I?' This is the beginning of the language of exile. Those who have never been 'displaced' can continue to ask themselves 'Who am I?' from their place of origin: the feelings of shame and guilt at the loss of identity often block acts of self-exploration and expression of personality. Being torn away from the familiar, taken-for-granted second skin that contains those wordless, all-embracing initial perceptions of the surrounding world is a kind of loss that is not easy to negotiate rationally. In the life of a baby and a small child, the familiar is the 'world'. Exile can mean losing one's world. Learning the language of exile means having to manage, live with, attempt to repair the loss and accept being a 'foreigner', 'étranger' (the word in French means 'foreigner' but comes from the word *étrange*: strange, bizarre). Being a foreigner is 'not being' like others. One way of dealing with the language of exile is over-adaptation, being more normal than 'normal', not to stand out from the crowd. Because of the divergence of what one is and what one seems to be as a foreigner, the language of exile teaches acute self-observation early on. Lost childhood implies precocious maturity, together with the desire to 'never grow up', the edict of Peter Pan.

'Lost childhood' of immigration reveals itself most intensely through the person's relationship to space and time. The omnipotence of those intimately and secretly guarded feelings, sounds, smells of the early skin is a strange place in psychic economy. The lost world, the abandoned native land becomes an enormous beach on which to deposit one's most precious desires and illusions. The Neverland, (of primary narcissism) is capable of capturing one's most far-fetched and fabulous phantasies, especially because it resembles the origins of time and the symbiotic totalitarian space of original oneness. The real world of daily drudgery is a pale comparison next to this colourful island of make-believe. This secret place is where the lost child can curl up and feel safe and, because it was once real, the illusion that it still exists are infinitely tempting. The Neverland has to be cultivated, nurtured and kept hidden. This is why it can be so resistant to change in analysis.

This is a timeless, wordless, staggering space where the lost child can revisit an idealized image of self, untransformed, without conflict. A space that cannot be symbolized or represented through words; it is more a taste than a sound, imbued by pure pleasure. The omnipotent Neverland blocks the self in a kind of narcissistic projection of what was, in a hidden attempt to preserve the past. It represents the struggle against the death of the infantile ideal of primary narcissism. The Neverland is always a hiding place for 'mother'. Although Peter Pan has banned the word from the island, all its inhabitants, including Captain Hook, are secretly yearning for their mother.

The sensual pleasure and pain that can be procured in this idealized space are undoubtedly what contributes to its resistance to change. Emotions and feelings remain locked within this split-off part of the psyche. The lost object is incorporated, immobilized and sealed off from the passage of time. This desperate strategy leaves little space for life in the here and now or for projecting into the future. The tendency is to withdraw libidinal energy from the present and invest in memories of the past in a kind of delicious, masochistic, painful nostalgia.

The lost child can also have the opposite reaction: no nostalgia, no dependence, no looking back, no history. All investment is in the present, in what is concrete. Only facts count; to act in the here and now is the most important. The immigrant becomes 'hyper-adapted' to the new world.

Then there is the lost child who is always elsewhere, who needs to leave everything and everyone in order not to experience loss. To love is to love at a distance, to keep things 'intact' so that nothing is destroyed. Time must be stopped! The image of the self and the object remain fixed to the land that was left behind. Pain is not attached to departure; nostalgia is not about leaving but rather about returning to find that things have remained unchanged in Neverland. The self is threatened by homecoming, a reunion that abolishes the necessary distance with the frightening and desired primary object. Therefore, the lost child provokes 'breaking up' whenever he can in order to create a viable distance with the loved one and to bury the original, intolerable separation that was never mourned. To leave is to love, to better find oneself as subject of one's own creation.

Louise, the lost child

Louise was six years old when she, her little brother and her mother fled the war-torn country of her birth. The children were not to know about the war; the adults invented stories to mask the dead bodies lying by the side of the road, the gunshots going off everywhere. Louise believed them. She also believed the stories her mother told about her own family and childhood. Louise learned the truth much later when she discovered her mother's adoption papers. They found refuge in France with the mother's adoptive French family. Then the news came: her father was murdered on his own land, the family farm. It was perhaps by one of his workmen – they never did find out. Her brother went back years later to search for the truth, but Louise preferred to forget. She even wanted to abandon her father's name, her name.

Louise was in her early forties when she came to see me. She had been married and divorced and shared her son and daughter with a wealthy, protective husband. Completely immersed in her work as the manager of an important cultural institution, she consulted me when management problems started getting out of hand. Face-to-face therapy was a mutual decision. For her, there was no question of lying on the couch; she needed to see me to make sure that I would not hide something from her. I sensed that her fear of regression might push her into acting out and could sabotage our work rather quickly.

The bomb exploded about two years later. I received a message that she could not come to her session; she had been taken to the police station for 48-hour questioning. It turned out that one of her collaborators had denounced her to the police for theft. They filmed her putting money into her purse on the occasion when she stood in for the cashier. Although she was the manager, she did everything in her power to be 'one of the boys'; she just wanted to be accepted, to be loved. She completely ignored the need for boundaries and structure in an organisation and would play favourites with her secretaries, thus creating passionate jealousy among them. She gave money to one of the workers when he was in dire straits. This employee happened to be a citizen of her country of origin and was confused about whether the money was a loan or a gift. Louise's entire libido was invested in the workings of the organisation and in herself as the omnipotent leader, navigating on all levels, regardless of the rules. The workplace was the subject of most sessions. She rarely spoke of her children, and there was no word of a relationship with a man. She disclosed that she slept with her teddy bear dressed in her son's baby clothes.

The omnipotent 'false self' adjusts to the environment but keeps the authentic, injured self withdrawn from reality, as if this part of the self were waiting to be revived, repaired and reconnected with the situation from which its development was discontinued. Sandor Ferenczi's article on the 'Confusion of Tongues between Children and Adults' (1949), as well as his *Clinical Diary* (1932), are essential documents for us to learn about the tact, care and sensitivity with which we must proceed in the analysis of early childhood trauma.

What is the essence of an 'authentic' relationship between the therapist and patient within the psychoanalytical frame? The frame is essential as it provides freedom for both persons in the analytical relationship, promoting a symbolising process rather than action or 'doing good'. The frame is first of all within the analyst. According to Freud, the analyst can only take their patient to where they have been in the psychoanalytic process, identified with their own analyst. This poses the question of the analyst's personal analysis, continuing attention to their internal economy and psychical functioning. The analyst's own story, psychic processes and the metaphors they live by are fundamental tools in working with patients.

Metaphors function like dreams as they offer an internal space to re-actualize past experience and conflicts. Like Winnicott's transitional space, metaphors allow one to take distance, differentiate and be able to play with one's internal and external worlds, thereby developing the capacity to symbolise. The process of 'metaphorisation' between mother and child is crucial at the beginning of psychic development. In the early symbiotic relationship, the child feels itself existing in the mother's eyes, mirrored in her gaze. According to Piera Aulagnier (1975), this process of 'specularisation' is a kind of appropriation that consists in recognising oneself in the other person's psyche, thereby creating the conditions for metaphorical thinking. The psychoanalytical frame that includes the analysts 'psychic gaze' and capacity for metaphorisation is an important element of the psychoanalytical process.

Metaphor is a kind of transference from one location to another that enables us to redefine the world in our way, taking account of what we see and what we feel to be important. Psychoanalysis is the dynamic of free association, a creative process of translating feelings and experiences into words, into new words.

I will now attempt to illustrate how we were able to create metaphors for working through childhood trauma with Louise. Having been torn away from the omnipotence of her childhood paradise where one could be queen of the orange groves, did she try to recreate this all-powerful feeling in her post as director of the institution? I needed to embed myself in her childhood environment. I tried to see, feel and hear her laughing and playing on the vast paternal farm of endless fields basking in the sun. Listening to her story, I am able to see the little girl with dark brown hair running freely, her baby brother trotting behind; she is chasing the chickens, catching butterflies, stroking the kitten curled up on the porch. The figure of a beautiful but cold, distant woman also appears – her mother scolds but later saves the little girl. It takes a long time before the man appears – he has an orange in his hand. Who is he giving it to? Is it to the little girl? Is it to the mother? She remembers, she feels, she cries: 'I wanted the orange to be for me! It was for me; my father gave me the orange. He loved me'. The vigour of this declaration came as a surprise to both of us, proving the power of the loss of her father that she had denied until now. The orange became the metaphor that we could use to find her way back to her father, to accept his name and, eventually, to accept a man whom she could love.

Conclusion

To conclude, I wish to evoke Donald Winnicott's image of the mother/infant relationship at the very beginning of life, that of the hungry baby with predatory urges and ideas and the mother with instinctual urges and wishes to be attacked by a hungry baby. The two do not come into a relationship with each other until mother and child 'live an experience together'. According to Winnicott, 'the central organizing thread of psychological development from its inception is the experience of being alive and the consequences of disruption to that continuity of being' (Winnicott, 1958).

As psychoanalysts, we accompany patients in their quest for 'aliveness' and continuity of being, and our work consists of how best to enable maturational processes in order that patients can experience life as subjects of desire and continue life as creative human beings. Is there a metapsychological map to guide this analytical process?

The clinical example here illustrates how a concrete object from childhood serves as a metaphor to bring two unlikely situations together: the context of early childhood linked to trauma and the psychoanalytical relationship. It is an unexpected alliance, just as awareness of unconscious processes is often astonishing. This link is thereby transforming familiar ground, constructing something new and not yet known. The creative capacity of the metaphorical process can thus be installed within the psychoanalytical relationship to shed new light on existing ways of being from a totally different perspective. Such a transfer of meaning facilitates the emergence of a new awareness of unconscious forces within the 'omnipotent' psychic dynamic. Omnipotence goes hand in hand with denial – it is a matter of 'all or nothing'. Initially, Louise had to deny her father to the extent of annihilating his name. Metaphoric thinking can help stretch existing boundaries and open up unexpected connections, thus transforming existing totalitarian visions of reality. The orange enabled Louise to relive the love of her father. It can also empower the creativity of the analyst: with Louise, just after the traumatic incident of the police arrest, I found myself wanting to fall asleep during our sessions. I experienced all kinds of emotions, from anger with myself to guilt and disbelief of the causes of my drowsiness until I decided to dare to share this fact with her. 'We need to understand why, when you speak, I want to fall asleep', I said bluntly. 'It is because I am not *speaking true*.' she answered. Not only our relationship but also our work changed from then on.

References

Aulagnier, P. (1975). *La violence de l'interprétation*. Paris: Presses Universitaires de France.
Barrie, J.M. (1906). *Peter Pan in Kensington Gardens*. London: Hodder and Stoughton.
Ferenczi, S. (1913). Stages in the development of a sense of reality. In Barossa, J. (Ed.), *Selected Writings of Sandor Ferenczi*. London: Penguin Books Ltd., 1999.
Ferenczi, S. (1926). The problems of the acceptance of unpleasure: Advances in the knowledge of a sense of reality. In Barossa, J. (Ed.), *Selected Writings of Sandor Ferenczi*. London: Penguin Books Ltd., 1999, 70.
Ferenczi, S. (1932). *The Clinical Diary of Sandor Ferenczi*. Ed. J. Dupont. Cambridge, MA: Harvard University Press, 1988.
Ferenczi, S. (1933). *Thalassa: A theory of genitality*. New York: W.W. Norton and Co., 1968.
Ferenczi, S. (1949). The confusion of tongues between the adult and the child. *International Journal of Psychoanalysis*, 30: 225–230.
Kelley-Lainé, K. (1997). *Peter Pan: The Story of Lost Childhood*. London: Element Books.
Kelley-Lainé, K. (2022). *Peter Pan the Lost Child*. London: Phoenix.
Winnicott, D. (1958). *Collected Papers: Through Paediatrics to Psycho-Analysis*. London: Tavistock.

In the adolescent . . .

Chapter 4

Omnipotence in adolescence

Sara Flanders

Phillip Gutton has articulated vividly the paradoxical rupture of puberty, an event for which he hypothesises no one is ever truly ready. It is a shock, a trauma, this event which marks the second phase of human sexuality, the transformation from child to adult. This bi-phasic sexuality (Freud, 1895, 1905, 1923) alongside the long period of infantile dependence, are the sources, Freud asserted, of the vulnerability and complexity of human sexuality and human identity. The abrupt and final intrusion of pubertal sexual development is always a rupture, breaking into whatever identifications and relationships to reality a child has developed, through the hard work of the Oedipus and the achievements of latency. Gutton writes:

> The pubertal is quite the antithesis of a movement of separation. A force directed against separation fuels the child's frenzy towards his parents. It is important to realize that the pubertal primal discovery of the new 'sexual aim' is 'diverted' by its very mental image: sexuality may have found its aim, but it has not found an appropriate object.
>
> (1998: 136)

The confused 'frenzy' towards the parent, precisely as the parent becomes incontrovertibly sexually alive in ways not subjectively experienced in childhood, is what Gutton calls the 'pubertal scene'. The shock of helplessness awakens the infantile vulnerability and dependence, driving a reaching out to the parent who might hold (Winnicott, 1971) or contain (Bion, 1962) the threat of disintegration or, in Kleinian terms, might mitigate the panic of the paranoid intrusion on whatever peaceful life had been achieved, or already painfully compromised, in latency.

The 'pubertal scene' catches some adolescents in a paradox that forecloses their development, when the reality of the changing body confronts them with the task of adapting to an intolerable fact of life (Money Kyrle, 1971), the fact of sexual maturation and a new realisation of separation-individuation (Blos, 1967). The intolerance for the reality of living in a separate, sexually identified body has its precursors in infancy and childhood (Mahler, 1968). Some kind of omnipotent

DOI: 10.4324/9781003185192-7

phantasy (Klein, 1940), an historical failure to negotiate reality, usually lies behind the more extreme traumas of helplessness when facing the arrival of puberty. One way out of the conundrum lies in a new, often more dangerous invocation of omnipotence (Laufer and Laufer, 1984): suicide is a specific threat in adolescence. More common and less destructive, what a research group at Brent Adolescent Centre has called repetitive compelling behaviour (unpublished) is symptomatic action: cutting, starving, bulimia, compulsive masturbation, compulsive risk taking, drug addiction, etc. Activity driven by an omnipotent phantasy is aimed to hold on to a sense of omnipotent control before the overwhelming and contradicting fact of physical development. Physical development is the reality that cannot be integrated, the repudiated reality a feature of the 'psychotic functioning' of adolescence (Laufer and Laufer, 1984; Bronstein, 2020). The anxiety awakened by the 'clamouring of the life drive', the 'turmoiling body' of adolescence (Lombardi, 2017; Ferrari, 2004) reawakens earliest emotional experience. Such moments are often passing, the ego recovers, adapts to change, helped by internalisation of a containing good object. But sometimes omnipotent defensive activity entrenches itself; it will not be a temporary phase, a moment in the adolescent process. Rather, it will become part of an effort to stop time, omnipotently arrest the changes heralding the loss of childhood dependency, a loss that will not be accepted, will not be mourned (Klein, 1940), will not be owned as history (Baranger and Baranger, 1988). The therapeutic process, aimed at retrieving and integrating a psychic history, hopefully subverts the necessity for omnipotent defences, helping the adolescent to find containment (Bion, 1962) of the renewed anxiety of separateness through the relationship to the therapist.

Needless to say, there is wide scope for parental collusion with the refusal of the changes which mark the breakdown (Laufer and Laufer, 1984) of adolescent development. Parents often cannot support the adolescent process. Moreover, the quality of what Ladame has noted as the failure of the adolescent preconscious (Ladame and Catipovic, 1998) often finds its origins much earlier, in infantile experiences: for example, in the defensive negations (Green, 1999) of the projections (Williams, 1997) of an invasive object, a parent who, in infancy, perhaps unconsciously but often psychotically, could not bear the otherness of the infant whose life it is her task to nourish, to gratify, to support. Too much invasion or, conversely, too little presence, leaving an infant or child with no other defence than omnipotent phantasy. The two adolescents I will use as illustrations also struggled with the absence of a good enough father. . . . That would be a father who supports and mitigates the necessary 'disillusionment' of a growing infant, helps negotiate the separation and mourn the loss of an illusion of omnipotence (Winnicott, 1971) so necessary in earliest relations with the mother and so damaging if not does not yield to a sense of reality.

Mary

Mary was a troubled 18-year-old whose dominant symptoms showed themselves in a bulimic eating disorder and a recurrent succumbing to suicidal mentation, a preoccupation with suicide which emerged whenever she was confronted with a conflict that presented her with a need to navigate something regarded as new. This is a capacity that develops out of experience (Solms, 2021), the development of mind, including an ability to recognize errors (Solms, 2021), to test reality, and adapt to it rather than instantly react in an action, the tactic of the primitive mind. The capacity is tested in the adolescent process, which is the adaptation to the pubertal changes. But the panic induced by the changes and the newly disturbed relation to the primary object can shut down an ability to think, leading to a regression to omnipotent action. In the beginning of her treatment, it became clear that Mary regarded the demand to think when facing some kind of emotional disturbance as a sign of her precipitant failure. The unexpected was her fault, not her challenge. The resort to the thought of an action – suicide – was her first idea when presented with a new experience. There was no middle ground, no transitional space (Winnicott, 1971), and little curiosity. As Ladame writes, one could see in the lack of elaborated thought, a 'failure of the preconscious' (Ladame and Catipovic, 1998), a failure in the realm of an ability to work, in the Freudian sense, (1915) and to play (Winnicott, 1971), to phantasise or symbolise. Against a despair of tolerating and attending to her emotional situation, she erected the defence of the eating disorder. At no time did she attempt suicide, nor did she, like many, attack her body through, for example, cutting. She did begin first, symptomatically, to vomit and then later to binge before vomiting. Bingeing and vomiting together became her omnipotent defence, the belief she was magically ridding her mind of despised emotions, an apparently empowering defence, her magical balancing rod pole as she walked a tightrope towards adulthood.

Mary had been known to psychotherapy services since early adolescence, and manifestations of maternal paranoia meant she was referred to boarding school, enforcing her separation from the immediacy of maternal disturbance. She was not happy with this, but I am certain it was a powerful element in her survival, the 'brick mother' (Rey, 1994) of boarding school which also served a paternal function, coming between her and her loving but paranoid and intrusive mother. Mary was the child of a disturbed woman who nonetheless functioned in the world; she had always worked; she cared for her only daughter; she agreed to the boarding school referral partly out of an awareness of her difficulty confronting her daughter's development, her newly apparent otherness. Mary was seen irregularly by a child psychotherapist who stayed in touch with her in boarding school, arranging for her to be referred to psychoanalytic psychotherapy when she graduated at 18 and left secondary school (Bellman, 1997). Upon her graduation, Mary was pleased to get away from boarding school. She had pined for the maternal care she looked forward to receiving at home, most palpably expressed through her mother's cooking. This is the food on which she binged before vomiting, until sufficient work had been done to facilitate a more representational relationship to emotions and to desire, some greater capacity to elaborate the overwhelming emotions for which she had no tolerance and no words when she started therapy (Ladame and Catipovic, 1998).

Mary had been waiting a long time before she started therapy, and the consequent idealisation, which had been a support, created a problem from the start of the therapy. The idealisation almost inhibited her completely in the room with me. *Après coup*, I came to understand the paralysis of those sessions, the mind-numbing deadness, as her way of staying in the room with me, the consulting room and myself carrying the projections linked to the powerful, intrusive mother she clung to, the mother of Gutton's pubertal scene (1998). The idealized therapy of the future, what had sustained her in boarding school, had been the raft to which Mary had clung when she was miserable and lonely. But the process of idealisation also carried the problematic of the rejection of reality – the reality, above all, of the adolescent's own 'turmoiling body' (Ferrari, 2004; Lombardi, 2017), as well as the bodies of others. My presence in the flesh challenged the repudiated flesh of adolescent breakdown, the body which she needed to stifle. My adult presence, I eventually understood, recreated the incestuous presence of her mother's body. So we had paralysingly controlled sessions. When I found something to say about the silence, the control, the state of mind barely perceptible, I saw Mary gesture with a visible gagging movement that looked like an attempt to swallow regurgitation. I eventually understood the food for thought I struggled to offer was contaminated by the still-alive pubertal situation in the transference.

While Mary showed in her repudiating gesture, her defence against an intrusive paranoid object, hers was not completely the 'no entry' defence so brilliantly described by Gianna Williams when considering the anorexic defences of a girl abused since childhood, at war with her adolescence, therefore refusing all entry, particularly thoughts experienced as too penetrating and a sexuality understood to be invasive (Williams, 1997). Mary's defence was not so complete, but it did, I believe, disclose the earmarks of infancy, the problematic of a loved child, certainly I imagine a well-fed child, attempting to take in both the food and the worldview of her paranoid mother yet protect herself from the invasive force of maternal projections, the violence of the maternal inner world (Williams, 1997).

A paranoid mother does not live in the world of uncertainty, a many-faceted reality, where there are different points of view (Lacan, 1953; Britton, 1989). The complexity of reality is not easily tolerated in the mind of a paranoid mother: hence, the prescription of boarding school in adolescence (Bellman, 1997). But paranoid certainty is attractive to the floundering adolescent, and it was one to which Mary aligned herself, leaned on, then struggled to escape. I learned, through the process of her development in therapy, of the seductiveness of a belief in the omnipotence which is expressed in the certainties of a paranoid mother. Such certainties provoke excessive anxiety and excessive hope, even an excessive excitation which would be re-enacted in the frenzied bingeing and vomiting symptom, the omnipotent act. In her development, Mary did not have much space to lay the foundations to 'become a subject' (Cahn, 1998), the achievement of a separate, thinking identity which is one hallmark of having achieved the developmental task of adolescence (Cahn, 1998). And yet she came, in a reverent, too-abject state before her idealised but also profoundly disappointing, decidedly not omnipotent therapist. We survived encounters in which I offered thoughts as hypotheses, rather than certainties. At the same time, I came to understand how blamed she felt if I offered a thought she had not thought of already. As her therapist, I only gradually achieved the capacity to be experienced as 'good enough', unintrusive enough to be trusted with revelations enabling her to reimagine a history, to help her gain, for example, the strength openly to contact her father, from whom her mother had separated when she was four and with whom her mother had forbidden contact.

The history of the symptom she had developed, and of which she was very ashamed, came out of the endeavour to indulge in but also extricate herself from her mother's seductive plan for her. It was not without some ingenuity. She described the beginning of both vomiting and bingeing as growing out of a context determined by her mother, who devised the notion that Mary would form a sexual bond with the son of her mother's good friend, someone who lived in the mother's country of origin, where the mother hoped to return with Mary in tow. She entertained, as parents might often entertain such phantasies, that the two children, young adolescents, might form a relationship so that they could all live together in the country of the mother's origins, a *menage a quatre*, symmetric, no abandonment, no separation. The vomiting emerged in the early stages of this togetherness, according to the history emerging in her therapy, when Mary recalled becoming paranoid about the food offered by the boy's mother. Her conscious fear was that the food would make her fat; it would make her ugly. In a context in which her own sexual attractiveness was meant to catch a boy whose mother connived with her own, the food which became dangerous was that of the boy's mother. Consciously, at this point, it was not the sexually controlling phantasy of her mother that she had to restrict. It was the destructive attack of the boy's mother. Mary's paranoia found a new object, a displacement from her mother constructed from her own phantasy life combined with maternal phantasy. At no time did she express consciousness of an anxiety, for example, that getting 'fat' might mean owning an adult body or a body like her mother's, a body that could grow 'fat' with pregnancy, as is often the case in anorexia.

The bingeing came later. This boyfriend came to visit Mary in London. At some point in the night, as both the mother and the boyfriend slept, she crept to the kitchen and suddenly found herself in a wild, ecstatic binge. By the time she came to therapy as an 18-year-old, the bingeing and vomiting had become her way to control the confused vulnerability, the excitement, the self-hatred, the claustrophobic entrapment. The act, apparently omnipotent, did not actually achieve psychological separation but rather maintained a tense, confused irresolution of the pubertal conflict. Psychological separation requires mourning, and Mary was still locked in the pubertal scene, the paranoid clinging to the incestuous object. In the wild binging, which certainly conveyed, in her telling, the force of both adolescent sexual excitement and the feeling of being overwhelmed, the breakout from claustrophobic pressure and yet the safety from engagement with another sexual being, she had found a symptom to express and control, to keep her in her arrested state. She could stay in the phantasy established by the mother, experience herself in control of the wild desires provoked, keep reality at bay.

The arrangement seemed to freeze the problematic of the pubertal crisis: Mary finding a way to maintain a clinging hold on a parental object and allow, at the same time, for an entry into sexual life. To have her cake and eat it. It is a process that bypasses the mourning which is a crucial element of the adolescent process and a crucial path towards the renunciation of omnipotent illusion (Winnicott, 1971). And it did not really work. She was terrified of being found out, the boy after a time rejected both her and the mothers' plan. In essence, the symptom did not help her extricate herself from the incestuous object from whom she could not separate. It took me some time to realise that I, too, before whom, as she later put it, she 'wrapped herself in silence', stood for the incestuous maternal object, and the inhibited silence of our early sessions was to do with the need to keep absolutely quiet the object relation that could explode into something as out of control as the binging frenzy.

Interestingly, Mary eventually did not shrink from interpretations linking feelings in relations to me with the incestuous feelings for her mother. Entering the consulting room furious, she had been beeped at as she sought a parking place in front of the consulting room; she eventually associated to a memory vividly disclosing the oedipal refusal at the heart of her conundrum. The memory, still linked with a sense of outrage, was to her experience on her mother's honeymoon, roughly at a time corresponding to her own puberty, when to her dismay, she was not welcome in her mother's bed. Given her still-palpable outrage and what looked like an hysterical indifference to the inappropriateness of the situation, she took little time to realize her absurd position when it was pointed out. It was as if she might have known it all along or that she was relieved, finally, to be helped out of the maternal bedroom. I recall being surprised by this inhibited, conformist and controlling girl, facing her incestuous homosexual wishes in the consulting room as if she was being released from a prison for which she was given the key to walk away. An acceptance of reality diminished the demand on omnipotence, as did a sense that she had been caught up in something mad and, in fact, not entirely of her own making.

As emotions were allowed more space, the control diminished. She found herself more able to talk to me. Mary and her mother found a *modus vivendi*, one that I think was overdetermined; her mother continued, as long as Mary was a patient, to cook what always sounded like lovely food. Mary ate exactly half; she left half on the plate. She did not take it all in . . . and for the most part, did not binge or vomit. She came to two sessions per week, rather than one. She established a sexual relationship with a boy, whom she saw twice per week; she gained a promotion; she used the sessions to develop, to separate, to distance herself from her disturbed maternal object; but one could see, at the age of 21, that there was a decidedly concrete element threading its way through her evolution. Representation of thoughts and feelings gained greatly, but action still carried some of the burden of containment. Some acceptance of the fundamental mourning associated with the conversion to symbolic functioning (Segal, 1986) was accompanied by a now-diminished but surviving allegiance to the omnipotence ascribed to action. And I did not challenge, nor really understand at the time, this compromise, this vestige of an omnipotent defence: Mary enjoying her mother's food but also rejecting it, in action, not, however, quite symbolically, still fighting the implications of being taken over, fused, unseparated. She no longer quite had her cake to eat and keep as well. But the primitive origins of the response to emotional states through action rather than symbolic functioning did not disappear (Solms, 2021). I am not sure if one could say that it had become a sort of play but, perhaps, a game.

It is to be noted here, and actually in many cases that I could enumerate, that the severe disturbances of puberty, the developmental problems underlying adolescent breakdown, the leaning on omnipotent defences, rest with failures not only in early mother-child relations, the intrusive violence of maternal projections, or the chaos engendered by too much abandonment, physical and emotional, but also in the failure of the paternal function, that function which actually limits the power of the maternal imaginary (Lacan, 1953; Bailly, 2009), the mother-child immersion in early infancy. The lack of a paternal function, in reality or in the mind of the mother, interferes with the gradual giving up of omnipotence (Winnicott, 1971) and the development of separation and individuation (Mahler, 1968). Outlining the historical function of the father in the case of Mary illustrates vividly the problems she faced, left alone as she was for too long with a mother who actually forbade her contact with her father. She recalled her parents' separation vividly; her father was escorted out of the house by police when she was four years old, and then her mother forbade contact with him. Again, there is the omnipotence in action wielded by a paranoid mother, who was, in fact, the violent one in the marital relationship and who could not lend herself to sympathy with a child's need for a father. Mary's father, in fact, rather than being a violent persecutor, feared the violence of his ex-wife, both in Mary's childhood and later, when she turned to him while in therapy with me. In fact, he had not completely disappeared from her life when she was a small child: he appeared to her through the fence of the school playground, his contact with her remaining a secret . . . their secret. Something was maintained of an ordinary relationship, perversely forbidden, confused with a taboo. The actual separation between mother and father and, by mother's design, between daughter and father, took place at the moment the oedipal crisis would be at its height, the time when, in normal circumstances, a child gives up the erotic possession of the parent of the opposite sex but keeps the protective and facilitating father.

The role of the psychoanalytic therapist in the case of adolescent breakdown is often to revivify and support a collapsed paternal function, a function whose origins lie deep in the history of any individual. The part played by the father, or the symbolic father (Lacan, 1953; Bailly, 2009), the father in the mind of the mother, had failed to support the child's experience of his or her separateness, had left the mother and child locked in a timeless world that is then too drastically blown apart by the pubertal scene. The developing child was driven back into the arms of the incestuously coloured parent and into the necessity of omnipotent solutions to the problematic of the implications of the reality of the changing body. As has been shown, Mary's father presented himself secretly to his daughter. When divorced from her mother, the father at the school boundaries, keeping his memory and reality alive in the child's mind, did not challenge the maternal dominance in Mary's world. Such that Mary, accompanying her mother on her honeymoon with a stepfather, still occupied the paternal place in bed.

And then, in therapy, as Mary emboldened herself to challenge her mother, to turn openly to her father, she asked him about the possibility of living in his home. Again, he let her down. Just as Mary had to swallow, in the psychotherapy process, the awareness of the incestuous phantasy binding her to her mother, she had to swallow the repeated failure of her father to help her out of it. Claiming that he did not want to risk the powerful wrath of Mary's mother, he said he was sorry; he could not provide her with a place to be. He invoked past experience; he was not prepared to risk her mother's vengeance. His palpable fear underlined the psychotic power of her mother's paranoid violence, a third aspect of reality that Mary had to face, a liberating but painful realisation supporting again the process of differentiation but also representing a substantial personal cost. The father's fears, whatever his true motivation, highlighted the great difference between his ex-wife's entitled possession of her daughter and his correspondingly tepid defence of reality. He was no match for the power of his ex-wife's psychotic violence, and so he left his daughter, this time with the ally of a therapist and her own developing drive towards a life of her own, to renegotiate it.

The process of Mary's therapy discloses a trajectory of remarkable development, a testament to a wonderful adolescent wish to grow, to develop, to overcome the limitations of a psychological structure that is not on its own adequate to the demand on the mind for work (Freud, 1915) that is the requirement of the adolescent process. If her omnipotent defences manifested themselves in childhood as a suspension of normal oedipal processes, the preservation of an illusion of her inseparability from her mother, those which were invoked in adolescence, did not take over her entire existence; the chaos had been bound by the bulimia. And it is important to hold in mind the function performed by the child psychotherapist's role supporting a boarding school placement. A negative capacity (Green, 1999), a no-entry defence (Williams, 1997) could be made real, more constant, and less destructive in the boarding school barrier. She was not continually provoked by a maternal incapacity to support her separateness, although she was very lonely and unhappy during much of this period. The omnipotent defences I encountered in her therapy were more organised, more boundaried; she only gave herself over to a manic enactment of an omnipotent defence (Klein, 1940) when bingeing and vomiting secretly. Her action, her taking 'arms against a sea of troubles', did not spread to anti-social or suicidal behaviour. Mary was deeply conformist; she became an excellent employee; she never missed sessions, even when most alienated. Nor did Mary ever disclose that imaginative creativity that can be so much in evidence in some adolescent struggles to adapt with authenticity to adulthood. Courage she did disclose in facing up to the intolerable conundrum of a prolonged and incestuous dependency or later, with a new young boyfriend, surprisingly risking rejection with an entirely sensible insistence on his taking an AIDS test if he wished not to use condoms. And she arrived at a capacity for enjoyable sexual intercourse, interestingly with a young man from her mother's country of origin. She kept her obsessional personality, but she achieved an adolescence.

Case 2 – Cassie: violence as omnipotent defence

Mary was, in most ways, a 'good girl', and she did not terrify her therapist with the sort of acting out that a risk-defying adolescent can employ. Mary was 18, not 13, like the young patient, Cassie, I will describe here, and Mary's three years of therapy took her into young adulthood, whereas Cassie was still only 18 when her therapy finished, as planned. She was seen, like Mary, in an adolescent clinic. At the centre of her symptoms was another pubertal scene, again complicated by the now-familiar issue of the mother's bed: Cassie's mother, unlike Mary's, who was older and less well educated, was also, like Mary's, from a foreign country. There she had met and then separated from Cassie's African father. She moved to England, where she married and lived for six years with a white Englishman and, after leaving him, conceived a boy through a brief liaison. Mother and two children – one mixed race, the much younger baby brother, a white 'angel' – lived together in a white household, which also included her mother's father, who had emigrated early in Cassie's childhood.

Just as Cassie was approaching puberty, her mother became involved with a lesbian woman who took up residence, first in the mother's bed and then in the home. Indeed, this serious professional woman was the first genuine oedipal rival Cassie ever met, the white 'husband' of six years having been no proper rival, never in Cassie's memory having slept with her mother. Cassie had no memory though had heard many stories of her own black father who was castigated for delinquency, sexual profligacy, and violence and, of course, lived in a foreign country. She called her mother's white husband of six years 'Father', she carried his name, and she had believed him to be her father, which she recalled later with astonishment as her deeper ownership of her own racial difference gathered meaning for her. It seems that she never saw him after he left her home. The setup before the entry of mother's lesbian partner confirmed an omnipotent, infantile phantasy, rather like Mary's: the phantasy of being her mother's partner, one which was totally disrupted by the facts when her mother took a lover as her daughter approached puberty. The upheaval sent Cassie into paroxysms of disorganising rage, the symptom that drove her referral to an adolescent centre where psychotherapy could be offered. In no way prepared by her history for the dilemma Gutton (1998) has described at puberty, her move towards integrating her own sexual and racial identity would present her and her therapist with a tall order. Happily, it was supported for some years by the concerned child psychotherapist meeting with the beleaguered mother and partner.

When I first met Cassie, she was a slim, pretty, mixed-race child, rather than adolescent, not at all a precocious 13. She wore clothes with an artful insouciance: different-coloured ribbons or socks, a charming, harlequin-like style that I thought then, and think now, represented an effort to integrate above all the racial strands that contributed to her identity, so different, so unique in her household. This sartorial flair betrayed the aesthetic talent she eventually disclosed, expressive, charming, genuine, although thoroughly inadequate to the demands made on it. Little had been made of her difficulty with school, where her intelligence had not been appreciated, but I could see she was very intelligent, though driven about by uncontained drives, libidinal and aggressive, paranoid above all. Cassie was all action. Classroom demands barely served as intermittent interruption to the battles of the playground she reported to me in the beginning. She had no reliable friendships at this point. However, the battle over who had the most crisps or sweets at lunch time described a less intense version of the battles which raged for her at home. The litany of minor but incessant skirmishes at school was interrupted in one of her early sessions by a description of an incident at her home: it began in a relatively benign discussion about the new paint colour to be chosen for the walls of one of the communal rooms in the house. A well-meaning attempt to include her by her mother's partner exploded into a terrible row. Cassie, angry, distressed, and confused by her rage, found herself crying out that she 'wanted her father'. The exasperated adult countered, 'Your father does not want you'. Brutally humiliated and enraged, Cassie went to the kitchen, held a knife to the gathering family members, including her grandfather, and challenged them not to touch her before she left the house. As had been required before, the women called police, who returned Cassie eventually to a home they deemed orderly and middle class, not in need of their involvement. But the apparent order only covered the chaos of Cassie's tormented confusion and the weakness of the structure into which the mother's lesbian relationship had intruded. It had been a chaotic structure, a confusing and fragile generational arrangement, in which the girl's omnipotence had been allowed to thrive and become linked with a phantasy of her centrality to her emotionally elusive mother's well-being. And Cassie needed omnipotent phantasy: she had often been moved about, as on a chess board, between beloved carers, suddenly, inexplicably gone, or a reliably present if weak father figure, who appeared and disappeared without explanation. More a failure of thoughtful empathy than an intrusive control, as in Mary's case, her mother seemed to take for granted her small daughter's resilience and failed, as far as I could understand, to empathise with a small child's need for her experience of radical change to be mediated by recognition, thought, solace. As happened while she was in therapy, to the much-older Cassie, her mother would meet distress with gratification; for the adolescent, she would buy new clothes in which Cassie looked brilliant. But Cassie complained, influenced by the careful attention to continuity of time and place in the therapy, of a childhood in which her mother didn't explain or interpret the changes in her life. She was especially indignant as she recalled the loss through death of a black child minder in her remembered childhood. Such parenting stayed teasingly apparent while Cassie was in therapy. Correspondingly, Cassie sought the gratification of her mother's affectionate attention, and she brought an aesthetically appealing and endearing quality to the consulting room, repeating the tactic which sometimes found a receptive object in the mother.

The teasing provocation, most vividly the mother's move to a white female partner at the time of her mixed-race daughter's puberty, exacerbated the dilemma described by Gutton: in as much as Cassie resembled, in her racial appearance, the estranged father she had never known, she would be likened more and more to the violent father who she now realised was hers, whose violence became consciously linked by her and by her white family with her own. He was more obviously negated as a sufficient partner to a woman. She and he were in the same boat. Was it her blackness which drove mother to her new partner? Would her attack on the lesbian couple mirror his in phantasy? The identification with the father's rejection and his violence would be an enduring problem in the therapy. It would be exacerbated by her adolescent power: she grew to tower over all in the house and over her white therapist as well. The adolescent capacity for effective violence (Laufer and Laufer, 1984), the responsibility of owning and living with greater physical strength, was burdened with the ongoing violent emotionality and the fact of her size. She could never retrieve a past identity as the beloved little girl of early childhood, the delusion of an encapsulated omnipotence, a validation of inseparability, and the oedipal triumph of the child. Her efforts to make herself into the small, endearing, and beautiful little girl she no longer was met the constant reality of her soon-towering height. And the identification with the violent paternal object did not help her separate from her mother, but drove her back to her in an indignant, betrayed, sexualised fury.

Omnipotent defences, of which violence is one, aim to obliterate differences, obviate disillusionment and helplessness, take control. And yet violence lost her the love she craved. Early after the incident with the police, she had come to therapy reporting with great anguish a dream of being 'Saddam Hussein', a dream which she associated to a school trip to the War Museum, and a frightened identification with the violence of Hitler. She was horrified at her own violence, and then she elaborated that Hitler had wanted, like her, to be an artist. Like her! She had wanted to be an artist. Had her mother's partner, asking her about the colour of the walls she would paint, referenced this ambition? She had certainly indicated that Cassie could contribute, but she had also confirmed that it was in her gift, not Cassie's control. Clearly, Cassie was indignant and humiliated. She became violent, a Hitler, a Saddam Hussein, a powerful omnipotent killer in phantasy, and she was frightened of the future. Homicide, like suicide, is an omnipotent action, an illusion of control and power, defending a vulnerability overwhelmed by feelings of helplessness, anger, and confusion. Murderous violence as a potential act, rather than phantasy, enters the adolescent's domain, arriving with the adult body, the aggression as well as sexuality suddenly changing the field of possibility. It was with great sadness, but also with great relief, that Cassie's capacity for guilt and thought entered the therapy, along with a vision of a potential future, a field where omnipotence can be framed, its destructiveness expressed and contained and therefore modified, the field of art. These were early, hopeful times in the therapy.

The framed space (Bleger, 1967; Green, 1999; Milner, 1988) of the psychotherapeutic setting created a holding space (Winnicott, 1971) that opened up a field of representation and thinking that Cassie was able to use creatively. She produced pictures. For example, in one phase, as she studied for GCSE exams, she brought, bound in a thick binder, many coloured drawings of women and costumes, some very accomplished, and including pictures of women of colour – Michelle Obama, for example – along with other drawings of Caucasian women, like her mother, not like her, using the field of drawing to make real the differences and desires she struggled to assimilate. She spoke of this; we both acknowledged the fact that in her notebook there were co-existing pictures of beautiful adult women, white and black. At the same time, it emerged that she could learn; she began to do well at school; poignantly, she went to a tutor who helped her with her mother tongue. She met this woman regularly, on her own, as she met me. She learned, or recovered, something of her mixed cultural background, her early childhood, her first language, and, at the same time, won respect for her mind at school and, at least superficially, at home.

But the trajectory was not straightforward. When she began to do better at school, eventually achieving much higher marks than expected, she was accepted at an ambitious secondary school far away from home, far away then from the small group of friends she actually made of the former acrimonious playground enemies, the school fellows of her first years of treatment, and far away from the therapy that had supported her. And she grew. She was nearing six feet when she suddenly seemed unable to get to sessions on time, pretending in the consulting room that she did not know how to tell time, this asserted as she stared at the clock in the room. I interpreted her sudden aversion to time, her wishing not to know about time and changes in time, and linked it to the periods she did not yet have; she was the only girl left among her friends who had not started her periods. As if invited, her period soon arrived with a surprising immediacy, as if just waiting for the release of an interpretation, and with it, a momentary respite from struggle. This momentary acceptance did not last. As Anna Freud (1937) predicts, we entered another phase, one in which the omnipotence would reassert itself as the panic linked to sexual adulthood intensified. A roller coaster ride of manic and risky behaviour opened up and was exacerbated when her success meant she transferred to a sixth form college that involved hours of travel and a culture much more challenging and less contained than at her previous smaller school. After her periods, after her success in exams, then after this transfer, the noisy business of more wild anxieties, urgent excitements, and aggressive drives barrelled through the frame of the sessions. In addition, the demands of A levels at the new and challenging and distant college provoked forces difficult to tame, the work which

Omnipotence in adolescence 65

she did in art now was too raw, too expressive, for the tame A-level syllabus. And there was a confusion in the demands of the A-level syllabus and the use that had been made of her drawing in therapy.

Cassie moved socially into wider circles, into clubbing, drugs, more violent encounters driven by anxiety, aggression as much as sexual yearning. She went truly out of control. She cut herself several times, a classical omnipotent reaction to the bleeding of menstruation, taking bleeding momentarily back into her control. She cut sessions. She erupted violently at home, where she physically intimidated everyone, including her misogynist and racist grandfather. Gone from her artwork was the abundant catalogue of beautifully dressed women, as well as the generous sharing, the conversation about difference, race. She was an action painter, sculptor, creator, but the aggression refused containment. The omnipotence of the drives (Freud, 1908, 1930) were what she would lean on, manic attempts before terrors of breakdown. At home, her bullying was sometimes rampant. On holiday with her mother and her partner, she found herself strangling herself with her scarves when her mother went off with her partner.

The age of 18 marks an entry into adulthood proper, as registered by, for example, the definitions guiding the National Health Service, but generally also marked by the taking of A-level exams, the end of secondary school. Such a firm definition would not be observed by an adolescent centre, but in Cassie's case, the limits of the psychotherapy contract within an adolescent institution meant that her therapy ended at the age of 18, after five years. I do not know if her acting out, which intensified greatly at the approach of an ending she could not control, might have been ameliorated by an extension of therapy. I think the limits of what psychotherapy could do, even if it were extended, were also informing her behaviour as the therapy ended, and the disillusionment with some kind of idealized result weakened her belief in the setting and what could be achieved (Bleger, 1967). And there was the increasing intensity of a legitimate anguish about race. She needed to find a way to love her blackness, and she was surrounded by whiteness, including her therapist.

As she and I worked, sporadically, towards an ending, Cassie found her way into an auxiliary space to continue, hopefully, with a development that would retrieve her ability to work, reaffirm a space for thinking, play, and independence. Importantly, it would ensure a relation to reality, the fundamental counterbalance to omnipotent phantasy. Cassie found an apprenticeship in a place of work where her boss was young and black, where she would be taken on to be educated to become a stylist, where young women who looked like her held positions of respect. One would be her boss, a place where her creativity, unlike in fine art, where she tried to express the powerful emotions she struggled with, could nonetheless find expression. She would not be omnipotent; she would not even have a blank canvas. She would have to fit in; she would have to observe a schedule; she would have to do menial things as well as be helped to fulfil at least some of her talents. A beautiful young woman, she had a knack for creating beauty. In the hairdressing salon, she found a frame and a setting, which she compromised getting wildly drunk before her first day, therefore not turning up. But she had also found a mentor who identified with her and wanted to help her and let her know that she was committed to helping her. Someone different from her white mother, her mother's white female partner, and her white therapist. Someone who looked more like her. Someone who offered a possibility in reality and one that would develop incrementally. A step towards a future that had an outline and a self-sufficiency, certainly not a field for omnipotent action. And she had found it herself.

References

Bailly, L. (2009). The paternal metaphor: The role of the father in the unconscious. In *Lacan*. Oxford: One World.
Baranger, M., Baranger, W. & Mom, J.M. (1988). The infantile psychic trauma from us to Freud: Pure trauma, retroactivity, and reconstruction. *International Journal of Psychoanalysis*, 68: 113–128.
Bellman, D. (1997). Pre-therapy in working with adolescents. In Laufer, M. (Ed.), *Adolescent Breakdown and Beyond*. London: Karnac, 1997.
Bion, W. (1962). *Learning from Experience*. London: Karnac.
Bleger, J. (1967). Psycho-analysis of the psycho-analytic frame. *International Journal of Psychoanalysis*, 48: 511–519.
Blos, P. (1967). The second individuation process in adolescence. *Psychoanalytic Study of the Child*, 22: 162–186.
Britton, R. (1989). The missing link: Parental sexuality in the Oedipus complex. In *The Oedipus Complex Today*. London: Karnac Books.
Bronstein, C. (2020). Psychosis and psychotic functioning in adolescence. *International Journal of Psychoanalysis*, 101 (1): 136–151.
Cahn, R. (1998). The process of becoming-a-subject in adolescence. In Perret-Catipovic, M. & Ladame, F. (Eds.), *Adolescence and Psychoanalysis*. London: Karnac.
Ferrari, A. (2004). *From the Eclipse of the Body to the Dawn of Thought*. London: Free Association Books.
Freud, A. (1937). *The Ego and the Mechanisms of Defence*, London: Hogarth.
Freud, S. (1895). Studies on hysteria. *Standard Edition*, II: 1–307.
Freud, S. (1905). Three essays on the theory of sexuality. *Standard Edition*, VII: 123–246.
Freud, S. (1908). Civilized sexual ethics and modern nervous illness. *Standard Edition*, IX: 177–204.
Freud, S. (1915). *Instincts and Their Vicissitudes. Standard Edition, XIV*. 117–140.
Freud, S. (1923). *TheEego and the Id. Standard Edition, IXX*. 48–82.
Freud, S. (1930). Civilization and its discontents. *Standard Edition*, XXI: 64–145.
Green, A. (1999). *The Work of the Negative*. London: Free Association Books.
Gutton, P. (1998). The pubertal, its sources and fate. In Perret-Catipovic, M. & Ladame, F. (Eds.), *Adolescence and Psychoanalysis*. London: Karnac.
Klein, M. (1940). Mourning and its relation to manic depressive states. In *Love, Guilt and Reparation*. London: Hogarth, 1975.
Lacan, J. (1953). The function and field of speech and language in psychoanalysis. In *Ecrits: A Selection*. London: Tavistock, 1977.
Ladame, F. & Catipovic, M.P. (1998). Normality and pathology in adolescence. In *Adolescence and Psychoanalysis: The Story and the History*. London: Karnac.

Laufer, M. & Laufer, E. (1984). *Adolescence and Developmental Breakdown*. London: Yale.

Lombardi, R. (2017). Body and mind in adolescence, in body-mind dissociation. In *Psychoanalysis*. New York and London: Routledge.

Mahler, M. (1968). *On Human Symbiosis and the Vicissitudes of Individuation*. New York: International Universities Press.

Milner, M. (1988) The framed gap. In *The Surpressed Madness of Sane Men*. London: New Library of Psychoanalysis.

Money Kyrle, R. (1971). The aim of psychoanalysis. In Meltzer, D. (Ed.), *The Collected Papers of Roger Money Kyrle*. London: Clunie Press, 1978.

Rey, H. (1994). *Universals of Psychoanalysis in the Treatment of Psychotic and Borderline States*. London: Free Association Books.

Segal, H. (1986). Notes on symbol formation. In *The Work of Hannah Segal*. London: Free Association Books.

Solms, M. (2021). *The Hidden Spring*. London: Profile Books.

Williams, G. (1997). The 'no entry' system of defences: Reflections on the assessment of adolescents suffering from eating disorders. In *Internal Landscapes and Foreign Bodies, Eating Disorders, & Other Pathologies*. London: Duckworth.

Winnicott, D.W. (1971). *Playing and Reality*. Tavistock: London.

Chapter 5

Customising the body
From omnipotence to autonomy

Alessandra Lemma

Breasts removed, noses resculpted, breasts augmented. These are all medical interventions, but they are not in the service of restoring a loss of function or curing physical illness. They are pursued in the quest of 'enhancement' or of finding a more hospitable embodied form for the articulation of identity. Some have questioned where such melioristic or 'custom-made' body trends will take us. As clinicians, one reason we are concerned by the drive to modify the body when it is a presenting feature in the patient is that the engineering of mood or self-esteem through bodily changes is often surface deep and does not address the more fundamental disquiet in the psyche. Moreover, altering the 'given' body and redesigning it according to one's specification raises the concern that omnipotent phantasies are fuelled and sustained through an enactment on and through the body.

In this chapter, I focus on psychoanalytic work with patients who are preoccupied with, and deeply distressed by, the appearance of their bodies. They may see 'ugly' in the mirror, or they may see an alien reflection that is not experienced as 'me'. This may lead them to undertake cosmetic and surgical procedures to embellish the body or to align the body with their subjective sense of transgender identity. This clinical work has taken place during a socio-cultural period of unprecedented technological and medical advances that have turned us ever more into specular objects and made it comparatively easier access to the 'tools' to change our bodies.

The culture of bodily enhancement and customisation provokes debate and concern. Enhancement is about the quest for more, for better, sometimes for 'the best'. Some philosophers caution that 'playing God' undermines core human values and risks distorting human nature (e.g., Sandel, 2007). There is a concern that easy pleasures will corrupt us and that there is nothing like the confrontation with loss and guilt to make us stronger and wiser. Psychoanalysts, too, are predisposed to view the culture of body modification with some considerable suspicion, squarely focusing on the risks associated with the enactment of an omnipotent phantasy. I share this concern in many cases, as I will illustrate through my work with a patient who pursued cosmetic surgery. However, in this chapter, I also want to consider a) that there are developmentally appropriate omnipotent phantasies and b) that there are some individuals for whom the modification of the body represents their best possible adaptation. In such cases, I suggest that the decision to modify the body may be understood as a 'cognisant adaptation' because it is not based on an unconscious enactment. Drawing on both psychoanalysis and applied ethics, I conclude by briefly outlining a clinical-ethical framework for working with patients whose primary presentation is their drive to modify the appearance of the body.

The perfect match and self-made phantasies

For some patients, the pursuit of body modification is fuelled by an omnipotent phantasy. When I refer to omnipotence, I am working to the definition by Almond: 'Omnipotence is a subjective state – a sense of complete control and influence – that the individual tries to bring about through action and/or fantasy' (2005: 3). Furthermore, omnipotence, as I use the term here, denotes a state of mind that thrives on idealisation of the self (i.e., grandiosity) and on denigration of the other (i.e., sadism). With respect to body modification, this can take two forms: the perfect match phantasy and the self-made phantasy (Lemma, 2010). In the *perfect match phantasy*, the body modification serves the function of creating the perfect, ideal body that, in phantasy, will guarantee the object's love and desire. Whereas the perfect match phantasy concerns the *fusion* of an idealised self with an idealised object, the *self-made phantasy* expresses an *envious attack* on the object. Here, the object's independence is intolerable, and a profound grievance towards the object fuels the envy. The individual retreats into phantasising that it can create itself, thereby circumventing the object and, hence, any experience of dependency. Through modification of the given body, the individual creates the illusion that all ties to the object are severed. The need to sever ties might be due to the experience of an object that is felt to be unavailable or rejecting or whose separateness is experienced as intolerable.

Circumventing the reality of one's origins inevitably also entails a denial of the reality of the parental couple. The attack on the parental couple is implicit in the self-made phantasy. In many of these cases, it is indeed possible to discern the absence of what Birksted-Breen (1996) refers to as the 'penis-as-link': that is, the absence of the linking and structuring role of the knowledge that mother and father are linked and form a creative couple. When all is going well developmentally, acceptance of this reality allows the individual to come to terms with the fact of both difference and complementarity and, hence, to accept her own insufficiency as well as her need for the other. However, a pathological response to this reality is found in the enactment, through the modification of the body, of a phantasy that reassures the self of its omnipotence and self-sufficiency. This psychic position might well be termed 'phallic' in the sense that being the phallus represents a psychic state of complete self-sufficiency and, hence, is an attack on otherness and functions as a defence against dependency.

Decisions to modify the body that are driven by an omnipotent state of mind are typically very unstable and unlikely to yield positive outcomes for the individual, as I will illustrate through my work with Ms A., whom I saw for three times weekly psychoanalytic therapy, face-to-face, over a period of five years.

The case of Ms A.

Ms A. was a very attractive, meticulously groomed woman in her late fifties. She was referred for severe depression that began just as her divorce was finalised after several years of an acrimonious legal battle. Her husband had left her for a younger woman, and Ms A. had been determined to fight him. The hatred she felt for him and the fight of the divorce, had staved off the latent depression, but once it was all finalised, she collapsed. She felt hopeless about the possibility of meeting anyone else given her age, and she became suicidal, requiring admission to hospital.

A depressed, aggrieved state enveloped Ms A. I struggled to engage her. At first, the sessions seemed like a rerun of the legal battle. She spared no one in the process: her husband had betrayed her; her daughter had abandoned her to live abroad; her friends had deserted her; her body was failing her. It was not long before I, too, was added to this list of disappointments and recriminations.

As I explored her early childhood, Ms A. described distant relationships with both her parents. Her mother was felt to have been 'devoted' to her father and a socialite for whom appearances mattered. Her father, too, had also been 'devoted' to her mother. I sensed that she had felt bitterly excluded by the parental couple.

Ms A.'s desperate state of mind was palpable. She was tormented by thoughts of her husband with his new younger wife. Part of the torment was fuelled by the dominant version in her mind of the couple: for example, she imagined them mocking her as they enjoyed luxurious holidays together. She would go over such phantasies in her mind again and again, and torture both herself and the couple with her hatred in the process.

I would now like to give some excerpts from three sessions spanning a three-week period during which time she resolved to pursue surgery on her eyes.

After a few months in therapy, Ms A. arrived for her last session of the week in a very disgruntled state of mind. She pointed to her eyes and said: 'Look, what *she* has done!' (her emphasis).

I was confused as I could not really see anything untoward. I said nothing. I felt Ms A. stiffen in her posture, and I recognised in myself the by-then-familiar feeling that I had somehow disappointed her. I was mindful, too, that this was a Friday session and that the weekend break often stirred her rage towards me, turning me into someone who did something 'bad' to her by exposing her need for me.

Ms A. begrudgingly explained to me that she had been for her Botox injections (she had been having Botox every four months approximately, though I had not known this before) and that the female doctor who had administered the injections had done this wrong. Now her eyelids were droopy. As she spoke, she was very angry and told me that she was thinking of suing the doctor. She contrasted the failings of this doctor with the 'mastery' of the cosmetic surgeon who had performed a face lift on her when she was in her early forties.

I said that she seemed to feel not only angry but also deeply humiliated by what had happened, and she now comforted herself with the possibility of exposing this doctor for *her* failure.

Ms A. angrily replied: 'Words can never make me feel better'. She added that the only comfort she had ever gotten was from looking good. It was then that she told me for the first time about her extensive reliance on all manner of cosmetic procedures, virtually on a weekly basis (for example, dermabrasion, Botox, facials, teeth whitening).

By the following Monday session, Ms A. was calmer, yet very detached, and she announced, casually, that she would be missing two or three weeks the following month as she had booked herself in for a blepharoplasty (to rectify drooping eyelids).

As she spoke about the surgery, this had the quality of a trance-like state: she told me that the surgeon was '*the best*'; his waiting list was closed, but he made an exception *for her*; the operation was not dangerous, 'no different to having some tooth fillings', she said; and she had made sure she would get the most senior anesthetist so she would feel '*no pain*'.

I eventually said that she was letting me know she now felt very safe in a part of her mind where she could rely on feeling special, where she would be taken care of by doctors who were devoted to her. In this place, she no longer felt exposed and humiliated as she had done after her Botox injections on the Friday. I added that I thought the weekend break had also left her feeling exposed to her need for me, for which she hated me, and that she was now making it clear to me that she did not need me.

Following a brief pause, Ms A. replied that that there was nothing really for us to talk about. She was clear that the surgery was something she had to do, and she reverted to talking about the surgeon and how experienced he was.

It proved impossible to engage Ms A. in thinking with me about the meaning for her of the proposed surgery and what was happening transferentially. I experienced her to be so safely tucked inside a narcissistic cocoon that the other person (me) ceased to exist. Later in the same week, Ms A. reported this dream:

> I can see the beach. I am swimming in calm waters. The sea is clear and beautiful. I can see beautiful, colourful fish swimming underneath me. The sea is warm, like a blanket. And then suddenly I can hear terrible screams, and a little girl is drowning.

Ms A. reluctantly responded to my interest in her associations to this dream by saying that the sea reminded her of a beach her parents loved. They would go there on holiday at least once per year. They were both keen swimmers and would swim far out, leaving her behind on the beach to play on her own. She was then silent and then remarked that she felt good today because the weather outside was warm.

I took up how, in the dream, she felt very safe, tucked under a warm sea blanket but that this was only a part of the story: there was also a very frightened little girl screaming for help.

Ms A. then added that the best thing about the dream had been the way she had felt 'light' and 'at peace in my body'.

I said that it seemed very hard to listen to the little girl's screams. Ms A. replied that the little girl struck her as 'very small', and then she pointedly added that she was not actually 'screaming'.

I felt very dismissed by her tone, as if I was making too much of the girl's struggle to remain afloat, and yet I was quite sure that Ms A. had herself used the words 'terrible screams'. I said that it seemed imperative that neither of us paid attention to the fact that a little girl was drowning and was not being rescued.

Ms A. casually replied that fear had to be 'overcome, not succumbed to', and with that statement, I felt she bolted the final lock and shut me out. She cancelled the following session, interestingly due to a sore throat, which left me wondering about the drowning girl whose screams had been so hard to hear in the session.

In the first session of the following week, Ms A. seemed more agitated and indicated that the weekend had been stressful because her daughter was being 'difficult'. Ms A. said that her daughter 'owed' her a visit, and she berated her daughter for not suggesting that she would come over to see her. She then told me this dream:

> I am shopping in [a country] I think. . . . I see this beautiful fur coat. It's on sale . . . half price, and I tell my husband that it's a real bargain. My husband says I have one already; why do I need another? . . . And then he says, 'It's just another scam to get people to buy things they don't need'. I feel terrible. It's so soft, and I feel cold, but he simply doesn't understand. He leaves the shop. . . . He hates shopping. I stay, and the shop assistant is no longer there, and I just take the coat and run out with it. The alarm starts ringing, and there is so much noise. I start to feel dizzy . . . can't walk. . . . I fall over, I think . . . then I wake up in the dream and I am in a strange place I don't recognise. I feel sweat pouring down my face, but I say to myself – you are not there anymore.

As she recounted this dream, Ms A. became very anxious and distressed. I observed how anxious she seemed. I said that she was letting me know how urgently she needed to wrap herself up in a luxurious state of mind where she would command the devotion that she felt no one was prepared to give her. And yet, I added, a part of her recognised that the fur coat was a kind of scam to get her to buy into something that was not what she really needs. I then linked this to her upcoming blepharoplasty.

Ms A. went on to say that there were times when she looked at photographs of how she used to be when she was younger, and all she could see was a very depressed face – nothing beautiful about it. She now had nothing left – her life was over – why not make herself feel better at least in the only way she knew how to?

I said that my thoughts about her dream had left her feeling exposed to this very depressed, damaged part of her, and she was now saying to me: 'How could you do this; can't you see this is all I have?'

I will not go into this session further, but it is worth noting that when Ms A. resumed talking, I felt more connected to her than I had done for some weeks. Significantly too, I thought, rather than hiding away from me during the weeks' convalescing post-surgery (which had been her plan), in the following session she asked me if she could still attend her sessions. I saw her, in fact, shortly after the operation, her face bruised and swollen.

From the start of my work with Ms A., I felt that she demanded absolute 'devotion'. Anything short of that left her feeling bitterly disappointed, as if she was thrust back into an intolerable Oedipal scenario in her mind in which a devoted, passionate couple shamefully excluded her. This gratifying union, from which she felt so brutally rejected, was where she desired to be and what she felt was owed to her. Significantly, she had never enjoyed her mother's positive cathexis of her bodily self: her own appearance had been criticised by the mother who always seemed to feel that the daughter could 'look better'.

The 'failed' Botox left Ms A. feeling raw and exposed to the anticipated harsh, mocking glare of an excited couple she felt was forever excluding her. She managed this humiliation by phantasising about suing the doctor over whom she now triumphed and then resolving to modify a part of her body: not insignificantly, perhaps, her eyes. Once she had taken this decision and conjured up the image in her mind of how her eyes would look, in the transference, I was made to feel insufficient (as she often felt), unlike the other doctors who were 'the best'. Cocooned in her idealised couple with the surgeon and now able to make herself look as she wished to her specification, Ms A. reversed her humiliation and triumphed over the object.

The surgery promised Ms A. an all-enveloping, unbroken psychical skin. She now felt less vulnerable, more in control and, crucially, she felt desirable. The idealisation of the psychic system, of which the omnipotent phantasy is a core component, was central to her psychic equilibrium. This was apparent in the way she configured the events to come in her mind and presented them to me: the surgeon was 'the best', she was special, and she was safe (she would feel no pain, she said). She felt omnipotent: she could imagine an idealised object looking at an ideal version of her (i.e., the perfect match phantasy), and she could now create this experience without my help (i.e., the self-made phantasy).

The anticipated surgery sustained her. It was important not simply in terms of its promised outcome (i.e., she would look so much better) but also in terms of the *process of transformation* itself: she was special, and she was, in her mind, elevated as the special patient who accessed the best surgeon, and she would be taken care of – unlike the experience of being my patient, shut out of my office in between sessions. For Ms A., in that moment, the surgery provided her with an opportunity to avail herself of the loving gaze and touch of a surgeon/father/mother who would make beautiful her felt-to-be-ugly self and so guarantee that she would not be overlooked. Importantly, she was fully in control of this, thereby protecting her from an intolerable experience of smallness and dependency. The decision to modify the body – a 'cure' she could access without any intervention from me – provided her with an experience of power in relation to me and enabled her to deny any dependency on me.

Omnipotence or omnipotentiality: A reading of Luca Guadagnino's (2020) We Are Who We Are (HBO)

Ms A.'s case illustrates that in cases where there has been an undercathexis of the bodily self by the (m)other, there may be not just the yearning for an idealised mother who will look at the self with admiring, loving eyes, but also an accompanying sense of grievance about the felt deprivation and, hence, a need to omnipotently triumph over the object. Omnipotent action, such as Ms A's decision to have cosmetic surgery, may create a temporary sense of superiority, power, and triumph over the object. However, in some cases, omnipotent action creates a sense of potentially broadened efficacy (Novick and Novick, 2005) that is adaptive and needs to be distinguished from the toxic omnipotence I have just described. The adolescent state of mind provides the best example of this, by far.

Adolescence is a developmental phase during which the conviction that anything is possible, right here, right now, and that this is down to me and only me illustrates the operation of an omnipotent state of mind. Indeed, the adolescent state reads like a checklist for narcissistic pathology, but as Waddell (2006) points out, its fluidity and the experimentation that accompanies it caution us to view this kind of narcissism and the omnipotence that it exposes somewhat differently. The appreciation of the 'culture of experimentation' (Waddell, 2006) that characterises the adolescent organisation was well captured earlier by Pumpian-Mindlin's (1969) concept of *omnipotentiality*. Omnipotentiality refers to the developmentally appropriate experimentation through the extension of one's possibilities and limits (mental and physical): it is a 'trying on for size' of different versions of one's self.

Omnipotentiality is a helpful way of understanding what drives body modification in some individuals, particularly during adolescence and early adulthood. Here, the intention to modify the body is not in the service of triumphing over the other, but rather, it denotes a developmentally necessary drive to differentiate from the object and to articulate identity. Decisions to modify the body that are underpinned by this state of mind require appreciation of the developmentally appropriate, fluid nature of the underlying intentionality, even when the 'means' chosen for the purpose of self-definition may carry risks. If the disregard for reality or for the object that characterises this state may be considered 'aggressive', this is about a ruthless focus on the self rather than an act of violence or sadism towards the object.

Luca Guadagnino's (2020) coming-of-age TV drama, *We Are Who We Are*, is possibly one of the best portraits of omnipotentiality with all the attendant potential and risks. I will use this as a way of illustrating the difference between omnipotence and omnipotentiality. Set in 2016, the drama follows a group of American teenagers growing up on a US military base in Chioggia near Venice. The narrative focuses mostly on the friendship between Fraser and Caitlin. Fourteen-year-old Fraser is a compelling mixture of intelligence, social awkwardness, and slavery to fashion. He is drawn to Caitlin, the seemingly self-confident daughter of one of the American lieutenants. At first, she is irritated by the attention Fraser gives her, but when Fraser gifts her two items of male clothing, she realises he is the only one who understands that she is wrestling at the gates of her assigned gender.

Deploying the ephemera of summer, from the rumpled T-shirts on the sand to the hastily shed flip-flops, Guadagnino details the rapidity of adolescent identifications and their shedding. As winter sets in, the intoxication of being able to push the body to its limits and to defy any binary gender categorisations is brutally shattered by the news that a former member of the teenagers' group has died in action in Afghanistan. This loss acts as a sobering reminder that the body may be reconfigured in many ways, but its ultimate limits cannot be denied. The brutal reality of death – of a young person dying well before their time – stands in stark contrast to the omnipotence the teenagers have been thriving on up until that point.

Despite its declarative title, *We Are Who We Are* presents its characters in flux, trying on and shrugging off different identities in search of their authentic selves. Fraser and Caitlin do this primarily though the modification and presentation of their bodies, and this experimentation seems essential and appropriate. As Pumpian-Mindlin noted:

> The free exercise of this omnipotentiality is a necessary and salutary occurrence in youth. The wider the range of exploration, the more adequately prepared is the youth to relinquish his omnipotential strivings.
>
> (1969: 224)

Fraser's tufty peroxide hair, chipping black nail varnish, outlandish clothes, and attraction to a male soldier could be read as a rejection of heterosexuality, and yet he defies all labels. As does Caitlin. She doesn't enjoy kissing her boyfriend but tries to do so because she thinks she ought to. When a friend pulls Caitlin to one side to offer her some sanitaryware as she emerges from the sea, blood streaming down her thigh, Caitlin looks perplexed. She cleans herself with a tissue that she then carefully buries in the sand, as if she needs to quite literally bury this new sign of the biological sex that she cannot yet integrate into her representation of her body in her mind.

Beyond the confines of the army barracks, Caitlin experiments secretly with a version of herself as 'Harper'. She tucks her long trademark hair into a cap and flirts with a local Italian girl, exhilarated when she 'passes' as a boy. This might lead us to conclude that she is gender-fluid, but significantly, labels don't appear to have currency in Guadagnino's narrative – in fact, when Caitlin, breasts in a binder and with a glued-on moustache, is asked if she is a 'transman', she seems confused as if she is really not sure who she is. It is clear that a label is not going to solve this problem.

Fraser, wise through books and the internet, is also palpably ill at ease in his body. As for his sexuality, he has only ever kissed a mirror (literally) – a poignant illustration of how his intellectual all-knowingness and omnipotence shelters a body that cannot yet be receptive to the other but can only relate to its own mirror image. It is clear that Fraser hasn't figured out his own sexuality yet, and he explores it by proxy through assisting Caitlin's modification of her own body. He helps her shave her long hair and glue hair shavings to her upper lip. In one particularly intimate scene, she stands close behind him while he urinates, using his body as a surrogate for the one she thinks she might prefer. As she holds his penis, she expresses how much she enjoys this experience.

Avoiding any judgement, Guadagnino steers a fine line between supporting experimentation and committing the body to more permanent changes. Caitlin is encouraged by Fraser's mother to see the army base's endocrinologist and therapist to discuss her 'transness'. We see Caitlin at first espousing this offer with some relief that she is finally understood, only to later reject this decision, literally flushing it down the toilet as she disposes of the leaflet given to her for the appointment.

Guadagnino uses the instability of the parents' military careers – at any moment, they will have to uproot and start over or go to war – to signal how the adolescents' lives are governed by impermanence. This impending displacement fuels their *carpe diem* spirit. But it is also a nod to how the urgent sense of possibility – the adolescent omnipotent grasping at all possible identities – can also be just as quickly discarded and replaced by another version that seems better fitting.

In my work with transgender adolescents – who represent by far the most significant increase in referrals in my practice in the past eight years – I am confronted daily with versions of Fraser and Caitlin. Some of these young people go on to socially and/or medically transition, and the body is modified in significant ways. In some cases, this seems to provide a stable adaptation. By contrast, others fervently declare themselves to be 'trans', but in the therapeutic work, it is their experience of puberty and sexuality as traumatic that emerges over time as central to understanding why they have turned to the modification of the body to create an illusion of bodily omnipotence. In these cases, the trauma seems to be managed through a precarious 'trans' identification (Lemma, 2018), an unshakeable omnipotent belief that 'I can control this body and do what I want with it'. Whilst this state of mind is also present in omnipotentiality, it is the *rigidity* of the psychic omnipotent position that distinguishes it from omnipotentiality. Whereas the characters in Guadagnino's drama experiment with their bodies, the drama illustrates that such experimentation, whilst carried out with conviction, does not lead to relentlessly pursuing one course of action on the body.

The state of omnipotentiality is about the importance of experimentation without *permanent commitment* to any one option. Here, omnipotent phantasies of the modification of the body are flirted with and provide the developmentally necessary possibility of experimenting with how one feels in bodies that are carefully customised. A premature foreclosure of this experimentation through permanent bodily modifications may inhibit this exploration and unwittingly pressurise the young person to 'commit' before they can try on for size a few more versions of who they feel they are/want to be. Striking the right balance between supporting the 'potential' in omnipotentiality and protecting the individual from destructive enactments through the body can be very challenging and is not always successfully achieved. This challenge is not restricted to work with adolescents.

Body modification as adaptation to trauma

I now want to consider yet another function of body modification: namely, those cases in which the modification of the body is neither in the service of experimenting with so-called 'potentiality' nor can be conceptually reduced to the enactment of an omnipotent phantasy. Rather, it represents an individual's best adaptation post-trauma in an 'all things considered' sense. I will illustrate this briefly with work with a transgender patient, but I am not presenting this as an explanation of transgender identification, which is far more variegated in its underlying meanings and functions (Lemma, in press).

In my work with some patients who are intent on modifying the body, this decision appears to be very clearly connected to traumatic events in childhood. The psychoanalytic inclination is to address the trauma in the hope that this might relieve the pressure to act on the body. Addressing the trauma is essential. However, in some cases, as I will briefly illustrate through my work with Kay, the therapist is challenged to consider that insight may not be sufficient to render obsolete the need to modify the body. Or, to frame this differently, insight provides the patient with a foundation for determining whether the modification of the body offers something of value to them – a value that can only be assessed relative to the individual's value system and psychological needs.

Kay, then in her mid-twenties, first came to see me because she wanted to undergo a double mastectomy so as to align her natal female body with her subjective sense of transgender identity. Kay was depressed and struggling in many aspects of her life. She detailed a long history of significant discomfort in her body, feeling that since she was a child, she had disliked, as she put it, her 'feminine form'. She described herself as gender-fluid and said that she had always wished that she had been born a boy. Over time Kay became insightful about the origins of her bodily discomfort and was able to connect it to traumatic events in her childhood. In therapy, she explored the motivations for her wish for surgery, recognising that some people might view it as an extreme measure, but for her, it felt 'right'. She felt that the surgery would help her feel 'more myself' in her body.

For Kay, the image of herself with a flat chest made her feel 'better' – she felt more confident and 'more me'. She could see that if she had not had the childhood she had, she might have felt differently, but she thought this was beside the point: her past had shaped not only what she did not like (her breasts) but also what she preferred (to be flat chested and to look androgynous). She was clear about the risks of surgery and that she could potentially regret this, but for her, these were risks worth taking.

After over two years of twice-weekly psychotherapy, Kay resolved to pursue a double mastectomy. Kay said that she had no doubts that pursuing surgery was the right decision for her. She was aware, she said, that I seemed committed to helping her to go on exploring this decision, but as far as she was concerned, she had spent two years doing this, and her decision remained the same. She said that she now felt better overall. She was satisfied that we had addressed her motivations from 'every possible angle'. I detected some exasperation on her part with what she (accurately) perceived to be my bias towards more exploration.

As I reflected on my work with Kay, I was starkly confronted with how I had been in the sway of my need to rescue her from a decision that *I* evidently struggled with. Kay challenged me to view her decision to pursue surgery as denoting what I can best describe as a *cognisant adaptation* to who she felt herself to be and aspired to be, given her history. Kay was meaningfully connected to her history of trauma and how this shaped her relationship to her body. Even so, in her mind, the representation of her flat-chested body was one that made her feel safe and confident, and it was therefore aspired to. The projected bodily representation of the 'body-to-be' (a flat-chested body that she felt would not signal 'sexy woman', but 'strong'), rather than the 'body that holds the memory' (a visibly woman's body, for Kay) had been an essential and adaptive defence to the traumatic circumstances in early childhood.

This type of clinical presentation distinguishes itself from a traumatic adaptation in which the patient is unaware of the ongoing impact of the trauma on their decisions. By contrast, Kay illustrates how a patient can have insight into the links between the trauma and the desire to modify the body (i.e., not be in denial) and yet resolve to pursue the modification of the body. Another patient might well have chosen to persevere with more exploration, but the fact that Kay chose surgery, cognisant of her own history and of the risks associated with her choice, challenges us to recognise that an individual can make an informed choice about an imagined bodily form that bolsters their feelings of safety and preserves their adaptation in the outside world such that surgery is, for them, a price worth paying. Kay's case illustrates how, despite the reduction of the original conflict that brought the traumatic adaptation into being, defences that were once essential to psychic survival may persist and support a good-enough adaptation in external reality (Joffe and Sandler, 1968). Understanding this difference clinically is important.

If my work with Kay had stopped at the time that she resolved to pursue surgery, I suspect that I would still be wondering if Kay had made the best possible decision *for her* or whether I had simply not been able to help her enough. However, Kay stayed in therapy for another four years post-surgery. I could observe that the surgery did help her feel at home in her body and accommodate its history. She was able to finally enjoy a close sexual relationship and be more comfortable in group situations, and she developed a fulfilling professional career.

Faced with patients who want to modify their bodies in more or less extreme ways, it is helpful to keep in mind that what the therapist privileges in their view about what makes a life go well may be at odds with the patient's view. Changing the body does not necessarily entail denial or omnipotent triumph over the internal object relationships. For Kay, changing the body was a way of adapting to her history, not denying it, and the therapy helped her reach a stage when she was able to meaningfully consent to the medical intervention she sought.

Of course, adaptation could take a very different form, but then we would be talking about someone other than Kay. This is the key point: we have to engage with each patient singularly and without a pre-ordained outcome at the back of our minds. At its best, that is how psychoanalysis is oriented. But I have observed in myself and in colleagues that decisions by the patient to change the so-called given body can be provocative, confronting the analyst with a tension between their values and definition of psychic health and the patient's desires and values. The risk is then that the words, values, and intentions of the patient in the service of articulating a viable identity are not given the same weight as those of the analyst.

Conclusion: Towards psychoanalysis as an ethics of autonomy

It is difficult to think and to write about the body and its sometimes extreme, sometimes violent modification without somehow implying that there is a normative relationship to the body from which only a few individuals deviate. Yet psychically, there may be no difference between the individual who has cosmetic surgery and the one who 'only' invests in anti-ageing creams. It is the underlying phantasy that will either distinguish them or reveal that even if the means differ, the psychic ends are shared. The psychic investment that we have in our body, its form, and its appearance is key to understanding the subjective experience of embodiment. The body is the primary site of inscription and meaning arising from external forces as well as internal, unconscious ones.

In an era when enhancement and modification of the body are commonplace, the question of what changing the body (or not) means psychically is inescapable.

Our perception of human limits and capacities is now problematised. Treating body parts as mere unwanted contingencies or using the modification of the body as a means to reinvent ourselves invites us to consider whether the underlying driver is an omnipotent phantasy. The case of Ms A illustrates that compromising awareness of our suffering through omnipotent solutions can lead to acting on the body that ultimately only creates further suffering. However, I have suggested that consideration of omnipotentiality during adolescence helpfully reminds us that there is a developmentally appropriate omnipotence. I have further suggested that the case of Kay sheds light on how, for some individuals, the modification of the body is not necessarily an enactment of an omnipotent phantasy but may be a cognisant adaptation that enhances well-being. Embodiment is a challenge for us all, and for some patients, this challenge requires a modification of the given body that facilitates an adaptation, not based on denial but rather based on a realistic assessment of who they are, of their resilience, and of what they desire going forwards.

Psychoanalysis is principally an ethics of renunciation. Notwithstanding important nuances across theorists, the analytic notion of health is rooted in the importance of delaying (e.g., pleasure), of giving up, of accepting our ultimate helplessness and the reality of loss. This orients the analyst in a very particular way to requests for modifying the body. From this vantage point, enhancement and modification of the given (healthy) body, in whatever form, can only be viewed suspiciously at first. Whilst a patient may well be deluded or in the grip of an omnipotent organisation when they seek to modify the body, I have suggested in this chapter that this is not invariably so. Although Kay's case is not, in my view, representative of the majority of the patients who seek significant forms of body modification, the exceptions are always very instructive.

My work with adult transgender patients in particular has prompted me to reflect more broadly about what position may be most helpful when working in this highly complex and emotional area for both patient and analyst. No doubt, other analysts would reach different conclusions or positions. For me, the therapeutic journey with patients who feel the need to modify their bodies through surgery has focalised that the primary aim of analytic work lies not in any predetermined outcome congruent with the analyst's definition of psychic health, but in the protection of the analytic space so that the patient can discover the unconscious determinants of their choice(s). This provides the foundations for a more realistic assessment of whether their decision to modify the body and the risks/costs associated with it are worth taking. This enhances their autonomy in relation to the choice (or not) to modify the body (Lemma and Savulescu, submitted).

How does this relate to the original concern in this chapter about omnipotence? I suggest that working with patients who modify their bodies invites consideration of omnipotence from the standpoint of autonomy: when we are in the grip of omnipotence, we are not able to function autonomously. This is because an omnipotent state of mind is not rooted in reality. Autonomous functioning requires that we have access to a realistic appraisal of the internal and external influences that bear on what we think we want for ourselves (Lemma and Savulescu, submitted). This evaluation requires access to both conscious and unconscious 'facts' (i.e., possible *unconscious* drivers). Once these unconscious influences become objects of conscious reflection, we can take steps to reduce or accommodate their effect on our behaviour and decisions. Although unconscious factors pose a threat to autonomy, the more we understand the extent to which we *are* unconsciously motivated and influenced, the better equipped we are to function autonomously. Yet, as Kay helped me understand, functioning autonomously *may* result in decisions to modify the body that are not inevitably driven by omnipotence but represent a more viable, even 'better', way to live for the individual.

References

Almond, R. (2005). Omnipotence and power. In Ellmann, C. & Reppen, J. (Eds.), *Omnipotent Fantasies and the Vulnerable Self*. New York: Jason Aronson.

Birksted-Breed, D. (1996). Phallus, penis and mental space. *International Journal of Psycho-Analysis*, 77: 649–657.

Joffe, W. & Sandler, J. (1968). Comments on the psychoanalytic psychology of adaptation, with special reference to the role of affects and the representational world. *International Journal of Psycho-Analysis*, 49: 445–454.

Lemma, A. (2010). *Under the Skin: A Psychoanalytic Study of Body Modification*. London: Routledge.

Lemma, A. (2018). Transitory identities: Some psychoanalytic reflections on transgender identities. *International Journal of Psychoanalysis*, 99 (5): 1089–1106.

Lemma, A. (in press). *Transgender Identities: A Contemporary Introduction*. London: Routledge.

Lemma, A. & Savulescu, J. (submitted). *To Be, Or Not to Be? The Role of the Unconscious in Transgender Transitioning: Identity, Autonomy and Well-Being*.

Novick, J. & Novick, K. (2005). Omnipotence: Pathology and resistance. In Ellmann, C. & Reppen, J. (Eds.), *Omnipotent fantasies and the vulnerable self*. New York: Jason Aronson.

Pumpian-Mindlin, E. (1969). Vicissitudes of infantile omnipotence. *Psychoanalytic Study of the Child*, 24 (1): 213–226.

Sandel, M.J. (2007). *The Case Against Perfection: Ethics in the Age of Genetic Engineering*. Cambridge, MA: The Belknap Press of Harvard University Press.

Waddell, M. (2006). Narcissism – an adolescent disorder? *Journal of Child Psychotherapy*, 32 (1): 21–34.

In the adult . . .

Chapter 6

On three forms of thinking

Magical thinking, dream thinking, and transformative thinking

Thomas H. Ogden

In broad strokes, the current era of psychoanalysis might be thought of as the era of thinking about thinking. It seems to me that many of the most interesting and generative questions with which analysts are currently working have less to do with the symbolic content of dreams, associations, play, and other behavior and more to do with what work we do psychically with our lived experience. In other words, our attention as analytic clinicians and analytic theorists has been increasingly focused on *the way* a person thinks, as opposed to *what* he thinks. To my mind, the two most important contributors to this movement in psychoanalysis are Winnicott, who attended more to the capacity for playing than to the symbolic content of play, and Bion, who explored in his writing the process of dreaming/thinking far more extensively than he discussed the symbolic meanings of dreams and associations.

In this chapter, I will demonstrate some of the ways in which this shift in emphasis from symbolic content to thought process has altered the ways I approach my analytic work.

I conceive of the three forms of thinking that I will be discussing – magical thinking, dream thinking, and transformative thinking – as coexisting, mutually creating, preserving, and negating aspects of every experience of thinking. None of these forms of thinking is ever encountered in pure form.[1] Neither is there a linear relationship among these forms of thinking, such as a "progression" from magical thinking to dream thinking. Rather, I see these forms of thinking as standing in dialectical tension with one another, just as I view the relationship between the conscious and unconscious mind; the paranoid-schizoid, the depressive, and the autistic-contiguous positions (Klein, 1946; Ogden, 1989); the psychotic and the nonpsychotic parts of the personality (Bion, 1957); the basic assumption groups and the work group (Bion, 1959); the container and the contained (Bion, 1970); primary and secondary process thinking (Freud, 1911); and so on. Moreover, none of these forms of thinking is a single, unitary way of thinking; rather, each "form of thinking" represents a rather wide spectrum of ways of thinking. The particular variation of the form of thinking that an individual may employ is always in flux and depends on his level of psychological maturity, the intrapsychic and interpersonal emotional context of the moment, cultural factors, and so forth.

DOI: 10.4324/9781003185192-10

The forms of thinking on which I will focus by no means encompass the entire spectrum of ways of thinking. For example, I will not address operational thinking (de M'Uzan, 1984, 2003), autistic thinking (Tustin, 1981), psychic foreclosure (McDougall, 1984), or "phantasy in the body" (Gaddini, 1969), to name only a few.

In order to provide a sense of the trajectory of this chapter, I will briefly introduce the three forms of thinking before delving into each clinically and theoretically. (In the tradition of Bion, when I speak of thinking, I am always referring to thinking and feeling.) I use the term *magical thinking* to refer to thinking that relies on omnipotent fantasy to create a psychic reality that the individual experiences as "more real" than external reality – for example, as seen in the use of the manic defense. Such thinking substitutes invented reality for actual external reality, thereby maintaining the existing structure of the internal world. Moreover, magical thinking subverts the opportunity to learn from one's lived experience with real external objects. The psychological cost paid by the individual for his reliance on magical thinking is a practical one: magical thinking does not work in the sense that nothing can be built on it except for additional layers of magical constructions.

I use the term *dream thinking* to refer to the thinking we do in the process of dreaming. It is our most profound form of thinking, which continues both while we are asleep and in waking life. Though it is primarily an unconscious mental activity, it acts in concert with preconscious and conscious thinking. In dream thinking, one views and attributes meaning to experience simultaneously from multiple vantage points: for example, from the perspectives of primary and of secondary process thinking, of the container and of the contained, of the infantile self and of the mature self, and so on (Bion, 1962a; Grotstein, 2009). Dream thinking generates genuine psychological growth. Such thinking may be done on one's own, but a point is inevitably reached beyond which one needs another person with whom to think/dream one's most deeply troubling emotional experience.

The third of the forms of thinking that I will discuss, *transformative thinking*, is a form of dream thinking that involves a radical alteration of the terms by which one orders one's experience: one transcends the categories of meaning that have previously been felt to be the only possible categories with which to organize one's experience. In transformative thinking, one creates new ways of ordering experience in which not only new meanings but also new types of feeling, forms of object relatedness, and qualities of emotional and bodily aliveness are generated. Such a fundamental change in one's way of thinking and experiencing is more striking in work with severely disturbed patients but occurs in work with the full spectrum of patients.

In the course of the discussion that follows, I will present clinical examples that illustrate some of the ways in which conceptualizing forms of thinking in the ways I have described is of value to me in talking with myself – and, at times, with the patient – about what I think is occurring in the analytic relationship and in other sectors of the patient's internal life and life in the world.

Magical thinking

Beginning with Freud (1909, 1913), omnipotent thought has been a well-established concept in psychoanalytic theory. Freud (1913) credits the Rat Man with coining the term *omnipotence of thought* (p. 85). I will make a few observations that capture something of my sense of the differences between magical thinking and the other two forms of thinking that I explore in this chapter.

Magical thinking has one purpose and one purpose only: to evade facing the truth of one's internal and external experience. The method employed to achieve this end is the creation of a state of mind in which the individual believes that he creates the reality in which he and others live. Under such circumstances, psychic reality eclipses external reality: reality is "the reality not of experience but of thought" (Freud, 1913: 86). Consequently, emotional surprise and encounters with the unexpected are, as much as possible, foreclosed. In the extreme, when the individual fears that the integrity of the self is in danger, he may defend himself by means of virtually all-encompassing omnipotent fantasies that so disconnect him from external reality that his thinking becomes delusional and/or hallucinatory. In this psychological state, the individual is unable to learn from experience and incapable of distinguishing between being awake and being asleep (Bion, 1962a): i.e., he is psychotic.

To the degree that psychic reality eclipses external reality, there is a progressive deterioration of the individual's capacity to differentiate dreaming and perceiving, symbol and symbolized. As a result, consciousness itself (self-awareness) is compromised or lost. This leads to a state of affairs in the analytic setting in which the patient treats his thoughts and feelings not as subjective experiences, but as facts.

Magical thinking underlies a great many psychological defenses, feeling states, and forms of object relatedness. I will briefly discuss only three. Mania and hypomania reflect the hegemony of a set of omnipotent fantasies: the individual relying on the manic defense feels that he has absolute control over the missing object, and therefore, he has not lost the object; he has rejected it; he celebrates, not grieves, the loss of the object because he is better off without it; and the loss is not a loss because the object is valueless and contemptible. The feeling states associated with these omnipotent fantasies are concisely summed up by Klein (1935) as feelings of control, contempt, and triumph.

Projective identification is also based on omnipotent fantasy: the unconscious belief that one can split off dangerous and endangered aspects of oneself and put them into another person in such a way that that aspect of oneself takes control of the other person from within. (The act of "containing" [Bion, 1970; Ogden, 2004a] a projective identification involves the "recipient's" transforming the "projector's" magical thinking into dream thinking, which the projector may be able to utilize in dreaming/thinking his own experience.)

Similarly, envy (which protects the individual from disturbing feelings such as abject emptiness and desolation) involves the omnipotent fantasy that one is able to steal what one lacks from another person and spoil what remains of what is envied in that person.

The qualities of magical thinking just discussed all reflect the use of omnipotent fantasy in the service of creating the illusion (and, at times, delusion) that one is not subject to the laws that apply to others, including the laws of nature, the inescapability of time, the role of chance, the irreversibility of death, and so on. One may speak cruelly to another person and then believe that one can literally "take back" the comment (recreate reality): for instance, by renaming it a joke. Saying something makes it so. One's words are felt to have the power to substitute a newly created reality for a reality that is no longer convenient. More broadly, history can be rewritten at will.

Magical thinking is very convenient – simply saying something obviates the need to face the truth of what has occurred, much less do anything about it. But as convenient as magical thinking is, it has one overriding drawback: it does not "work" – nothing can be built on it or with it except additional layers of magical constructions. Such "thinking" has no traction in the real world that exists outside of one's mind. Rather than constituting a form of genuine thought, it is an attack both on the recognition of reality and on thinking itself (i.e., it is a form of anti-thinking). It substitutes invented reality for actual reality, thus collapsing the difference between internal and external reality. The belief, for example, that one can use an indiscriminate "forgive-and-forget" approach to interpersonal experience only to serves not further blind the individual to the reality of the nature of the emotional connection that exists between himself and others but also further blinds him to who he himself is. He increasingly becomes a fiction – a magical invention of his own mind, a construction divorced from external reality.

Nothing (and no one) can be built on or with magical thinking because omnipotently created "reality" lacks the sheer immovable alterity of actual external reality. The experience of the otherness of external reality is necessary for the creation of genuine self-experience. If there is no *not-I*, there can be no *I*. Without a differentiated other, one is everyone and no one.

One implication of this understanding of the central role of the recognition of otherness in the development of the self is the idea that, as important as it is for the analyst to understand the patient, it is equally important for the analyst to be a person who is different from the patient. The last thing in the world any patient needs is a second version of himself. The solipsistic aspects of a patient's thinking – the self-reinforcing nature of his ties to his unconscious beliefs – lead to a limitation of the patient's ability to think and to grow psychologically. What the patient (unconsciously) is asking of the analyst – even when the patient is explicitly or implicitly claiming that he has no need of the analyst – is a conversation with a person other than himself, a person who is grounded in a reality that the patient has not created (see Fairbairn, 1944; Ogden, 2010).

A patient who was reduced to omnipotence[2]

Ms. Q told me in the initial interview that she had come to me for analysis because "I am unusually talented in wrecking everything in my life – my marriage, the way I treat my children, and the way I do my work." Despite the intended irony of this statement, it felt to me to be more a boast than an admission of failure or a request for help. It seemed to me that Ms. Q was putting me on notice that she was no ordinary person ("I am unusually talented").

In the first week of Ms. Q's five-session-per-week analysis, something quite striking occurred. Ms. Q left a phone message saying that, due to a change in her work schedule, she was unable to attend the meeting we had scheduled for the following day, but she would be able to attend the session just after the one we had scheduled: i.e., she could meet an hour later. She ended the message by saying, "I'll assume that's all right with you unless I hear from you." I had no choice but to return her phone call. In my phone message, I said that I expected her at the time we had agreed upon. Had I not returned her call, she would have arrived at the same time as the patient to whom that later session belonged, which would have created an intrusive situation for the other patient and me when the three of us met in the waiting room.

The patient arrived twenty minutes late for the session she had asked to change. She offered facile apologies and explanations. I said to her, "It seems to me that you don't believe I've genuinely made a place for you here, and so you feel you have to steal one. But I don't think that such things can be stolen." I strongly suspected that the fear of not having a place of her own had been a lifelong anxiety for the patient, but I did not say this to her.

Ms. Q said that she did not think it was so complicated as that and went on to tell me more about events at work. I said to her, "I guess I'm not to have a place here with you unless I fight for it." The patient behaved as if I had said nothing.

Ms. Q spoke in a rather flippant way about her life. In talking about her "formative years," she said that she had had a "perfectly normal childhood" and had "perfectly reasonable parents" who were highly successful academics. "I can't blame it all on them." I imagined that what the patient said was true in a way that she was not at all aware of. That is, she had been a "perfectly" behaved child (compliant and fearful of her emotions), and her parents were "perfectly reasonable" in the sense that they were little able to be receptive to, or expressive of, feeling. This inference was borne out over time, both in the transference-countertransference and in the patient's accounts of her childhood.

Closely linked with Ms. Q's efforts to control me and steal from me and from my other patients was her belief that I had the answers to her problems – her inability to be a mother, a wife, a friend, or a productive member of her profession. My "stubbornness" in not giving her solutions to her problems puzzled and enraged her.

I gradually became aware of a way in which the patient had been relating to me from the very beginning of the analysis, but which had become less disguised and more provocative as time went on. The patient would regularly misrepresent feelings, behaviors, and events that had occurred either within or outside the consulting room. This was most striking when Ms. Q distorted something that she or I had said in the current session or in a recent one. After almost two years of feeling controlled in this way, I said, "I think that by presenting yourself and me with story after story that you know to be untrue or misleadingly incomplete, you ensure that everything I say or think is of no interest or value to you. Reality is only a story that you create and recreate as you choose. There is no real me or real you that lies outside your control. Since you can create any reality that suits you, there's no need to actually do anything to make the changes in your life that you say you want to make."

As I said this to Ms. Q, I was aware that I was angry at her for the ways she undermined me and the analytic work. I was also aware that my pointing out that she was failing to conduct herself in a way that I approved of would likely force her into an even more highly defended state. (That is, in fact, what ensued.) But it was not my anger that was most disturbing to me at this point. I was speaking in a chastising way that felt quite foreign to me.

A few sessions later, I closed my eyes for a few minutes while sitting in my chair behind the couch (as I often do while working with patients in analysis). After a while, I suddenly became very anxious. I opened my eyes but, for a few moments, did not know where I was, what I was doing, or whom, if anyone, I was with. My disorientation did not lift even after I saw a person lying on the couch. It took me a few seconds more to deduce where I was, who the person on the couch was, and what I was doing there (i.e., who I was). It took several more moments before this deductive thinking was succeeded by a more solid sense of myself as a person and as Ms. Q's analyst. This was a disquieting experience that led me, over time, to become aware of my own fears of losing myself in the psychological-interpersonal experience in which Ms. Q continuously reinvented reality and reinvented herself and me. It seemed to me that Ms. Q was showing me what she could not tell me (or herself): i.e., what it felt like to invent and reinvent herself and to be invented and reinvented by another person. I was reminded of Ms. Q's parents' demands on her and her own efforts to be "a perfect child," a child who made no emotional demands on her parents, a child who was not a child.

I said to Ms. Q, "I think that your distortions of reality, and particularly your inventions of yourself and me, are efforts to show me what you don't feel able to convey to me in words. It seems to me that when you were a child, you felt you were the invention of someone else's mind, and you continue to feel that way. I think that you've been afraid to tell me or to tell yourself the truth because that would endanger what little you have of yourself that feels real. To tell me the truth would be to leave yourself open to my taking from you what feels most real about you and replacing it with my own version of you." Ms. Q did not reflexively dismiss what I said with a sardonic quip or other form of contemptuous dismissal, as was her wont. Instead, she was quiet for the few minutes that remained of the hour.

In the following day's session, Ms. Q told me a dream: "I was playing tennis – in reality, I don't know how to play tennis – and the ball rolled to a far corner of the series of courts on which we were playing. There was a kind of trough at the edge of the far court that was filled with brand-new tennis balls, but I didn't know how to take more than one or two with me. I can't remember what happened after that. I woke up in the morning feeling all right – not great, not terrible."

I said, "In telling the dream, you told me and yourself right away that in the dream, you are playing tennis, but in reality, you can't play tennis. It seems that it felt important to you that we both know what is real and what isn't. The ball rolled to a far corner where there's a trough. You find a great many new tennis balls in it – it seems like an exciting treasure, but you can only take one or two with you. On the other hand, the tennis balls that you already have are enough. When you woke up, you didn't feel cheated of a treasure, nor did you feel like a thief, as you have felt so often in the past. You felt all right."

Ms. Q said, "That's right. I didn't really care that I couldn't take all the tennis balls. I didn't want them or need them. Finding the tennis balls in the trough didn't feel like discovering a treasure; it just seemed strange. When I was a kid . . . actually, I was in high school . . . I shoplifted things I didn't want and threw them away as soon as I got outside the store. It makes me feel queasy remembering that. I knew I didn't want the stuff, but I couldn't stop myself."

In the course of the succeeding year of analysis, Ms. Q's creation of her own reality greatly diminished. At times, when she was engaged in distorting reality, she would interrupt herself, saying, "If I continue talking in this way, it will be pointless because I'm leaving out an important part of what happened that I'm embarrassed to tell you."

In the portions of the analysis that I have discussed, the patient relied heavily on magical thinking in an effort to create (and destroy) reality, including herself and me. The alternative to creating reality, for her, was not simply an experience of helplessness but a sense of losing herself, a feeling of having herself stolen by someone else. Moreover, she felt ashamed of not being able to hold on to a sense of herself that felt real and true to her.

The patient's distortions of reality (her magical creation of her own reality) angered me because of the way in which they contributed to what felt like a theft of meaning from the analytic dialogue and a theft of my sense of self. What I initially said to the patient regarding her magical thinking was excessively accusatory and, consequently, unusable by her. It was, however, of value to me in alerting me to the way in which I did not recognize myself in the way I was talking. This understanding, in turn, created a psychological space in which a reverie experience was generated (by the patient and me), in which I experienced a frightening feeling that I did not know who I was, where I was, or who was with me.

Talking with Ms. Q about what I believed to be her feelings of losing herself in her endless reinventions of reality provided an emotional context (a containing way of thinking) that allowed her to dream (with me) an experience of being herself in the world without the need for magic. The patient, both in the tennis ball dream and in talking with me about it, was able to be accepting of herself as she was. Reality was not a threat; it served as a grounding otherness. My otherness and the otherness of external reality were made more immediately present as I "retold" the tennis ball dream in a form that was other to her own telling of it.

In hearing my telling of the dream, Ms. Q, I believe, saw something like herself (herself at an observable distance) in "my dream." The patient made use of the external reality (the otherness) of my version of the dream in a self-defining way, as reflected in her quietly correcting my version of the dream in places where she felt she did not recognize herself. For example, she told me that finding the multitude of tennis balls "didn't feel like discovering a treasure"; rather, she found it "strange" (that is, foreign to the person she was becoming).

While this section of the chapter has focused on magical thinking, the work of coming to understand something of what was occurring in the analytic relationship involved a good deal of dream thinking on both the patient's part and mine. I will further describe this aspect of the analysis in the next section of this chapter. (As I mentioned earlier, one's thinking always involves the full spectrum of forms of thinking. What varies is the prominence of one form, or combination of forms, at any given moment.)

Dream thinking

Dream thinking is the predominantly unconscious psychological work that we do in the course of dreaming. We dream continually, both while we are awake and while we are asleep (Bion, 1962a). Just as the light of the stars in the sky is obscured by the glare of the sun during the day, dreaming continues while we are awake, though it is obscured by the glare of waking life. Dream thinking is our most encompassing, penetrating, and creative form of thinking. We are insatiable in our need to dream our lived experience in an effort to create personal, psychological meanings (which are organized and represented in such forms as visual images, verbal symbols, kinesthetically organized impressions, and so on) (Barros and Barros, 2008).

In dream thinking, we view our lived experience from a multiplicity of vantage points simultaneously, which allows us to enter into a rich, nonlinear set of unconscious conversations with ourselves about our lived experience. That multitude of vantage points includes the perspectives of primary and secondary process thinking; the container and the contained; the paranoid-schizoid, depressive, and autistic-contiguous positions (Ogden, 1989); the mature self and the infantile self; the magical and the real; the "psychotic" and "nonpsychotic" parts of the personality (Bion, 1957); getting to know what one is experiencing (Bion's [1970] "K") and becoming the truth of what one is experiencing ("O"); the "projector" and the "recipient" of projective identification; and so on. The multilayered, nonlinear "conversations" constituting dream thinking take place between unconscious aspects of the personality, termed by Grotstein (2000) "the dreamer who dreams the dream" and "the dreamer who understands the dream" and by Sandler (1976) "the dream-work" and "the understanding work." Such thinking would result in massive confusion if it were to occur consciously while one was attempting to go about the business of waking life.

The richness of dream experience and dream thinking is captured by Pontalis (2003) in his description of waking up from sleep:

> I must separate myself brutally from the nocturnal world, from this world where I felt and lived more incidents than anywhere else, where I was extraordinarily active, where I was more awake than one ever is in what we call the "state of wakefulness" (p. 15).... Dreams think and they think for me.... Waking up we would like to recover the beautiful, distressing, and disturbing images that visited us in the night and already these images are fading. Yet we also feel that what we are losing then is much more than these images; it's a realm of thought that progresses continuously [p. 18].... [Dreaming – and, I would add, dream thinking] unfurl[s] in all directions (p. 50) ... unaware of its destination ... carried away by the sole power of its movement.
>
> (p. 19)

As discussed earlier, the problem with magical thinking is the fact that it does not work: it substitutes invented reality for the reality of who one is and the emotional circumstances in which one is living. Consequently, nothing of substance changes in oneself. The strength of dream thinking lies in the fact that it does work: it does give rise to psychological growth, as reflected, for instance, in the way one consciously and unconsciously goes about making changes in the way one relates to other people and in one's other engagements with the real external world. In this sense, I view pragmatism as a principal means of taking the measure of the value of any aspect of the workings of the mind (as is true of the workings of the body). A fundamental question regarding any given form of thinking is always: Does it work? Does it contribute to the development of a sense of an emotionally alive, creative, self-aware person, grounded in the reality both of himself and of the external world?

Beginning in earliest infancy and continuing throughout life, every individual is limited, to varying degrees, in his capacity to subject his lived experience to dream thinking: i.e., to do unconscious psychological work while dreaming. When one has reached the limits of one's ability to dream his disturbing experiences, one needs another person to help one dream one's undreamt dreams (Ogden, 2004b, 2005). In other words, it takes (at least) two people to dream one's most disturbing experience.

In earliest life, the psychological-interpersonal phenomenon that I am describing takes the form of the mother and infant together dreaming the infant's disturbing experience (as well as the mother's emotional response to the infant's distress). The mother, in a state of reverie, accepts the infant's unthinkable thoughts and unbearable feelings (which are inseparable from her response to the infant's distress) (Bion, 1962a, 1962b; Ogden, 1997a, 1997b). The mother, who in this way enters into a subjectivity that is co-created with the infant, Winnicott's (1956) "primary maternal preoccupation"; Bion's (1962a) and Rosenfeld's (1987) intrapsychic-interpersonal version of projective identification; and Ferro's (1999) "bi-personal field," or what I call the "intersubjective third" (Ogden, 1994a, 1994b) brings to bear on the infant's unthinkable experience her own larger personality and greater capacity for dreaming. In so doing, she and the infant together dream something like the infant's disturbing experience. The mother communicates to the infant his formerly undreamable/unthinkable experience in a form that he is now more fully able to dream on his own. A similar intersubjective process takes place in the analytic relationship and in other intimate relationships, such as the parent-child relationship, marriage, close friendships, and relationships between siblings.

In saying that it takes (at least) two people to think one's most disturbing emotional experience, I do not mean to say that individuals are not able to think on their own. Rather, I am saying that one inevitably reaches a point in one's thinking/dreaming beyond which one cannot go. At that juncture, one either develops symptomatology in an (often futile) effort to gain some measure of control over (which is not to say resolution of) one's psychological difficulties, or one enlists another person to help one dream one's experience. As Bion (1987) put it, "The human unit is a couple; it takes two human beings to make one" (p. 222).

It must be borne in mind that not all forms of mental activity that appear to be dreaming – for example, visual images and narratives experienced in sleep – merit the term *dreaming*. Post-traumatic nightmares that are repeated night after night achieve virtually no unconscious psychological work and, consequently, do not constitute genuine dreaming (Bion, 1987). In other words, such "dreams" are dreams that are not dreams in that they leave the dreamer psychically unchanged. Again, the measure of whether a dream is a dream is whether it "works": i.e., whether it facilitates real psychological change and growth.

The ordinary rescued from the magical

As I mentioned in connection with my work with Ms. Q, dream thinking was done at several critical points in that analysis. I will focus here on one of these instances: my use of my reverie experience that occurred during a session in which I listened to the patient while my eyes were closed. In that reverie, I was, in an important sense, dreaming *with* Ms. Q an experience that she had been unable to dream on her own (much less put into words for herself or for me). The reverie itself was a form of waking dreaming in which I not only lived the experience, but – even as I was in the grip of it – I was also able to form questions that addressed the essence of the emotional situation: Where am I? Who am I? With whom am I?

On "waking" from the reverie, I was able to engage in more conscious aspects of dream thinking. This involved my conceiving of my experience of having momentarily lost myself as constituting an unconsciously co-created version of Ms. Q's experience of losing herself as a consequence of her use of omnipotent fantasy to invent and reinvent herself and me.

The thinking I have just described involved apprehending and putting into words multiple levels of meaning that were alive in the emotional experience. I treated my reverie experience both as an experience of having co-created a dream with Ms. Q and as an experience that had personal meanings that were unique to each of us. My own experience of the reverie was one in which I briefly lost touch with my sense of who I was, while Ms. Q's experience of losing herself was lifelong and, at times, quasi-delusional.

As I have said, I view dream thinking as a form of thinking that is primarily unconscious, although it operates in concert with preconscious and conscious thinking. The co-creation of the reverie experience itself was principally an unconscious phenomenon that generated preconscious and conscious imagery (as is the case with dreams that one remembers after waking from sleep). In relating my reverie experience to Ms. Q's experience of herself, I was primarily engaged in conscious, secondary process thinking, but that type of thinking would, I believe, have been stale and empty had I not been speaking *from* my experience as a participant in the reverie.

An important measure of whether or not the thinking that Ms. Q and I did was genuine dream thinking lies in the degree to which it facilitated the work of helping the patient become more alive and responsive to her experience in the real world, better able to accept herself as she was, and more capable of thinking and talking about her experience with herself and with me. It seems to me that my use of my reverie experience to talk with Ms. Q about *her* experience of losing herself reflected psychological change in me: i.e., in my own increased capacity to contain the patient's unthinkable/undreamable experience (as opposed to evacuating it – for example, in the form of a chastising intervention). My talking with Ms. Q about her experience of losing herself contributed, I believe, to her dreaming her tennis ball dream, a dream in which she had little interest in, or use for, magical thinking. Her psychological growth was reflected in her capacity to dream that dream and in her enhanced ability to talk and think with me (and herself) about it.

The type of dream thinking that I have described here involved a form of self-reflection in which I drew my own experience and my conception of the patient's experience into relation to one another: i.e., I made use of my experience of losing myself to make an inference regarding the patient's experience of losing herself. The category of meaning (the experience of losing oneself) remained relatively constant. As will be seen in the following section of this chapter, dream thinking at times involves a radical shift in the structure of the patient's and the analyst's thinking. This form of dream thinking, which I refer to as *transformative thinking*, may precipitate what Bion (1970) refers to as "catastrophic change" (p. 106), a change in nothing less than everything.

Transformative thinking

The idea of transformative thinking occurred to me in response to a passage from the King James translation of the Gospel of John, which was discussed in an essay by Seamus Heaney (1986). I will treat the writing in that passage as a literary text, not a religious text, and as such, I will treat the figures and events depicted in the story not as expressions of theological meaning but as expressions of emotional truths arrived at by means of a particular form of thinking. Because the thinking is *in* the writing, I will quote the passage in its entirety:

> And the scribes and Pharisees brought unto him a woman taken in adultery; and when they had set her in the midst,
>
> They say unto him, Master, this woman was taken in adultery, in the very act.
>
> Now Moses in the law commanded us, that such should be stoned: but what sayest thou?
>
> This they said, tempting him, that they might have to accuse him. But Jesus stooped down, and with his finger wrote on the ground, as though he heard them not.
>
> So, when they continued asking him, he lifted up himself, and said unto them, He that is without sin among you, let him first cast a stone at her.
>
> And again, he stooped down, and wrote on the ground.
>
> And they which heard it, being convicted by their own conscience, went out one by one, beginning at the eldest, even unto the last: and Jesus was left alone, and the woman standing in the midst.
>
> When Jesus had lifted up himself, and saw none but the woman, he said unto her, Woman, where are those thine accusers? hath no man condemned thee?
>
> She said, No man, Lord. And Jesus said unto her, neither do I condemn thee: go, and sin no more.
>
> [Gospel of John (8:3–11)]

In this story, Jesus is brought into a situation in which a woman has been taken "in the very act" of adultery. He is asked whether he will obey the law (which demands that the woman be stoned) or break the law (by putting a stop to the stoning that is about to take place).

Jesus, instead of replying to the question, "stooped down, and with his finger wrote on the ground as though he heard them not." Instead of accepting the terms as they were presented (Will you obey the law or break the law?), Jesus opens a psychological space in which to think in the act of writing. The reader is never told what he wrote. Jesus's writing on the ground breaks the powerful forward movement towards action and, in so doing, creates a space for thinking both for the characters in the story and for the reader/listener.

When Jesus stands, he does not reply to the question that has been posed. He says something utterly unexpected and does so in the simplest of words – a sentence in which all but two of the fifteen words are monosyllabic: "He that is without sin among you, let him first cast a stone at her." Jesus does not address the question of whether to obey the law or break the law and instead poses a completely different, highly enigmatic question: How does one bring to bear one's own experience of being human, which includes one's own sinful acts, on the problem of responding to the behavior of another person? And further, the passage raises the question of whether any person has the right to stand in judgment of another person. At the end of the passage, Jesus renounces any intention of standing in judgment of the woman: "Neither do I condemn thee."

The final words of the passage, "go, and sin no more," are tender while, at the same time, demand honest self-scrutiny. Language itself has been altered: the meaning of the word *sin* has been radically transformed in the course of the story, but into what? In relation to what moral order is sin to be defined? Is the woman free to commit adultery if her own morality does not deem it a sin? Are all systems of morality equal in their capacity to prescribe, proscribe, and take the measure of the way human beings conduct themselves in relation to themselves and one another?

My purpose in discussing this piece of literature is to convey what I mean by transformative thinking. It is a form of dream thinking that involves recognizing the limitations of the categories of meaning currently thought to be the only categories of meaning (e.g., obey the law or break the law) and, in their place, creating fundamentally new categories – a radically different way of ordering experience – that had been unimaginable up to that point.

The biblical story I have just discussed constitutes one of the most important narratives – and instances of transformative thinking – of the past two thousand years. No doubt it would have been forgotten long ago had it been less enigmatic, less irreducible to other terms (such as the tenets of a new set of secular or religious laws to be obeyed or disobeyed) or even to abstract principles, such as no person has the right to pass judgment on another person. Had the story merely substituted one binary choice for another or introduced a new prescription, the thinking achieved in the writing would not have been transformative in nature and, I speculate, would not have survived as a seminal narrative of Western culture. The story, like a poem, cannot be paraphrased and mined for meanings that stand still.

We, as psychoanalysts, ask of ourselves and of our patients no less than transformative thinking even as we recognize how difficult it is to achieve. Our theoretical and clinical work becomes stagnant if at no point do we engage in transformative thinking. It is this striving for transformative thinking that makes psychoanalysis a subversive activity, an activity inherently undermining of the gestalt (the silent, self-defining terms) of the intrapsychic, the interpersonal, and the social cultures in which patient and analyst live.

Each of the major twentieth-century analytic theorists has introduced his or her own conception of the transformation – the alteration of the way we think and experience being alive – that is most central for psychological growth. For Freud (1900, 1909), it is making the unconscious conscious and, later in his work (1923, 1926, 1933), movement in psychic structure from id to ego ("Where id was, there ego shall be") (1933: 80). For Klein (1948, 1952), the pivotal transformation is the movement from the paranoid-schizoid to the depressive position; for Bion (1962a), it is a movement from a mentality based on evacuation of disturbing, unmentalized emotional experience to a mentality in which one attempts to dream/think one's experience and, later (1965, 1970), a movement from getting to know the reality of one's experience (K) to becoming the truth of one's experience (O). For Fairbairn (1944), therapeutic transformation involves a movement from a life lived in relation to internal objects to a life lived in relation to real external objects. For Winnicott (1971), crucial to psychological health is the psychic transformation in which one moves from unconscious fantasizing to a capacity to live imaginatively in an intermediate space between reality and fantasy.

My focus in this section of the present chapter is not on the validity or clinical usefulness of each of these conceptions of psychic transformation, but on the nature of the intrapsychic and intersubjective thinking/dreaming that mediates these transformations. As will be seen in the next clinical illustration that I will present, the achievement of transformative thinking is not necessarily an experience of a sudden breakthrough, a eureka phenomenon. Rather, in my experience, it is most often the outcome of years of slow, painstaking analytic work that involves an expanding capacity of the analytic pair to dream aspects of the patient's formerly undreamable experience.

Transformative thinking – thinking that radically alters the terms by which one orders one's experience – lies towards one end of a spectrum of degrees of change-generating thinking (dream thinking). The clinical example that follows is taken from work with a patient who experienced florid psychotic thinking, both prior to the analysis and in the course of the analysis. I have elected to discuss my work with this patient because the transformative thinking that was required of the patient and me is more apparent and more striking than in most of my work with healthier patients. Nonetheless, it must be borne in mind that transformative thinking is an aspect of all thinking and, as such, is a dimension of my work with the full spectrum of patients.

A woman who was not herself

Ms. R sat stiffly in her chair, unable to make eye contact with me during our first consultation session. She was well dressed but in a way that seemed artificial in its perfection. She began by saying, "I'm wasting your time. I don't think that what is wrong with me can change. I'm not a person who should be in an analyst's office." I said, "The first thing you want me to know about you is that you don't belong here. I think you're warning me that both of us will no doubt regret having had anything to do with one another."

Ms. R replied, "That's right." After a minute or so, she said, "I should tell you something about myself." I said, "You can do that if you like, but you're already telling me, in your own way, a great deal about who you feel you are and what frightens you most."

Space does not allow for a discussion of the initial years of analysis. In brief, Ms. R spoke with great shame and embarrassment about how repulsive she felt; she continually readied herself for my telling her to leave. As we talked about these feelings, the patient slowly became more trusting of me. In a very unassuming way, Ms. R revealed herself to be a highly intelligent, articulate, and likable person.

Towards the end of the third year of this five-session-per-week analysis, Ms. R said, "There's something I'm afraid to tell you because you might tell me that I'm too sick to be in analysis. But you won't be able to help me if you don't know this about me, so I'm going to tell you." Ms. R haltingly went on to say that she had had "a breakdown" when she was in her thirties while traveling in Europe. She was hospitalized for a month, during which she had a hallucination that lasted for several days. "In it, a string was coming out of my mouth. It's very hard for me to say this because I'm afraid of getting caught in it again. I was terrified and kept pulling on the string in order to get it out of me, but the string was endless. As I pulled, I found that my internal organs were attached to the string. I knew that if I didn't get this string out of me, I would die, but I also knew that if I pulled out more of the string, it would be the end of me because I couldn't live without my insides." Ms. R said that she had felt unbearably lonely during the hospitalization and was consumed by thoughts of suicide.

She and I talked at length about the hospitalization, the experiential level of the hallucination, and her fear that the hallucination would frighten and alienate me and entrap her. I restricted myself to putting what she was saying into my own words in order to let her know that she was not alone now as she had been then. The hallucination seemed to me to be far too important an event to risk foreclosing it with premature understandings.

Ms. R also felt that I would have to know more about her childhood experience to be able to help her. She said, "I know I've been very vague in talking about my childhood and my parents. I'm sure you've noticed, but I couldn't bring myself to do it because it makes me feel physically ill to think about it. I don't want to get trapped there either."

Ms. R said that, as a child, she had "worshipped" her mother: "She was dazzlingly beautiful and extraordinarily intelligent, but I was as afraid of her as I was revering of her. I studied her way of walking, the way she held her head, the way she spoke to her friends, to the mailman, to the housekeeper. I wanted desperately to be like her, but I was never able to do it well enough. I could tell that she thought I was always falling short. She didn't need to say anything. It was unmistakable in the coldness of her eyes and in her tone of voice."

The patient's father was fully consumed with running the family business and was at home very little. Ms. R recalled lying in bed trying not to fall asleep so she might hear her father's voice and the sound of his movements around the house when he got home. She did not dare get out of bed for fear of displeasing her mother by "tiring her father out after his long day at work" (as her mother put it).

Gradually, in the course of growing up, the patient came to understand that her mother could not tolerate sharing her father's attention. Her parents seemed to her, even as a child, to have had an unspoken agreement that her father could spend as much time at work as he wanted to, and in exchange, her mother would run the house and the family as she pleased.

In this period of analytic work, the patient's lifelong, visceral sense of disgust for herself as a person and for her body (particularly its "female excretions") became so intense that Ms. R avoided as much as possible being around other people for fear that they would be repulsed by her odor. Being in my consulting room with me was almost unbearable for her. As she spoke about her "repulsive body" during one of these sessions, my mind wandered to a book that I was reading in which the narrator discussed the odor that clung to his own body and those of the other prisoners in the concentration camp in which he had spent more than a year. I thought, at that moment in the session, that not to be stained by the odor would have been far worse than being stained by it because being free of the odor would have meant that one was a perpetrator of unthinkable atrocities. A prisoner's terrible odor obliterated his individual identity, but at least it served to mark the fact that he was not one of "them."

In talking with me about her revulsion for herself and her body, Ms. R gradually began to recognize the depth and severity of her mother's "distaste" for her. "It was as if being a child was an illness that my mother tried to cure me of. Only now do I see that her teaching me how to be 'a young woman of culture' was insane. I was able to convince myself that this was what mothers did. On my own, I learned how to rid myself of the [regional] accent with which the other children spoke."

When the patient's periods began at age twelve, her mother left a box of Kotex and a detailed letter about "how to keep yourself clean." Not a single spoken word passed between them on the subject. The patient's mother became significantly colder and more disapproving of Ms. R after the patient entered puberty.

After several more years, during which the patient did considerable work with the understandings I have described, she began to experience left-sided abdominal pain that she was convinced was a symptom of cancer. When extensive medical tests failed to reveal a physiological source of the pain, the patient became extremely distressed and said, "I don't believe them. I don't believe their tests. They're not real doctors; they're researchers, not doctors." She then, for the first time in the analysis, sobbed deeply.

After a few minutes, I said, "It's terrifying to feel that doctors are not real doctors. You've put your life in their hands. But this is not a new experience for you. I think that you felt you had a mother who was not a real mother, and your life was completely in her hands. Just as you feel you are a guinea pig in the so-called doctors' research, I think that you felt you were merely a character in your mother's insane internal life."[3]

Ms. R listened to me intently but did not respond in words to these comments. Her sobbing subsided, and there was a visible decrease in the tension in her body as she lay on the couch.

The succeeding months of Ms. R's life, both within and outside the analysis, were deeply tormenting ones. During this period, she was again preoccupied with the string hallucination. The patient said she continued to feel the physical sensation of having her mother (who was now indistinguishable from the string) inside her, though the sensory experience no longer held the unmediated realness of a hallucination. Ms. R came to view her fear (and conviction) that there was a cancer growing inside her as a new version of the string hallucination.

Also, at this juncture in the analysis, Ms. R began to correct grammatical errors that I made – for instance, when I said, "people that" instead of "people who" or when I made an error in the use of the subjunctive. She subtly made her corrections by repeating the essence of my sentence but with the error corrected. I am not sure whether the patient was at all aware that she was doing this. Ms. R openly complained about television news broadcasters and the *New York Times* "butchering the English language." I became highly self-conscious regarding the grammatical correctness of my speech, to the point that I felt tongue-tied and limited in my ability to speak in a spontaneous way. I was able, over time, to understand what was happening as the patient's way of unconsciously forcing me to experience something of what it felt like for her to have her imperious mother inside her.

In a session in which Ms. R was feeling hopeless about ever being able to free herself of her mother's physical and emotional presence in her, I said, "I think that you feel today, almost as strongly as you did when you had the string hallucination, that you have only two choices: you can try to pull the string out of you – but that requires pulling out your own insides along with your mother, which would kill both of you. Or you can choose not to pull out the string, which means giving up your last chance to remove her from you. You would be giving up hope of ever becoming a person separate from her."

While I was saying this, I had a strong sense of emerging from a psychic state in which I had felt inhabited by Ms. R in a strangulating way. Something quite new and very welcome was occurring between the two of us at this point in the session, though I was unable to put it into words or images for myself or the patient.

Ms. R said, "As you were speaking, I remembered something that plagued me when I was in junior high and high school. I lived in a world of looming disaster. For instance, I had to predict exactly – to the tenth of a gallon – how much gas the car would take at the gas station. I was convinced that if I was wrong, my mother or father would die. But worst of all, there was a question that I could not get out of my head. I haven't thought about this for years. The question was: if my family and I were in a boat that was sinking, and everyone would drown unless one person was thrown overboard, and it was up to me to decide which one was to go, whom would I choose? I knew immediately that I would choose to throw myself into the water, but that answer was a 'wrong answer' – it was against the rules. So I would begin again asking myself the same question, and that went on over and over and over, sometimes for months."

I said, "As a girl, you were too young to know that it was not the answer you came up with that was wrong or against the rules – it was the very fact that the question had to be asked that was 'wrong' in the sense that there was something terribly wrong going on in your life and in the life of your family. I think that you've felt virtually every moment of your life, from the time you were a small child, that you have to decide who to kill – yourself or your mother."

Ms. R replied, "It was too awful – impossible – as a child to allow myself to know any of this. It's been there as a feeling, but I didn't have words for it. I felt she was everything. I knew that if I got her out of me, it would kill her, and I didn't want that, but I had to get her out; I didn't want to die. I'm so confused. I feel as if I'm in a maze, and there's no way out. I have to get out of here. I don't think I can stay."

I said, "The very first thing you wanted me to know about you in our initial meeting was that you and I didn't belong here together. Now I realize that, despite the fact that you couldn't put it into words, you were trying to protect both of us from yourself. If you allow me to help you, I'll be inside you, and you'll have to kill one or both of us. As a child, you were alone with that problem, but that's not true any longer."

Ms. R said, "There are times when I'm here that I know that there is a world made entirely differently from the one I've been living in. I'm embarrassed to say this – I can feel myself blushing – but it is a world in which you and I talk like this. I'm sorry I said it because I don't want to jinx it. I feel like such a little girl now. Forget I said anything." I said, "Your secret is safe with me." I had grown very fond of Ms. R by this point in the analysis, and she knew that.

It was only at this juncture, with the patient's help – her telling me she felt like a little girl – that I was able to put into words for myself something of the emotions I had sensed earlier in the session and was now feeling with far greater intensity. I was experiencing Ms. R as the daughter I never had, a daughter with whom I was feeling a form of tenderness and a form of loss (as she grows up) that is unique to the tie between a father and daughter. This was not simply a new thought; it was a new way of experiencing myself and Ms. R; it was a way of feeling alive both lovingly and sadly that was new to me.

In the next session, Ms. R said, "Last night, I slept more deeply than I've slept in a very long time. It is as if space has opened up in every direction, even downward in sleep."

As the analysis progressed, Ms. R was able to experience types of feeling and qualities of human relatedness that were new to her: "All my life, I've heard the word *kindness* being used by people, but I had no idea what the word meant. I knew I had never felt the feeling they were talking about. I now know what kindness feels like. I can feel your kindness toward me. I cry when I see a mother tenderly holding her baby in her arms or holding the hand of her child as they walk." She said she cried because she could now feel how little kindness she had been shown as a child. But more important, she thought, was the terrible sadness that she felt about having shown so little kindness to her own children. Ms. R had only occasionally spoken of her children up to this point in the analysis, despite the fact that all of them were having emotional difficulties.

Over time, the psychological-interpersonal shift that I have described became stabilized as a way of being and perceiving for Ms. R. The stability of the change was reflected in the following dream: "I was returning home from somewhere, and I found that people had moved into my house. There was a whole group of them, and they were in every room – they were cooking in the kitchen, watching TV in the living room; they were everywhere. I was furious. I yelled at them, 'Get the fuck out of here!' [I had never before heard Ms. R use profanity.] 'This is my house; you have no right to be here.' I felt good on waking up. In the dream, I wasn't frightened of the people who had taken over my house; I was irate."

I said, "The house is the place in which you live, a place that is yours and yours alone." Ms. R and I talked about the way in which the dream reflected her growing capacity to firmly lay claim to a place in which to live that is entirely hers, a place where she need not choose between killing herself or killing someone else who is occupying her. "In the dream, the people who had moved into my house were not going to die if I sent them away. They would simply have to find another place to live."

Ms. R had been living in a psychotic world generated by and with her mother (with the help of her father), a world in which the patient was, at every moment, unconsciously feeling that she had to choose between killing herself (giving herself over to being a projection of her mother's feelings of her own vileness) or killing her mother by insisting on becoming a person in her own right (albeit a person who had no real mother and no world that held meaning for her).

The thinking that I consider transformative thinking in my work with Ms. R was the thinking that the patient and I did together in the course of years of analysis – thinking that eventually led to a radical transformation in the way the patient and I ordered experience, creating a gestalt that transcended the terms of the emotional world in which she and I had lived. Ms. R, in this newly created way of generating and ordering experience, was able to feel feelings such as kindness, love, tenderness, sadness, and remorse, which up to that point had been only words that others used to refer to feelings she had never been able to feel. The intimacy and affection that Ms. R and I were now capable of feeling were alive for both of us when she spoke of a world in which "you and I talk like this." Even Ms. R's use of the words "you and I" in this phrase, as opposed to "we," conveyed a feeling of loving separateness, as opposed to engulfing, annihilating union. So simple a difference in use of language is communicative of the radical transformation in the patient's thinking and being.

The fundamentally new emotional terms that were created did not derive from self-hatred and pathological mutual dependence, but from Ms. R's wish and need to become a person in her own right, a person who was able to give and receive a form of love that she never before knew existed. It is a love that paradoxically takes pleasure in, and derives strength from, the separateness of the other person. Separateness in this new set of emotional terms, this new way of being alive, does not give rise to tyrannical efforts to incorporate or be incorporated by the other person; rather, it generates a genuine appreciation of the surprise, joy, sadness, and manageable fear that derive from the firm knowledge of one's own and the other person's independence.

While I believe that transformative thinking in this clinical account was a product of the entirety of the work with Ms. R, I also think that there were junctures in the work during which I sensed that Ms. R and I were engaged in something different from "ordinary" dream thinking. For example, as I have described, such a moment occurred in a session as I spoke to the patient about her hopelessness regarding the possibility of ever freeing herself of the need to make an impossible choice: whom to kill, herself or her mother? Though I could feel that a significant (and welcome) shift was occurring at that point, I was not able to attach words to, or even be clear with myself about, what I was feeling. As the session proceeded – a session in which a good deal of psychological work was done – the patient (unconsciously) helped me realize that I had come to experience her tenderly and sadly as the daughter I never had and never would have. Paradoxically, in the very act of becoming aware of that emotional void in myself, I was experiencing with Ms. R feelings of father-daughter love and loss (separation) that constituted, for me (and, I believe, for Ms. R), a new way of being with oneself and with another person.

This transformative thinking was inseparable from another level of transformative thinking in which the patient and I were engaged during this session: Ms. R's coming to feel and understand at a profound psychological depth her self-imprisonment in a world cast almost exclusively in terms of the dilemma that becoming a person separate from her mother required either murder or suicide. The patient was able to begin to experience a way of being that was cast in radically different terms. She began to experience separation (becoming a person in her own right) not as an act of murder, but as an act of creating a place in herself (and between herself and me) – a place in which she was able to experience a previously inconceivable sense of who she was and who she was becoming.

Concluding comments

The shift of emphasis in contemporary psychoanalysis from an emphasis on *what* the patient thinks to *the way* he thinks has, I believe, significantly altered how we, as analysts, approach our clinical work. I have discussed three forms of thinking that figure prominently in the portions of the two analyses I have discussed. The first of these forms of thinking – magical thinking – is thinking in name only; instead of generating genuine psychic change, it subverts thinking and psychological growth by substituting invented reality for disturbing external reality. The omnipotent fantasizing that underlies magical thinking is solipsistic in nature and contributes not only to preserving the current structure of the unconscious internal object world but also to limiting the possibility of learning from one's experience with real external objects.

By contrast, dream thinking is our most profound form of thinking. It involves viewing and processing experience from a multiplicity of vantage points simultaneously, including the perspective of primary and secondary process thinking; of the container and the contained; of the paranoid-schizoid, depressive, and autistic-contiguous positions; of the magical and the real; of the infantile self and the mature self; and so on. Unlike magical thinking, dream thinking "works" in the sense that it facilitates genuine psychological growth. While dream thinking may be generated by an individual on his own, there is always a point beyond which it requires two (or more) people to think/dream one's most disturbing emotional experience.

Transformative thinking is a form of dream thinking in which one achieves a radical psychological shift – a psychological movement from one's current conceptual/experiential gestalt to a new, previously unimaginable ordering of experience. Such movement creates the potential for generating types of feeling, forms of object relatedness, and qualities of aliveness that the individual has never before experienced. This sort of thinking always requires the minds of at least two people, since an individual in isolation from others cannot radically alter the fundamental categories of meaning by which he orders his experience.

Notes

1 Of the inseparability of forms of thinking, Freud (1900) wrote: "It is true that, so far as we know, no psychical apparatus exists which possesses a primary process only [i.e., without secondary process] and that such an apparatus is to that extent a theoretical fiction" (p. 603).
2 Bion once said to his analysand James Grotstein, "What a shame it was that you were reduced to omnipotence" (Grotstein, 2001). The connection between shame and omnipotent thinking that Bion subtly makes in this comment is a highly significant one: unconscious, irrational shame is a powerful force impelling one to give up on the real world and instead to create a world that is fully under one's control.
3 I also thought that Ms. R unconsciously experienced me as another doctor using her for my own purposes – perhaps using her as a subject for a lecture or paper – but I decided to wait to talk to her about that aspect of what I sensed was happening in the transference-countertransference until that set of thoughts and feelings was closer to her conscious experience of me. I believe that the patient would have experienced such a transference interpretation at that juncture as a substitution of my story for hers.

References

Barros, E.M. & Barros, E.L. (2008). Reflections on the clinical implications of symbolism in dream life. Presented to the Brazilian Psychoanalytic Society of Saõ Paulo, August.
Bion, W.R. (1957). Differentiation of the psychotic and non-psychotic personalities. In *Second Thoughts*. New York: Aronson, 1967, 43–64.
Bion, W.R. (1959). *Experiences in Groups and Other Papers*. New York: Basic Books.
Bion, W.R. (1962a). Learning from experience. In *Seven Servants*. New York: Aronson, 1977.
Bion, W.R. (1962b). A theory of thinking. In *Second Thoughts*. New York: Aronson, 1967, 110–119.
Bion, W.R. (1965). Transformations. In *Seven Servants*. New York: Aronson, 1977.

Bion, W.R. (1970). Attention and interpretation. In *Seven Servants*. New York: Aronson, 1977.
Bion, W.R. (1987). Clinical seminars. In Bion, F. (Ed.), *Clinical Seminars and Other Works*. London: Karnac, 1–240.
de M'Uzan, M. (1984). Les enclaves de la quantité. *Nouvelle Revue de Psychanalyse*, 30: 129–138.
De M'Uzan, M. (2003). Slaves of quantity. *Psychoanalytic Quarterly*, 72: 711–725.
Fairbairn, W.R.D. (1944). Endopsychic structure considered in terms of object-relationships. In *Psychoanalytic Studies of the Personality*. London: Routledge/Kegan Paul, 1952, 82–136.
Ferro, A. (1999). *The Bi-Personal Field: Experiences in Child Analysis*. London: Routledge.
Freud, S. (1900). The interpretation of dreams. *S. E. 4/5*.
Freud, S. (1909). Notes upon a case of obsessional neurosis. *S. E. 10*.
Freud, S. (1911). Formulations on the two principles of mental functioning. *S. E. 12*.
Freud, S. (1913). Totem and taboo. *S. E. 13*.
Freud, S. (1923). The ego and the id. *S. E. 19*.
Freud, S. (1926). Inhibitions, symptoms and anxiety. *S. E. 20*.
Freud, S. (1933). New introductory lectures on psycho-analysis. *S. E. 22*.
Gaddini, E. (1969). On imitation. *International Journal of Psychoanalysis*, 50: 75–484.
Grotstein, J.S. (2000). *Who Is the Dreamer Who Dreams the Dream? A Study of Psychic Presences*. Hillsdale, NJ: Analytic Press.
Grotstein, J.S. (2001). Personal communication.
Grotstein, J.S. (2009). Dreaming as a "curtain of illusion": Revisiting the "royal road" with Bion as our guide. *International Journal of Psychoanalysis*, 90: 733–752.
Heaney, S. (1986). The government of the tongue. In *The Government of the Tongue: Selected Prose, 1978–1987*. New York: Farrar, Strauss and Giroux, 1988, 91–108.
Klein, M. (1935). A contribution to the psychogenesis of manic-depressive states. In *Contributions to Psycho-Analysis, 1921–1945*. London: Hogarth, 1968, 282–310.
Klein, M. (1946). Notes on some schizoid mechanisms. In *Envy and Gratitude and Other Works, 1946–1963*. New York: Delacorte, 1975, 1–24.
Klein, M. (1948). On the theory of anxiety and guilt. In *Envy and Gratitude and Other Works, 1946–1963*. New York: Delacorte, 1975, 25–32.
Klein, M. (1952). The mutual influences in the development of ego and id. In *Envy and Gratitude and Other Works, 1946–1963*. New York: Delacorte, 1975, 57–60.
McDougall, J. (1984). The "dis-affected" patient: Reflections on affect pathology. *Psychoanalytic Quarterly*, 53: 386–409.
Ogden, T.H. (1989). On the concept of an autistic-contiguous position. *International Journal of Psychoanalysis*, 70: 127–140.
Ogden, T.H. (1994a). The analytic third – working with intersubjective clinical facts. *International Journal of Psychoanalysis*, 75: 3–20.
Ogden, T.H. (1994b). *Subjects of Analysis*. Northvale, NJ: Aronson; London: Karnac.
Ogden, T.H. (1997a). Reverie and interpretation. *Psychoanalytic Quarterly*, 66: 567–595.
Ogden, T.H. (1997b). *Reverie and Interpretation: Sensing Something Human*. Northvale, NJ: Aronson; London: Karnac.
Ogden, T.H. (2004a). On holding and containing, being and dreaming. *International Journal of Psychoanalysis*, 85: 1349–1364.
Ogden, T.H. (2004b). This art of psychoanalysis: Dreaming undreamt dreams and interrupted cries. *International Journal of Psychoanalysis*, 85: 857–877.

Ogden, T.H. (2005). *This Art of Psychoanalysis: Dreaming Undreamt Dreams and Interrupted Cries*. London: Routledge.
Ogden, T.H. (2010). Why read Fairbairn? *International Journal of Psychoanalysis*, 91: 101–118.
Pontalis, J.-M. (2003). *Windows*. Trans. A. Quinney. Lincoln, NE and London: University of Nebraska Press.
Rosenfeld, H. (1987). *Impasse and Interpretation*. London: Tavistock.
Sandler, J. (1976). Dreams, unconscious fantasies and "identity of perception." *International Journal of Psychoanalysis*, 3: 33–42.
Tustin, F. (1981). *Autistic States in Children*. Boston: Routledge/Kegan Paul.
Winnicott, D.W. (1956). Primary maternal preoccupation. In *Through Paediatrics to Psycho-Analysis*. New York: Basic Books, 1975, 300–305.
Winnicott, D.W. (1971). *Playing and Reality*. New York: Basic Books.

Chapter 7

The appeal of omnipotence

Michael Feldman

Freud described omnipotence as a characteristic of infantile thinking and of the magical thinking of primitive cultures (1913, 1920). He linked it with the state of what he called primary narcissism and the hallucinatory satisfaction of desire under conditions of frustration.

In Klein's studies of primitive defences and object relations, she included omnipotence of thought as an early defensive operation. One mechanism of defence against envy, for example, is to invoke an omnipotent phantasy of fusion between self and object that denies separation and dependence and an omnipotent control of the object by means of projective identification (1935, 1937, 1940).

From a different viewpoint, Winnicott (1960), describing the original and undifferentiated structure of 'baby and mother', focused on the baby's sense of omnipotence when all his needs are met, in contrast to the sense of impingement when frustration of his desires faces him with the limits of his control of reality and leads to a transitional object in the road from primitive omnipotence to the acknowledgment of frustration and dependency (In Kernberg, 1996).

Observations of the defensive functions of delusional grandiosity and omnipotence in schizophrenic, manic-depressive and paranoid psychoses emerged in the 1950s and 1960s and later in the observations on the importance of omnipotent control in the psychoanalytic treatment of the borderline conditions and pathological narcissism.

As Kernberg summarises it, 'The concept of omnipotence therefore, refers to a primitive phantasy, a mechanism of defence and a pathological psychic structure' (Kernberg, 1995: 1).

Omnipotence is the quality of having unlimited power. Monotheistic religions generally attribute omnipotence (in the sense of having unlimited power, usually also omniscience and, of course, immortality) only to the deity of *their* faith. What I want to discuss is the emotional appeal of a phantasy of omnipotence – what defences does it serve, what gratification does the individual derive from the phantasy of omnipotence, and what are the destructive aspects of such phantasies?

Freud, Klein, Ferenczi and Winnicott explored the manifestations of omnipotent thinking in the infant. In Freud's studies of obsessional neurosis, he repeatedly encountered the patient's phantasy that his or her destructive wishes or phantasies

DOI: 10.4324/9781003185192-11

would actually cause injury or death to an object – a rival, someone who has hurt them or someone they were jealous of, for example. He sees the person's belief in the power of their thoughts as a 'relic of the old megalomania of infancy' (Freud, 1909).

Winnicott has written about his views of infantile omnipotence. He describes the situation in infancy in which, if the mother is able to adapt to the infant's needs, this 'affords the infant the opportunity for the illusion that her breast is part of the infant' (Winnicott, 1953). The infant's need leads it to create this illusion over and over again. Winnicott believes that the mother's task is, in due course, gradually to disillusion the infant, challenging the omnipotent phantasy and establishing the mother, and her breast, as a separate object.

Klein, in her studies on early infantile development, pointed out that the infant was beset by powerful experiences both of gratification and of frustration and persecution. A simplified version of Klein's model suggests that, in the infant, there is a splitting of the object (initially the breast) into a gratifying version and a frustrating and persecuting version. The destructive elements of the self and the object have to be split off, disowned and projected. The gratifying elements are introjected and incorporated into the infantile ego. The idealisation of what has been incorporated serves as an important defence against early infantile anxiety, but the sense of possessing the ideal object internally can give rise to a delusion of infantile omnipotence. Repeated frustrating or damaging experiences may, of course, interfere with this development, and as I describe later, the propensity to retreat to omnipotent defensive structures remains (Klein, 1946).

I want to emphasise the extent to which omnipotent phantasies serve a vital defence against a desperate internal situation in which the individual feels helpless and impotent. This may involve the experience of the total loss of the object, linked to the phantasy of having damaged or destroyed the object, without the immediate prospect of restitution. The retreat into the phantasy of an omnipotent power may seem to be the only solution.

In his study of *Oedipus Rex*, Steiner (1985) describes how, in Sophocles's play, when Oedipus finally recognises the consequences of his actions – the murder of his father, his incestuous marriage, and his mother's subsequent suicide – he is devastated, filled with intolerable guilt and remorse. However, as Steiner (1990) points out, in *Oedipus at Colonus*, over time, instead of having to bear the reality of the terrible consequences of his actions, he deals with the anxiety and guilt that threatens him by appealing to authority – in this case, claiming divine authority and thus gaining the persuasive power and moral conviction that enable him to show a contempt for the truth. He does not deny the facts themselves; it is too late to pretend that he did not kill his father and marry his mother, but he denies responsibility and guilt and claims that these facts were wrongs inflicted *on* him rather than by him. The gods who singled him out to perpetrate the most awful acts now promise to make him a hero and elevate him to the status of near god. He no longer shows a respect for reality, and the retreat into omnipotence makes it irrelevant to feel shame or even to try to conceal his crimes.

Steiner suggests that this kind of relationship to reality is based on a retreat from truth to omnipotence. It involves identification with, and claims the support of, omnipotent figures, and it is their power to confer sanctity and to instil awe which demands respect. The truth does not have to be argued or justified, and shame and guilt are inappropriate. It is indeed the lack of shame which makes these alliances with omnipotent figures so dangerous since normal restraints on destructiveness and cruelty are rendered inoperative.

Segal (1972) described an elaborate delusional system in a borderline patient. Freud had understood the evolution of a delusional system as an attempt at restitution of a destroyed world following a psychic catastrophe. From childhood, Segal's patient had entertained secret grandiose delusions and marked obsessionality. He sought treatment, he said, as he had a mission in life to convert people to Christianity. He was convinced that he was a very special chosen instrument of God, but his symptoms interfered with the efficiency with which he could carry out this mission. Segal recognised that with her patient, her efforts to analyse and help him challenged his elaborate defence system. Far from recognising her as a helpful figure, he felt her work threatened him with a repetition of the catastrophic situation and had to be strongly resisted.

The concept of omnipotence has played an important part in some of the central legends of our culture. In the Book of Genesis, Adam and Eve are forbidden to eat of the fruit of the tree of knowledge of good and evil. If they did so, they were told, they would surely die. In Milton's great work, *Paradise Lost* (2000), he gives a wonderful description of the seductive power of the phantasy of omnipotence, represented by the Serpent. In the dialogue between Eve and the Serpent (in Adam's absence), he addresses Eve as 'Queen of the Universe' and argues that God's prohibition is merely an attempt to keep them low and ignorant. If they disobey God's instruction, they will *not* die; on the contrary, their eyes will be opened to the knowledge of Good and Evil, and they will be as Gods. Understandably, this appeal proved irresistible.

When God discovered their transgression, he said, 'The man has now become like one of us, knowing good and evil. He must not be allowed to reach out his hand and take also from the tree of life and eat and live forever'.

In all cultures, in order to protect the established order, it seems essential to preserve the vital distinction between man and God. Thus, it was necessary to keep Adam and Eve away from the tree of life. They were banished forever from the Garden of Eden, and God placed cherubim with flaming swords flashing back and forth to guard the way to the tree of life. This gives a powerful sense of the danger that is felt if man and woman were to attain the secret of eternal life and its omnipotence (Milton, 2000).

This theme of the seductive power of the phantasy of omnipotence and omniscience, the individual's attempt to identify with a powerful superior figure, is an enduring one. Money Kyrle (1968) refers to the 'spurious motivation of the craze for immortality which has bedevilled our species ever since it learned to talk'. He describes why 'the facts of life' are so difficult for us to accept. He suggests these 'facts' are fundamental unconscious assumptions. They all have to do with difference. First the difference between generations, second the difference between the sexes and third the reality of the passage of time and the inevitability of death. They are hated because they provoke envy and threaten omnipotence. A mythology is invented to deny them and to avoid facing our mortality and our dependence on others.

Probably all cultures have required the legend of an omnipotent figure or figures – all powerful, all knowing, with powerful ethical values – with which they have a complex set of relationships. This includes the phantasy or desire to join or identify with such a figure, to be monitored and controlled, rewarded and punished.

In the great Babylonian epic of Gilgamesh (George et al., 2003), probably written two or three thousand years before the Bible, Gilgamesh the King has almost unlimited power over the citizens of Uruk, but in due course, he becomes dissatisfied and restless, and with his close companion Enkidu, he becomes determined to attack the natural world (the great cedar forest) and the powerful figure of Humbaba guarding it. In retaliation for Gilgamesh's attack on the Bull of Heaven and the guardian of the cedar forest, Enkidu is condemned to die. Gilgamesh is thrown into despair at the loss of his close companion and, in his mourning, sets out to find the secret of eternal life for himself. In the end, he eventually learns that 'Life, which you look for, you will never find. For when the gods created man, they let death be his share, and life withheld in their own hands'. He has to abandon his search for omnipotence and immortality, accepting instead that he will live on in his works – the great creation of the walls of the city of Uruk.

In the prologue to Marlow's *Dr Faustus* (Marlowe, 1985), he is likened to Icarus, who flew too close to the sun and fell to his death when the sun melted his waxen wings. In the play, first performed around 1592, the learned doctor becomes dissatisfied with all his learning, and, driven by a desire for omniscience and omnipotent power, he decides to turn to the dangerous practice of necromancy, or magic. His incantations summon Lucifer, who strikes a pact with Faustus. Faustus is granted unlimited magical powers to have all his wishes fulfilled for a period of twenty-four years, after which he will give his body and soul over to Lucifer.

This is a repeated theme in literature and in legend – the human search for omnipotence and eternal life inevitably ends in disappointment or death. It is as if there is always a powerful internal authority representing parental prohibitions, which becomes a structure of the unconscious mind. This structure, identifiable as Freud's superego, can forbid actions or even thoughts – not only hostile thoughts directed towards parents and siblings, for example, but also against the search for knowledge, which unconsciously threatens the parental power and status.

Freud described the emergence of thought as related to the loss of omnipotence, the experience of frustration and the move from what he calls the pleasure principle to the reality principle. When the infant is subjected to peremptory inner needs such as hunger, his first response is by 'hallucinatory wish fulfilment' and the omnipotent phantasy of a need-satisfying object. Then he discovers that the hallucination fails to satisfy the need; Freud wrote:

> It was only the non-occurrence of the expected satisfaction, the disappointment experienced, that led to the abandonment of this attempt at satisfaction by means of hallucination. Instead of it, the psychical apparatus is driven to form a conception of the real circumstances in the external world and to endeavour to make a real alteration in them. . . . What was presented to the mind was no longer what was agreeable but what was real, even if it happened to be disagreeable. . . . This setting-up of the reality principle proved to be a momentous step.
>
> (Freud, 1911: 219)

Segal writes, 'To form a conception of the real circumstances and to endeavour to make a real alteration in them could be called a first step in thinking' (Segal, 1986: 221). She continues:

> So long as a phantasy is omnipotent, it is not a thought because it is not recognised as such. When a phantasy is recognised as a product of one's own mind, it moves into the realm of thought. One can then say, I phantasied this or that, or I thought such and such'. Thinking evolves from omnipotent phantasy, and a phantasy recognised as such and one that can be subjected to reality testing.
>
> Both the omnipotent phantasy-hallucination and thinking enable one to bear the gap between need and satisfaction: the absence and the need for a satisfying object. But while omnipotent phantasy denies the experience of need, thought, which admits the need, can be used to explore external and internal realities and deal with them. But because thought springs from and admits frustration, it can be attacked at its very inception.
>
> (Segal, 1986: 222)

A patient of Segal's referred to a dream in which a woman was giving the breast to a baby. The breasts were so close to the patient that he could fondle them. Then the woman went away, but she left the breast with the baby and the patient, who continued the sucking and fondling. The patient remarked that the baby must also be himself.

He began the next session reporting that the moment he set eyes on the analyst, he noticed she was wearing a white blouse and started thinking about her breasts. He then spoke about breasts and sucking different things, becoming more and more dreamy and remote. The analyst drew his attention to this and reminded him of the dream. The patient interrupted angrily, saying, 'Don't make me think. I don't want to think. I want to suck. I hate thoughts. When I have thoughts, it means I have nothing to suck' (Segal, 1986: 223).

What we describe as an omnipotent phantasy can be seen to be rooted in early infantile processes for dealing with hunger, pain and frustration. Gradually, as the early psyche develops the capacity for thinking, this can be used to bear the gap between need and satisfaction without resorting to phantasy-hallucination. This enables the infant to explore external and internal realities and to deal with them as best he or she can. However, as Segal points out, 'Thinking puts a limit on the omnipotence of phantasy and is attacked because of our longing for that omnipotence' (as we see in the clinical vignette of her patient and the phantasy of his possession of the breast).

I would like to conclude by referring to Ignes Sodre's fine study of the use of idealisation and omnipotence to deny painful reality. In her analysis of Flaubert's *Madam Bovary* and Thomas Mann's *Death in Venice*, she suggests that the main characters have their imaginations taken over by the seductive, delusional belief that they can create a timeless paradise of endless beauty through excessive, compulsive erotisation of a particular idealised relationship (Sodre, 2014).

This excessive idealisation is, of necessity, created from splitting off and projecting the unwelcome contents of reality associated with a relationship. In order to sustain omniscience, we need to project ignorance. To sustain omnipotence, weakness has to be projected. The important consequences of these mechanisms are the constant presence of whatever is felt to be painful and disturbing. This creates an ugly and threatening external world, with the constant threat of the projected elements returning and invading the mind.

This configuration is vividly represented in the great work of literature mentioned earlier, Milton's *Paradise Lost*. While Adam and Eve are blissfully 'Imparadised in one another's arms/The happier Eden shall enjoy their fill/Of bliss on bliss', Satan is consumed with envy and jealousy and seeks to seduce Eve away from dutiful obedience and towards endless joy in Paradise (Milton, 2000).

The transgression of Adam and Eve results, as we know, in them leaving paradise, having to face the realities of the outside world – work, the pain of childbirth, and eventual death.

It is not difficult to see the seductive appeal of omnipotence, which disavows the pain and frustration, the endless effort, that is inevitable in the external world if we are not able to retreat into omnipotent idealisation. Great works of literature, and of course our daily contact with patients (as well as ourselves), also make us aware of the destructive consequences of omnipotent ways of thinking that can lead us astray, prevent the creation of the life we want or present constant fear of the return of projections. Thinking may put limits to omnipotence, but thinking rewards us by enriching our relationship to our internal and external worlds.

References

Freud, S. (1909). *Notes Upon a Case of Obsessional Neurosis. S.E. 10.* 153–320.
Freud, S. (1911). *Formulations on the Two Principles of Mental Functioning. S.E. 12.* 213–226.
Freud, S. (1913). Animism, magic and the omnipotence of thoughts. In *Totem and Taboo. S.E. 13.* 1–161.

Freud, S. (1920). *Beyond the Pleasure Principle. S.E. 18.* 3–64.
George, A., Sandars, N.K. & Pasco, R. (2003). *The Epic of Gilgamesh.* Trans. Andrew George. New York: Penguin Classics.
Kernberg, O. (1995). Omnipotence in the transference and in the countertransference. *The Scandinavian Psychoanalytic Review*, 18: 2–21.
Kernberg, O.F. (1996). A psychoanalytic theory of personality disorders. In Clarkin, J.F. & Lenzenweger, M.F. (Eds.), *Major Theories of Personality Disorder.* London: Guilford Press, 1996, 106–140.
Klein, M. (1935). A contribution to the psychogenesis of manic-depressive states. In *Love, Guilt and Reparation and Other Works.* London: Hogarth Press, 1975. Reprinted Karnac Books, 1992, 262–289.
Klein, M. (1937). Love, guilt and reparation. In *Love, Guilt and Reparation and Other Works.* London: Hogarth Press, 1975. Reprinted London: Karnac Books, 1992, 306–343.
Klein, M. (1940). Mourning and its relation to manic-depressive states. In *Love, Guilt and Reparation and Other Works.* London: Hogarth Press, 1975. Reprinted London: Karnac Books, 1992, 344–369.
Klein, M. (1946). Notes on some schizoid mechanisms. In *Envy and Gratitude and Other Works 1946–1963.* London: Vintage, 1997, 1–24.
Marlowe, C. (1985). *Dr Faustus, the a-Text.* Nedlands: University of Western Australia Press.
Milton, J. (2000). *Paradise Lost.* London and New York: Penguin Books.
Money Kyrle, R.E. (1968). Cognitive development. *International Journal of Psycho-Analysis*, 49: 691–698.
Segal, H. (1972). A delusional system as a defence against the re-emergence of a catastrophic situation. *International Journal of Psychoanalysis*, 53: 393–401.
Segal, H. (1986). *The Work of Hanna Sega: A Kleinian Approach to Clinical Practice.* London: Free Association Books & Maresfield Library.
Sodre, I. (2014). *Imaginary Existences. A Psychoanalytic Exploration of Phantasy, Fiction, Dreams and Daydreams.* London: Routledge and New Library of Psychoanalysis.
Steiner, J. (1985). Turning a blind eye: The cover up for Oedipus. *International Review of Psycho-Analysis*, 12: 161–172.
Steiner, J. (1990). The retreat from truth to omnipotence in Sophocles' Oedipus at Colonus. *International Review of Psychoanalysis*, 12: 161–172.
Winnicott, D.W. (1953). Transitional objects and transitional phenomena. *International Journal of Psycho-Analysis*, 34: 89–97.
Winnicott, D.W. (1960). The theory of the parent-infant relationship. *International Journal of Psycho-Analysis*, 41: 585–595.

Chapter 8

A neuropsychoanalytic note on omnipotence

Mark Solms

The goal of this brief chapter, if readers will excuse the irony, is very modest. Using the concept of 'omnipotence' as an example, I aim merely to *illustrate* the kinds of new perspectives on psychoanalytic concepts that can be gained by also considering them from a neuroscientific point of view.

Omnipotence is a complex thing, with many manifestations in normal, pathological and developmental contexts. I want to focus on just one of these manifestations – one that is routinely overlooked by psychoanalysts – because it takes us to the nub of the matter I want to address. It is an incontrovertible fact that omnipotent states of mind can be induced artificially through the administration of stimulant drugs such as amphetamine, methamphetamine, cocaine and methylphenidate. Similar states can be produced iatrogenically by drugs like levodopa, which are routinely used in the treatment of Parkinsonian diseases. Perhaps the best-known examples of this type are the clinical states of mania and psychosis that Oliver Sacks accidentally induced in the group of encephalitis lethargica patients he described in his famous *Awakenings* (1973). The risk of triggering compulsively over-optimistic states in Parkinsonian patients – such as gambling and religiosity and the like, culminating, if left unchecked, in megalomania – is well known to every neurologist. How can we reconcile these medical facts with our psychological understanding of omnipotence?

Most psychoanalysts nowadays ignore such facts (they do not deny them; they just ignore them) because they experience them as challenging to their whole way of thinking.[1] If omnipotence is a narcissistic state of mind – as Freud would have it, a regression in libidinal cathexis from object love to self-love or, as Melanie Klein would have it, a retreat from the depressive position to the paranoid-schizoid position – then how can such complex psychodynamics be produced through the simple administration of a drug?

Neuropsychoanalysts like me, by contrast, are intrigued by such facts; we see in them an opportunity to learn something new about the clinical phenomena in question, bringing neuroscientific understanding of such phenomena into psychoanalysis and psychoanalytical understanding of them into neuroscience. For us, each such fact is a Rosetta stone.

DOI: 10.4324/9781003185192-12

Sigmund Freud sometimes used this bilingual approach. For example, he observed in his *Three Essays* (long before he introduced the concept of 'narcissistic neuroses') that:

> The neuroses, which can be derived only from disturbances of sexual life, show the closest clinical similarity to the phenomena of intoxication and abstinence that arise from the habitual use of toxic, pleasure-producing substances (alkaloids).
>
> (Freud, 1905: 216)

The alkaloid that would have been at the forefront of Freud's mind here was cocaine because he had extensive clinical experience with it and was intimately familiar with its psychological effects, even in his own case. For example, he wrote the following to his fiancée, Martha Bernays, in a letter dated June 2, 1884:

> Woe to you, my princess, when I come. I will kiss you quite red and feed you till you are plump. And if you are forward you shall see who is the stronger, a gentle little girl who doesn't eat enough or a big wild man who has cocaine in his body.

On the basis of observations such as these, it is not far-fetched to speculate that Freud's experience with cocaine may even have contributed to his broadened conceptualisation of sexuality: to his hypothesis of 'libidinal drive' as a generalized all-purpose pleasure-seeking force in the mind.

What cocaine has in common with the other four drugs listed earlier is that it stimulates a neurotransmitter called dopamine. There are three dopamine systems in the brain, but the one most pertinent for our purposes is the one that every neuroscientist would agree is the prime target of amphetamine, methamphetamine, cocaine and methylphenidate: namely, the so-called 'brain reward system'. This system, the technical name for which is the mesocortical-mesolimbic dopamine system, has many other descriptive labels, such as the 'self-stimulation' system, the 'wanting' system and the 'curiosity-interest-expectancy' system. The term I will use for it in this short chapter is the 'SEEKING' system. This is the name that Jaak Panksepp (1998) gave it in his authoritative taxonomy of the basic emotional drives found in all mammals (and therefore in humans, too).

Significantly, just as this dopaminergic system is the prime target for drugs which *stimulate* omnipotent narcissistic states, so, too, it is the prime target for drugs that have been the mainstay of the pharmacological approaches we have used for the past 70 years to *suppress* them: namely, anti-psychotics, the primary action of which is to reduce dopamine transmission in the SEEKING system.

So how does this system work, and what new light does it cast on our understanding of omnipotence? Here I will provide only a cursory answer, in line with the modest aims of this chapter; for a fuller account of the SEEKING system see Panksepp (1998) and Solms (2021).

SEEKING is said to be the most fundamental of all the mammalian drives. It is the basic reason we engage with the world at all. This is because, no matter what you need, it is typically to be found 'out there' in the world. Accordingly, the satisfaction of almost all our bodily and emotional needs is channelled (at least in part) through SEEKING. For example, if you are hungry, you can find food 'out there'; if you are thirsty, you can find water 'out there'; if you are scared, you can find safety 'out there'; and if you become separated from your caregiver, you can establish reunion with her 'out there'. In this way, through SEEKING, we find all manner of things that we need, like food, water, safety and caregivers.

Importantly, these needs coalesce in activating the SEEKING drive; they all trigger it into action in the same way. This is because they share the common denominator just mentioned: what is needed is 'out there'. Hence, the SEEKING *instinct*, our primary (innate) behavioural response to the SEEKING *drive*, is not food-seeking or water-seeking or safety-seeking, etc., but rather all-purpose exploratory or 'foraging' behaviour. This makes it equivalent to what Freud and Klein called the 'epistemophilic' instinct and perhaps what Bion calls 'K'. SEEKING always engages proactively with what is *not* known. (This is the origin not only of novelty-seeking but also of the thrill-seeking and even the risk-taking that it frequently entails.)

Think of a dog in an open field. While it excitedly explores the new terrain, it almost accidentally comes upon many of the things that it currently needs, such as food, water, playmates or sexual partners.[2] Through learning from such experiences, primary objectless SEEKING yields secondary, more specific, goal-directed forms of 'wanting' (see Berridge, 2003). In future, the animal will not eagerly explore every novelty in the same terrain, precisely because they will be novelties no longer. Now, instead, the animal knows where to focus its efforts – as it has learnt which type of scratch satisfies which type of itch in that particular place. This matching of itches with scratches, affective neuroscientists believe, is the very basis of cause-and-effect learning, which is so fundamental for all knowledge (Panksepp, 1998).[3]

I say we *can* find all the things we need 'out there', and the instinctual type of foraging behaviour that is triggered by SEEKING is predicated on that assumption. Sadly, however, this doesn't mean that we necessarily *will* find what we are looking for. This touches on another one of the most basic properties of the SEEKING drive. When activated, it generates confident feelings of agency and *optimism*. In a word, the SEEKING system operates on the basis of an overarching *wishful* prediction:[4] 'I can and will meet my needs out there in the world'.

Please remember: this is not a loose conjecture; it is solidly grounded in empirical evidence. By administering dopamine-boosting agents, we can artificially *produce* omnipotent feelings. Witness the dramatic narcissistic excesses of Sacks's 'awakened' patients and Freud's boast to his fiancée (quoted earlier) about imposing his will on her. By contrast, if we *block* dopamine, by means of a microelectrode inserted into the dopamine-producing substantia nigra, we can artificially generate the opposite feelings: hopelessness and helplessness:

> The patient's face expressed profound sadness within five seconds [of the electrode being activated].... Although still alert, the patient leaned to the right, started to cry, and verbally communicated feelings of sadness, guilt, uselessness, and hopelessness, such as 'I'm falling down in my head, I no longer wish to live, to see anything, hear anything, feel anything'.... When asked why she was crying and if she felt pain, she responded: 'No, I'm fed up with life, I've had enough.... I don't want to live any more, I'm disgusted with life.... Everything is useless, always feeling worthless, I'm scared in this world.' When asked why she was sad, she replied: 'I'm tired. I want to hide in a corner.... I'm crying over myself, of course.... I'm hopeless, why am I bothering you?' ... The depression disappeared less than 90 seconds after stimulation was stopped. For the next five minutes the patient was in a slightly hypomanic state, and she laughed and joked with the examiner, playfully pulling his tie. She recalled the entire episode. Stimulation [at other brain sites] did not elicit this psychiatric response.
>
> (Blomstedt et al., 2008: 254)

The state of mind elicited in this patient (with no psychiatric history of any kind) is the very opposite of omnipotence. It is characterized by a near-total lack of agency and therefore by *pessimism*, and it results in the opposite of SEEKING: anergia, abulia, anhedonia, defeatism, etc.

In natural situations, the most common cause of such feelings and behaviours (i.e., total or near-total shutting down of SEEKING) is prolonged separation from a caregiver: that is to say, loss of her. Initially upon separation, juvenile mammals (including human children) emit 'separation-distress vocalizations' (e.g., crying) and 'search' behaviours. Ethologists call this response the 'protest' phase of the separation-distress cascade. Then, if reunion is not established, the protest behaviour is followed by 'despair'. Here is Bowlby's (1969) classical description of the two phases of this response:

> [Protest] ... may begin immediately or may be delayed; it lasts from a few hours to a week or more. During it the young child appears acutely distressed at having lost his mother and seeks to recapture her by the full exercise of his limited resources. He will often cry loudly, shake his cot, throw himself about, and look eagerly towards any sight or sound which might prove to be his missing mother. All his behaviour suggests strong expectation that she will return. Meanwhile he is apt to reject all alternative figures who offer to do things for him, though some children will cling desperately to a nurse.
>
> [Despair] ... succeeds protest, the child's preoccupation with his missing mother is still evident, though his behaviour suggests increasing hopelessness.

The active physical movements diminish or come to an end, and he may cry monotonously or intermittently. He is withdrawn and inactive, makes no demands on people in the environment, and appears to be in a state of deep mourning.

The despair phenotype is, of course, the normal prototype for depression, as Freud (1917) discerned long ago: melancholia (i.e., depression) is a pathological form of mourning (i.e., grief). What we know today, on the basis of experiments and clinical observations of the kind described earlier, is how the transition from 'protest' to 'despair' actually works in the brain: falling mu opioid levels (which characterize 'protest') result in rising kappa opioid levels (dynorphin), which, in turn, shuts down dopamine, which produces 'despair'. That is, it shuts down SEEKING. There is a long evolutionary story as to why this happens, but that story need not concern us here.

These simple facts outline the essential functions of the SEEKING system and its relationship to omnipotence. I think they shed new light on what omnipotence *is*. It is, in a word, unconstrained SEEKING. The developmental sequence goes something like this.

The SEEKING drive activates an instinctual prediction (viz., foraging behaviour), which, to begin with, is excessively optimistic about our ability to meet our needs in the world – our ability to impose our will upon it. This yields thoughts like 'You shall see who is the stronger'. A shutting down of the SEEKING drive, by contrast, generates predictions which are excessively pessimistic – that is, thoughts like 'I'm tired. . . . I want to hide in a corner. . . . I'm hopeless. . . . Why am I bothering you?'

Here we have the two poles of Freud's 'pleasure principle' – through satisfaction and thwarting of the libidinal drive – and the mode of operation of his 'pleasure ego' (Freud, 1925), which functions on the basis that 'if something feels good, it is part of me, and if it feels bad, it is not' (i.e., splitting, through introjecting the pleasurable and projecting the unpleasurable). In other words, here we have the mode of operation of Melanie Klein's 'paranoid-schizoid position'. It is no accident, then, if everything bad is projected outside, that megalomania progresses to paranoia.

What the child (like the optimistic dog in an open field) is called upon to do – which is the great task of all mental development – is to learn from experience which of its needs can be met, where and how, and which cannot, where and how. Crucially, this includes a tolerance and acceptance of *loss*.[5] This is the middle ground of Freud's 'reality principle' – and the mode of functioning of his 'reality ego' (Freud, 1925) – the essential task of which is to constrain SEEKING through learning from experience.[6] In this way, the child gradually builds up what we (in contemporary neuroscience) call a viable 'predictive model' of how it can meet its needs in the environmental niche it finds itself in (see Clark, 2015) – a model which is far more context sensitive and therefore more efficient than the overly generalized instinctual prediction that we are born with, which seems to embody the (manic) Christian injunction: 'Seek, and ye shall find'.

Oliver Sacks (1973), as always, sums things up beautifully. Describing the ways in which his Parkinsonian patients overcame their drug-induced excesses, he shows they did so in much the same way as omnipotent inclinations must be overcome by us all:

> The weapons of use in the tribulations of L-DOPA are those we all use in conducting our lives: deep strengths and reserves, whose very existence is unsuspected; common sense, forethought, caution, and care; special vigilance and wiles to combat special dangers; the establishment of right relations of all sorts; and, of course, the final acceptance of what must be accepted. A good part of the tribulations of [Parkinsonian] patients (and their physicians) comes from unreal attempts to transcend the possible, to deny its limits, and to seek the impossible: accommodation is more laborious and less exalted, and consists, in effect, of a painstaking exploration of the full range of the real and the possible. Accommodation lacks the glamour of Awakening. It lacks its sudden, spontaneous, 'miraculous' quality. It does not come 'of itself' – easily and effortlessly. It is earned, worked for – with infinite effort and courage and trouble. It does not reflect some local change in the basal ganglia,[7] and can in no sense be regarded as a localized process: it is an achievement of character, of negotiation, in its widest possible sense. What is achieved in this way, with work and difficulty, is secure and enduring – unlike the facile 'flash' of 'awakening', which goes, as it comes, too easily, too quickly.

I hope readers will agree that nothing I have said here pours cold water on our classical psychoanalytical understanding of omnipotence. On the contrary, the classical notions help us explain some neuropsychiatric findings which would otherwise be difficult to understand (e.g., why should megalomania so frequently develop into, or so frequently be accompanied by, paranoia?). On the other hand, I hope that readers will agree also that the concept of SEEKING adds a new dimension to our understanding of omnipotence, one which enables us to integrate our own observations with those of our neurological and neuroscientific colleagues. This can only be a positive development because, as Charcot famously said: 'Theory is good; but it doesn't prevent things from existing'.

Notes

1 This did not apply to the first generation of psychoanalysts, most of whom were neurologists. See, for example, Smith Ely Jelliffe (1927).
2 The fact that LUST activates SEEKING led Freud to the erroneous conclusion that they are part of one and the same drive. SEEKING (not LUST) performs all the major functions that Freud attributed to the 'libidinal' drive. LUST is no more apt to trigger SEEKING than is any other need.
3 Cf. Freud's concept of the 'experience of satisfaction'.
4 Here is a first link with psychoanalysis. The wishful SEEKING system literally drives dreaming (see Solms, 2000, 2001, 2011).

5 Omnipotent patients have great difficulty in accepting that they cannot have their cake and eat it too: i.e., in relinquishing one option in favour of another. This inability to bear loss is closely related to the 'all-or-nothing' attitude that characterizes splitting; omnipotence entails the implicit belief that one can 'have it all'. This is also closely related to greed, of course (and its cognate, envy).
6 The *constraining* of SEEKING, which characterizes the depressive position is quite different from the *shutting down* of SEEKING, which characterizes depression (cf., the all-or-nothing of splitting, just mentioned). Moving on from 'despair' (i.e., what Bowlby calls 'detachment') requires acceptance of the loss.
7 The basal ganglia are innervated primarily by dopamine.

References

Berridge, K. (2003). Pleasures of the brain. *Brain and Cognition*, 52: 106–128.
Blomstedt, P., Hariz, M., Lees, A., et al. (2008). Acute severe depression induced by intraoperative stimulation of the substantia nigra: A case report. *Parkinsonism and Related Disorders*, 14: 253–256.
Bowlby, J. (1969). *Attachment*. London: Hogarth Press.
Clark, A. (2015). *Surfing Uncertainty: Prediction, Action, and the Embodied Mind*. New York: Oxford University Press.
Freud, S. (1905). Three essays on the theory of sexuality. In *Standard Edition of the Complete Psychological Works of Sigmund Freud*, 7. London: Hogarth, 125–243.
Freud, S. (1917). Three essays on the theory of sexuality. In *Standard Edition of the Complete Psychological Works of Sigmund Freud*, 14. London: Hogarth, 239–258.
Freud, S. (1925). Negation. In *Standard Edition of the Complete Psychological Works of Sigmund Freud*, 19. London: Hogarth, 235–240.
Jelliffe, S.E. (1927). The mental pictures in schizophrenia and in epidemic encephalitis. *American Journal of Psychiatry*, 6: 413–465.
Panksepp, J. (1998). *Affective Neuroscience: The Foundations of Human and Animal Emotions*. New York: Oxford University Press.
Sacks, O. (1973). *Awakenings*. London: Duckworth.
Solms, M. (2000). Dreaming and REM sleep are controlled by different brain mechanisms. *Behavioral and Brain Sciences*, 23: 843–850.
Solms, M. (2001). The neurochemistry of dreaming: Cholinergic and dopaminergic hypotheses. In Perry, E., Ashton, H. & Young, A. (Eds.), *The Neurochemistry of Consciousness*. New York: John Benjamins, 123–131.
Solms, M. (2011). Neurobiology and the neurological basis of dreaming. In Montagna, P. & Chokroverty, S. (Eds.), *Handbook of Clinical Neurology*, 98 (3rd series), *Sleep Disorders*, Part 1. New York: Elsevier, 519–544.
Solms, M. (2021). *The Hidden Spring: A Journey to the Source of Consciousness*. London: Profile Books.

Chapter 9

The relinquishment of omnipotence in a severely traumatised patient

Heinz Weiss

Introduction

The relinquishment of omnipotence is a necessary, albeit painful task in human development. When it activates feelings of deprivation, humiliation, and shame, it can assume a traumatic quality. But even when reality can be accepted, the pain of mourning and loss must be faced. If these feelings seem unbearable, the individual may turn to omnipotent illusions once again. Therefore, the loss of omnipotent beliefs may be something that we can tolerate only temporarily so that the 'joy of illusion and the pains of disillusionment are recurring experiences as we journey through life' (Steiner, 2020: 4).

Disillusionment and loss are even more difficult to bear if omnipotence is required to maintain a precarious psychic equilibrium. This is often the case when patients resort to pathological organisations of the personality to protect themselves against anxieties of a paranoid-schizoid or depressive kind. Under these circumstances, omnipotence is required to avoid fragmentation, confusion, or the confrontation with guilt and unbearable psychic pain.

Our understanding of pathological organisations is based on the work of Karl Abraham (1919, 1924), Melanie Klein (1935, 1940, 1946), Joan Rivière (1936), and others. Herbert Rosenfeld (1964, 1971) and Donald Meltzer (1968, 1973) have described them as operating like a narcissistic or 'mafia like' gang (Rosenfeld, 1971). In times of need, they try to seduce weak and needy parts of the self through the promise of protection and security. If the individual accepts the offer, they often find themselves lured away into a trap because the price to pay is allegiance and submission to the organisation's principles. It is particularly when the patient tries to free himself from its dominance that the sadistic cruelty of the pathological structure becomes obvious.

Sometimes the organisation is idealised in the beginning and presents itself as a secure place or 'safe haven', such as a cosy cave, a tropical island, or a sanctuary. At other times, the hopelessness and imprisonment are more overtly visible. In both cases, however, an addictive dependency owing to the seductive power of omnipotence may develop. As John Steiner (1993) has demonstrated, it is the complexity of these organisations and the dependency on omnipotence that make them relatively resistant to psychic change. He has described these states of mind as *'psychic retreats'*, and he also emphasized the narcissistic and perverse elements that are involved in their construction and maintenance. In continuation of Steiner's ideas, I have pointed out that 'timelessness' is another characteristic feature of pathological organisations; it is the denial of the experience of time that contributes to their rigidity and impedes the working through of mourning and loss (Weiss, 2009, 2020). Other authors have named these retreats *'bastions'* (Baranger et al., 1988) or *'traumatic defence organizations'* (Brown, 2005, 2006; Weiss, 2020).

What these structures have in common is that they serve initially as a 'protective shield' and become, in due course, prisons that are difficult to escape from. Another prominent feature is that during treatment, these organisations have a pervasive impact on the transference situation. Often the analysis gets stuck, and the patient seems 'difficult to reach' (Joseph, 1975). Behind the scenes, subtle re-enactments take place, difficult to recognise and disentangle (Steiner, 2000, 2006). By some means or other, the analyst then gets drawn into the pull of the pathological structure.

In this chapter, I will describe a patient who had built up such an organisation beginning in her childhood, in my view mainly to protect herself from fears of persecution and abandonment. I will examine how the omnipotent organisation was constructed as a shield against her early traumatic experiences, how it gained control over vast areas of her life, and how an addictive dependency on its operation developed.

I will explore how the pathological structure resurfaced in the transference situation and how the patient was overwhelmed with confusion and despair when faced with reality and depressive anxiety. As she finally made steps to leave her psychic retreat, she broke down as the omnipotence of her organisation collapsed, and she seemed to be exposed to persecution and guilt beyond repair.

After the breakdown, new developments emerged. However, as several authors have emphasised (O'Shaughnessy, 1981), the pathological structure did not entirely disappear. For a while, its remains coexisted with the new developments, and it was only when the patient could gradually face mourning and guilt that she was able to repair her damaged inner objects. I will show this by describing in more detail the ending phase of her analysis when she felt enabled to acknowledge the passage of time and made steps to leave her timeless universe. This was accompanied by a relinquishment of omnipotence on the part of the patient, but also on the part of the analyst who had to orient himself towards the limited but realistic aims that could be achieved.

Clinical material: Mrs. E

Mrs. E[1] was an intelligent, shy, somehow childlike 27-year-old employee who had sought analysis when what she had called her 'inner strength' was in danger of breaking down. A couple of months previously, she had married her husband who evidently seemed to love her. However, her state deteriorated quickly: she lost weight, could neither eat nor work, withdrew, and started to hurt herself as she had done frequently in the past. In her depression, she was absorbed in thoughts of accidents and incurable diseases and was convinced that her husband would find nothing loveable in her and therefore leave her.

History

Mrs. E's deteriorated state reflected the return of some of the devastating experiences of her childhood. As the elder of two siblings, she had been neglected and abused by a delinquent, alcoholic mother who was often drunk and largely absent. Repeatedly, she and her younger sister were left alone in the flat without food, and, as early as age two, she was admitted to hospital due to dehydration. The same happened when she was eleven. At that time, she refused to eat and wanted to die. She said she had hoped that in this way she would relieve her mother of the burden of her existence.

With the exception of times with her grandmother, a neighbourhood boyfriend when she was little, and occasional excursions with her father, there was little evidence of any significant good experiences during her childhood. As I learned in the course of her analysis, Mrs. E's mother had not only prostituted herself but also 'lent' the patient to a circle of paedophile men from the age of five onwards. Her father appeared as a weak, depressed figure in the background. He was often away, and he, too, had affairs with other women. After her parents' divorce when she was fourteen, she had taken over responsibility for her father and her younger sister.

Despite all these pressures, she was able to finish her school education and find employment as an officer with a large security firm. Everything in this company, down to the smallest detail, was regulated by rules, procedures, and instructions, meeting her needs for subordination and discipline. Some two years before her marriage, her father had died, and it was left to her to organize his funeral without any expression of sadness or grief, which she considered to be signs of 'weakness' and unforgiveable 'lack of discipline'.

Mrs. E tried to 'erase' her mother from her mind; her mother was not to know where she lived, whether or not she had married, or what name she now had. At the same time, however, she was convinced that she would end up like her mother and sink into chaos, overwhelmed by greed and cruelty, and indeed, she felt she was already exactly like her. This was the reason she felt she had not 'deserved' her husband and banned herself from the idea of having children of her own.

Before Mrs. E came to analysis, she had lived in a state of 'sedation' for many years, having been treated more or less unsuccessfully with neuroleptics, antidepressants, tranquilisers, and behaviour therapy. Her self-harming had started in childhood and went along with eating disorders, gastrointestinal problems, excruciating inner turmoil, states of derealisation, and often a wish to die.

The pathological structure

As I learned during Mrs. E's analysis, she had developed early in her youth a highly complex phantasy system to cope with the terrible experiences of her childhood. The system was based on submission, control, and self-discipline in relation to the central structure of a 'tower', a solid structure and a 'safe place' where she was imprisoned. As she described it, inside the tower, which served as a refuge, she was tormented and humiliated by a gang of anonymous, cruel men, who eventually got her into a state of 'belonging', making her feel close to her tormentors and absolutely secure under their protection. This idea comforted her and gave her some relief because the promise was that, if she was able to suffer their cruelty without complaint, she would be offered 'total security' and finally become part of them.

This phantasy formed an important part of her daydreaming, in particular at those times when she felt helpless and depressed. It gave her solace at night time and helped her go to sleep. By resorting to the omnipotent figures inside the 'tower', Mrs. E had created a timeless universe where the perpetrators of her childhood had been transformed into what she had come to call her 'best friends'.

Thus, the promise of the organisation was to turn persecution into security by establishing an identification with cruel, powerful objects if she was prepared to submit to their principles and relinquish her own life. Evidently, the 'tower' represented an idealised superego structure, offering 'order', a sense of identity, and freedom from feelings of guilt at the cost of a restricted life and chronic suffering. An important feature was that the structure was always available and did not change.

The emergence of the 'tower' in the transference situation

In the analysis, it took Mrs. E several months before she could tell me about her hidden phantasy world. This was because she feared that, by communicating her ideas, they would lose their power, and the men in the tower would see this as disloyalty and withhold their protection. In this way, the analysis was experienced as a threat to the security that was provided in her prison. However, at the same time, the analysis was seen as powerless and weak since I was to know about her torment but only as a witness, helplessly unable to change anything. In fact, the idea of a person 'who knows everything' that goes on in the tower but is unable to intervene was an important part of her phantasy.

During Mrs. E's analysis, the 'phantasy of the tower' was re-enacted in different ways. In a first phase, she followed my interpretations like demands or 'orders' she was expected to obey. She tried to read my mind, to follow my hidden expectations, and to avoid anything that could disappoint me. In doing so, she erected a new tower within the analysis, and I became identified with a powerful figure that demanded submission at the cost of psychic change. She suspected, for instance,

Figure 9.1 Maschikuliturm, Festung Marienberg, Würzburg, Germany
Source: Carina Weiss

that I had a plan for her she was expected to 'obey'. When I did not openly declare my expectations to her, she saw this as a particularly cruel strategy because this way, she could only 'get it wrong' while being completely at my mercy. If, however, I addressed her sadness and despair, she was confused because she saw these feelings as 'weakness' that was not 'allowed'.

From early on in the analysis, however, a more needy and childlike part of her, who wanted to be picked up and nurtured in her misery, was very palpable. Whenever this side of her came to the fore and she was able to express some gratitude, the 'men in the tower' became suspicious, insulted her, and announced they would punish her even more. They demanded that she had to lower her gaze when leaving the session, saying how pathetic and mean she was and that she did not deserve understanding or help. Thus, a seemingly irresolvable conflict of loyalty between her pathological organisation and her analysis developed. The men accused her of being base and worthless and threatened if she did not obey, they would let her fall into chaos and disaster.

The collapse of the pathological organisation and its consequences

This threat was realised in the second year of her analysis when some changes in Mrs. E's private life – a severe marital crisis and the death of her beloved grandmother – took place. Now she felt that her 'protective armour' (in her words) had broken down and that the men in the tower were no longer available. She felt desperate, helpless, and confused and asked herself where the analysis had taken her. Everything inside her seemed to collapse; the iron slogan in her life – 'You can, you should, you must!' – seemed no longer effective. She was preoccupied with a longing to die and overwhelmed by destructive impulses, feeling a strong desire to harm herself and 'to destroy everything'. When I linked this to our sessions and, in particular, to the imagery she had created of her mother and the lack of her protection, she experienced this as a devastating accusation and, at the same time, as confirmation of her worst fear: namely, that she might be exactly like her mother. She missed several sessions, and in the face of her destructiveness, I felt helpless and powerless, presumably similar to how she felt during her childhood.

She returned to tell me a dream: she was standing in front of her former school in which a fire had broken out. The fire brigade had come too late, and she looked at the immense devastation. Her classmates' charred bodies sat on the chairs, and she wished that she could have been burned and died with them.

In view of this destructive scene, I felt impotent as if I had 'arrived too late', like the fire brigade, and maybe was even responsible for the devastating fire which had erupted in her. Only now did it become clear to me to what extent her destructive powers were bound in the pathological organisation of the 'tower', and I began to doubt whether the treatment could extinguish the fire that had been ignited. This danger was real, but nevertheless, I thought that the desperate situation in which we found ourselves had probably been unavoidable if anything was to change at all.

Mrs. E seemed to sense my doubts and lack of confidence. She asked me what made me hang on to the treatment so tenaciously. At the same time, she expressed her dependency on the sessions as never before. On one occasion, she said that there was 'no way back', and she hoped that I knew what I was doing. I felt the responsibility she handed over to me but was full of doubt and did not myself know how things would turn out.

This situation reminded me of the dilemma described by Joan Rivière (1936) when the individual feels trapped between guilt and depression without hope or prospect of reparation, a situation which is sometimes experienced as if the only choice that is left is the choice between madness and death (Weiss, 2020: 83).

Subsequent developments

Nevertheless, Mrs. E overcame this crisis, and in the subsequent period of her analysis, some new developments emerged. She decided to stay with her husband, and together, they adopted two kittens, which she treated as if they were their children. The accounts of her kittens filled many sessions and conveyed a sense of family life. This was interrupted when one day she arrived in shock and despair because the younger kitten had fallen from the balustrade of her balcony, where a black bird had landed. The kitten subsequently died, and in this session, she was barely able to speak. Her voice was interrupted by brief animal-like shrieks and several times she cried: 'I have lost my daughter, ooh my little girl!' She was overwhelmed by sadness and guilt, but clearly realised that this loss could never be reversed. It took her several months to mourn the death of her kitten, but I think this indicated a change: she was no longer identified with a murderous mother who had killed her child but with a guilty mother who had lost her child.

The ensuing shifts between reparation and guilt dominated the subsequent years of her analysis, which I cannot report in detail. The 'men in the tower' had not totally disappeared but faded into the background and sometimes were resorted to when loss and feelings of uncertainty were hard to bear. They would then warn her 'not to go too far', but they appeared to accept her analysis in order to 'make her a better person'.

Subsequently, Mrs. E began to discover a 'zest for life', a feeling hitherto unknown to her, and made plans for the future. If something went wrong, however, her newly grown confidence was attacked by internal figures such as those represented in a dream of black birds with huge wings inviting her to fall into the peaceful land of silent deadness, which, like the 'tower', was also timeless and where the pains of life did not have to be faced. Of course, these 'black birds' reminded her of the loss of her kitten, frightened by a black bird that had landed on the balustrade of her balcony. In contrast to the beginning of her analysis, however, she now knew about the dangers of the peaceful deadness of this timeless world and tried to resist the seductive pull that emanated from it, reminding me of

Odysseus's struggle with the sirens. But even at those moments, she said, she felt, that 'there was a development that could not be reversed'.

The ending phase

It was in the seventh year of Mrs. E's analysis that a slowly growing, constant feeling emerged that her analysis would not go on forever and one day would come to an end. When she told me about this, she was anxious because the idea made her sad. Furthermore, she was afraid that articulating the thought would make it 'real', and this was painful because a part of her could not imagine that the analysis would ever end. What followed was a one-and-a-half-year-long exploration of her feelings connected with the idea of ending.

Her growing confidence that she could live her own life and deal with the feelings of mourning and loss had to do with a change in our relationship, in which she no longer saw me as the powerful authority to whom she had to submit or as the idealised figure who could 'rescue' her. More on the level, she would call me by name, sometimes argue with me, and look straight into my eyes at the beginning and the ending of the sessions. Often, she expressed a simple undisguised feeling of gratitude.

This more realistic stance towards the analytic endeavour involved an acknowledgment on her part that the damage and losses in her life could not be reversed, as well as an acknowledgment on my part that the effects of the analysis would always remain limited compared to the experiences she had undergone in her childhood.

Nevertheless, uncertainty and doubt sometimes re-emerged, in particular when the reality of the ending became more apparent. When she recognized how difficult it was to endure the passage of time, she would sometimes drift away into brief moments of derealisation. On a foggy afternoon, she described the soft falling of the leaves from the trees near my consulting room and said that it felt like a sensation of ease and comfort. Then she realized that next autumn, she would no longer be coming to see me.

In a dream, she pictured me as 'Professor Freud', sitting opposite the couch looking straight into her eyes. She associated 'Professor Freud' with a somewhat old-fashioned paternal authority with strange views about women. She would not like to see me like him, she said, although she liked the idea of a father she could trust. Then she added that she no longer saw therapy like the 'repair of a car' or as a magical healing via the gaze of a powerful authority. Nevertheless, there was also a wish 'that my father would somehow be around and see me'.

In another dream, she undertook a journey with her father, who now appeared much younger, although she knew that he was dead. She also said she still could not forgive her mother but asked herself what would have happened if her mother had had the chance to have analysis at her age.

All this was accompanied by feelings of mourning and uncertainty. Sometimes the 'black birds' reappeared, and it was not easy to resist their appeal. Timelessness was still an option, although she knew that finitude and loss had become irreversible. In one of these sessions, she said: 'Yes, I will end, but I wish to assure you that we still have material for another 1,000 sessions.' I had no doubt that this was true, as was her recognition that analysis could not go on forever. This seemed to indicate that the idea of ending was *her decision* and not just the result of an analysis which had dried out. She further admitted that for a long time she had believed as long as she continued to suffer, she would be allowed to come forever. Now she seemed to believe that there was no such thing as an endless analysis but also no endless suffering.

Then, after eight years, the last sessions came up. The impending end shook her. She again felt restless and anxious and had trouble with her bowels, feeling as if the ground was drawn away beneath her feet. Most of the losses in her life had been immediate, sudden, and confusing. It was unusual that now there was some time left for mourning. There was a phantasy of lying with ear plugs on the couch and falling into a long, soft sleep to avoid the pain of separation. What would the very last session feel like, the moment when she would say goodbye? It would be so difficult to put her feelings into words, including her sadness and her gratitude.

Three sessions before the end, she mentioned a dream in which she had already 'told' me the dream while she slept. The only scene that she remembered was that of a cosy wooden cottage in Scandinavia. She was sitting with a man at a table in front of the hut when snow began to fall. Then a storm came up. She tried to hold on to the table, but the wind swept her away, and the man did nothing but just let her go as if he was indifferent to her disappearance. She landed somewhere in the snow and was taken up by a group which passed by.

In this dream, the cosy wooden hut seemed to stand for her analysis, which she was going to leave. We were already sitting outside, but when the storm grew and swept her up, I did nothing to hold her back. To the snow she associated that she was born in winter and was sometimes called 'snowflake'. When she was a child, she would at times write down her dreams and tell them to her father, who would comment on them. But I asked myself whether she really saw me as indifferent to her leaving. Sleeping and snowfall were, of course, also reminders of the soft, timeless states of mind. But they were different from the dark land of the black birds.

She said she wanted to visit her father's grave, and now some of the feelings emerged to do with the mourning, which she had suppressed at the time of his death. She did not know whether her mother was still alive, but she thought that she would it find difficult to mourn her, although she felt some compassion for her.

Again, she felt sad, and she dreamed she would arrive late for her last session because she would be delayed by her dentist. He proposed to give her a brace to make her teeth fit more closely together, but she did not like this idea. It seemed connected to the 'men in the tower' demanding new 'procedures' from her.

Contrary to her expectations, she arrived rather nervous but in a bright mood to her very last session. There was a sort of woefulness but also a sense of humour when she mentioned her husband jokingly saying that she would certainly be back soon because 'It is no more than just saying goodbye!' Of course, it was not. She had noticed her heart beating, and during the session, she briefly wept. But then she remembered quite freely how she felt at the beginning of her analysis and spoke about the prospects for her future, although she was uncertain how things would turn out. When she said goodbye, she looked straight into my eyes, and in this moment, she must have realised that some sadness resided inside me which was difficult to put into words.

Some thoughts about termination – the relinquishment of omnipotence and the difficulty of accepting finitude

The description of the ending phase of Mrs. E's analysis is, of course, a highly condensed report of a long period of therapeutic work. Perhaps there was a romantic element in her relationship with me as her father-analyst in the final sessions. She could bring me dreams as gifts and expect me to understand her as the 'snowflake' – with a disturbing and difficult mother being left outside. What I wanted to illustrate, however, were the shifts between the return to timeless states of mind – the soft falling of the leaves, the ear plugs, the snow, and the idea of falling asleep – and Mrs. E's slow, steady acknowledgment of the reality of separation and loss, which is a prerequisite for the relinquishment of omnipotence.

For many years, Mrs. E was in the grip of an omnipotent organisation which had evolved from the traumatic experiences of her childhood. The organisation, represented by 'the men in the tower', provided her with a sense of identity and strength by protecting her from feelings of persecution and abandonment and had a pervasive influence on her life. It ruled her relationships at the cost of contact with others and emotional development. She believed she was bad and saw the sole justification of her existence in surviving to 'function for others'. Thus, she was unable to mourn her father's death and was confused about her husband's love.

As soon as she entered analysis, the pathological structure interfered with the transference situation, leading to a conflict of loyalty between the 'men in the tower' and the analysis. In the course of the therapy, her 'best friends' withdrew their protection, and the collapse of the organisation exposed her to confusion and despair. She felt an urge to die and was overwhelmed by destructive impulses. At this stage of her analysis, the loss of omnipotence was experienced as a shock and loss of orientation, and I, too, was filled with doubt and uncertainty how to proceed.

It was in the subsequent years that the need for punishment was gradually replaced by the working through of guilt (see Nunberg, 1926). This allowed for new freedom and a better contact with reality. However, as in the case described by O'Shaughnessy (1981), the organisation was not entirely dismantled when development occurred, but coexisted for a long period with the analysis, available when an omnipotent part of the patient felt the urge to stay in projective identification with powerful destructive objects to evade feelings of mourning and loss.

Despite her traumatic childhood, Mrs. E displayed an amazing capacity to take in the few good experiences that she found in her life. This ability was palpable from the very beginning of her analysis. It enabled her to deal with mourning and guilt and finally to leave the timeless universe of the 'tower' where suffering would go on forever. In other words, she had replaced obedience to the superego with a loyalty to reality, and this allowed her to repair her damaged inner objects.

It is the painful task of reparation (Klein, 1937; Rey, 1986, 1988) which brings us in contact with some fundamental aspects of reality which we find difficult to accept. Amongst these 'facts of life', Roger Money-Kyrle (1971) has attributed particular significance to the infant's dependency on the 'breast' as an external source of goodness, to the parental intercourse as a 'supremely creative act', and finally, to the 'recognition of the inevitability of time and ultimately death' (p. 443).

I think the relinquishment of omnipotence has to do with the recognition of all these elementary 'facts of life', but perhaps it is the reality of transience (Freud, 1916a) and loss, which is the most fundamental and the most difficult to acknowledge. After several years of analysis, Mrs. E realised that her treatment would come to an end just like the sufferings of her childhood could not go on forever. Paradoxically, she had to mourn the loss of the omnipotent security the 'men in the tower' offered in order to get access to the pains and joy that life in reality provides. This included a more realistic appreciation of what had really been bad in her life and could not be reversed, as well as a deeper appreciation and love of the good things and developments that also occurred.

Approaching termination often means for the patient the loss of an idealized illusion she or he had adhered to and for the analysts the loss of some omnipotent belief, which also has to be mourned and to be replaced by a more realistic judgement of what she or he could achieve. Of course, for Mrs. E, these achievements would always remain limited compared to the experiences she had lived through in her childhood. Nevertheless, she expressed a genuine feeling of gratitude and aroused some sadness in me when she looked straight into my eyes to say goodbye.

Termination is, therefore, perhaps one of the most crucial points in each analysis. It indicates that the actual experience of loss cannot be evaded and has to be faced in order to proceed with the process of mourning. Thinking about this, I felt reminded of a remark by Melanie Klein in her paper 'On Termination', in which she says that the last bit of mourning must be done by the patient when she or he is finally alone, without the analyst (Klein, 1950: 46). Sometimes this process goes on for quite a while, even after the ending.

'Why *must* analysis end?' was the insistent question of another patient when she felt that her analysis was inevitably coming to an end. She added: 'Can you please give me the reasons?' I did not know what to say and so asked my supervisor, who was at that time Hanna Segal. She said I could simply say: 'Because it *must* end'. When I was not content with her answer, she explained: 'It is only because all good experiences must come to an end that also the bad experiences cannot go on forever' (Segal, 2008, personal communication).

I think it is the awareness of this 'fact of life' that can sometimes help us come to terms with the difficult task of ending.

Note

1 A more detailed account of the clinical material from the first years of Mrs. E's analysis is presented in my book *Trauma, Guilt and Reparation: The Path from Impasse to Reparation* (Weiss, 2020: 63–98).

References

Abraham, K. (1919). A particular form of neurotic resistance against the psycho-analytic method. In *Selected Papers of Karl Abraham*. London: Karnac, 1979, 303–311.

Abraham, K. (1924). A short study of the development of the libido, viewed in the light of mental disorders. In *Selected Papers of Karl Abraham*. London: Karnac, 1979, 418–501.

Baranger, M., Baranger, W. & Mom, J.M. (1988). The infantile psychic trauma from us to Freud: Pure trauma, retroactivity, and retroaction. *International Journal of Psycho-Analysis*, 69, 113–128.

Brown, L. (2005). The cognitive effects of trauma: The reversal of alpha function and the formation of a beta screen. *Psychoanalytic. Quarterly*, 74, 397–420.

Brown, L. (2006). Julie's Museum: The evolution of thinking, dreaming and historicization in the treatment of traumatized patients. *International. Journal of Psycho-Analysis*, 87, 1569–1585.

Freud, S. (1916a). On transience. *S.E. XIV*, 303–307.

Joseph, B. (1975). The patient who is difficult to reach. In Giovacchini, P.L. (Ed.), *Tactics and Techniques in Psychoanalytic Therapy. Vol. 2: Countertransference*. New York: Jason Aronson, 1975, 205–216.

Klein, M. (1935). A contribution to the psychogenesis of manic-depressive states. In *The Writings of Melanie Klein*. London: Hogarth, 1975, 262–289.

Klein, M. (1937). Love, guilt, and reparation. In *The Writings of Melanie Klein*, vol. 3. London: Hogarth, 1975, 306–343.

Klein, M. (1940). Mourning and its relation to manic-depressive states. In *The Writings of Melanie Klein*. London: Hogarth, 1975, 344–369.

Klein, M. (1946). Notes on some schizoid mechanisms. In *The Writings of Melanie Klein*. London: Hogarth, 1975, 1–24.

Klein, M. (1950). On the criteria for the termination of a psychoanalysis. In *The Writings of Melanie Klein*. London: Hogarth, 1975, 43–47.

Meltzer, D. (1968). Terror, persecution, dread: A dissection of paranoid anxieties. *International Journal of Psycho-Analysis*, 48, 396–401.

Meltzer, D. (1973). Infantile perverse sexuality. In Meltzer, D. (Ed.), *Sexual States of Mind*. Strath Tay, Perthshire: Clunie Press, 90–98.

Money-Kyrle, R. (1971). The aim of psychoanalysis. In Meltzer, D. & O'Shaughnessy, E. (Eds.), *The Collected Papers of Roger Money-Kyrle*. Strath Tay, Perthshire: Clunie Press, 1978, 442–449.

Nunberg, H.G. (1926). The sense of guilt and the need for punishment. In Nunberg, H.G. (Ed.), *Practice and Theory of Psychoanalysis*. New York: International Universities Press, 1948, 89–101.
O'Shaughnessy, E. (1981). A clinical study of a defensive organisation. *International Journal of Psycho-Analysis*, 62, 359–369.
Rey, H. (1986). Reparation. *Journal of the Melanie Klein Society*, 4, 5–35.
Rey, H. (1988). That which patients bring to analysis. *International Journal of Psycho-Analysis*, 69, 457–470.
Rivière, J. (1936). A contribution to the analysis of the negative therapeutic reaction. *International Journal of Psycho-Analysis*, 17, 304–320.
Rosenfeld, H.A. (1964). An investigation into the need of neurotic and psychotic patients to act out during analysis. In Rosenfeld, H.A. (Ed.), *Psychotic States. A Psychoanalytical Approach*. London: Hogarth Press, 1965, 200–216.
Rosenfeld, H.A. (1971). A clinical approach to the psychoanalytic theory of the life and death instincts: An investigation into the aggressive aspects of narcissism. *International Journal of Psychoanalysis*, 52, 169–178.
Segal, H. (2008). Personal communication.
Steiner, J. (1993). *Psychic Retreats: Pathological Organizations in Psychotic, Neurotic and Borderline Patients*. London and New York: Routledge.
Steiner, J. (2000). Containment, enactment, and the analytic setting. *International Journal of Psycho-Analysis*, 81, 245–255.
Steiner, J. (2006). Interpretative enactments and the analytic setting. *International Journal of Psycho-Analysis*, 87, 315–320.
Steiner, J. (2020). *Illusion, Disillusion, and Irony in Psychoanalysis*. London and New York: Routledge.
Weiss, H. (2009). Das Labyrinth der Borderline-Kommunikation. In *Klinische Zugänge zum Erleben von Raum und Zeit*. Stuttgart: Klett-Cotta.
Weiss, H. (2020). *Trauma, Guilt and Reparation. The Path from Impasse to Development*. London and New York: Routledge.

Chapter 10

Possessed by a cruel God

The damaging effect of an omnipotent internal object

Carlos Tamm

In most religious belief systems, omnipotence is God's most important attribute. Adam's days on his own in Paradise, however, did not feel like divine perfection, leading God to consider: 'It is not good that the man should be alone; I will make him a helper fit for him' (Genesis 2.18 ESV, 1957). Later, as we understand, Adam and Eve longed for more, and their curiosity would lead them to the erotic experience, which in turn would result in the birth of mankind.

To be born is to come into a world of need and action, of experience and error, of learning and of ignorance. In many different phases of one's life, there can be found a yearning to try and recover this lost perfection of paradise.

Over time in my work, I have been struck by the realisation that many patients have certain beliefs that are tenaciously maintained, even when there is compelling evidence that contradicts them. These beliefs often take the form of rules or dogmas; they are not born out of experience but, on the contrary, seem to precede actual experience. In this sense, they define not how things are, but how things must be or shall be. The tenacity with which they are kept is defined by Britton: 'Belief rests on probability, not certainty, and yet it produces the emotional state that goes with certainty' (Britton, 2009: 8). It is as if what Bion calls a 'definitory hypothesis' (Bion, 1963: 29) had become a concept without going through the processes described by him on his grid (Bion, 1963, 1970, 1989) as notation, attention and inquiry, which were aborted by Ψ (resistance). Some primitive elements of this operation are present in culture, corresponding to areas of human experience that have not been subjected to proper inquiry. These powerful dogmas correspond to unconscious phantasies, behaviours or statements, repeated and perpetuated despite the abundance of evidence contradicting the supposed truth. Prime examples of these: it is considered that all parents feel only love for their children and are necessarily loved by them; siblings likewise have only loving feelings towards each other; children have no sexuality; and the list goes on. Beliefs in these areas have been treated not as ideas or possibilities but as necessary facts.

In religion, where we probably find the main instance of dogma, we might ideally find relief in the clear distinction between two different realms: when one is engaged in religious practices or takes part in a service or enters a temple, he

DOI: 10.4324/9781003185192-14

embraces all the dogmas involved in his adherence to that religion. However, when he is in the outside world, he understands that his beliefs do not matter to those who do not share them. In many religious traditions, however, there is not a clear distinction between the religious statement and the statement of an undeniable fact. It is as if it were impossible to view the belief from outside the belief system itself (Britton, 2009: 9).

The process by which a piece of evidence that might contradict a particular belief is easily dismissed is familiar to any practicing psychoanalyst. It was strikingly illustrated to me by Mr G, a very withdrawn and, at the same time, quite sensitive patient, in a session in which he was talking about all the joy he felt in his daughter's company, something that puzzled him. Twenty minutes later in the same session, he calmly said: 'You know, I'm this being who doesn't feel'. He expressed no conflict about the evident contradiction. My first intervention was to simply try and register the contradiction.[1] After a long pause, he said he understood what I said, but he didn't feel it as a contradiction; he had always been 'this person who doesn't feel'. He then added, very candidly, that what he felt before was 'probably a lie'. The splitting was clear, and to maintain his theory about himself, Mr G found a way to dismiss the evidence produced by his own feeling.[2]

Impossible tension

The case I will now discuss, Mr L, was a middle-aged man who presented accentuated obsessional traits and was in a state of visible despair when he first came to see me. He would occasionally hold his head in his hands, eyes wide open and teary, his face flushed, his voice trembling. It seemed that he was on the verge of giving up, which he made explicit.

Nothing in Mr L's life or circumstances could easily explain what was going on. His relationship with his wife was good, and there was no major concern about his children. He had a stable job and meaningful achievements in his field. There was, however, a fierce and almost unbearable pressure in his mind of implacable and relentless self-accusations and tormenting criticism that reduced his self-image to that of a wrecked failure.

Despite many years of experience in his profession, every time Mr L needed to perform a task, he feared it might be a complete disaster, and he would make a fool of himself, to his public disgrace. That made work and preparations extraordinarily tormenting, making it extremely hard for him to concentrate. He slept poorly and was in a permanent state of great anxiety. He had no idea what to do about it or if it would ever improve. It was clear to me that if he did not fear for his life and the consequences for his family, particularly his children, he would not have allowed himself the 'indulgence' of believing that he could seek help and be deserving of it. It is important to note that despite coming to see an analyst, Mr L was not at all convinced that his apprehensions were unjustified, or that he was too harsh on himself. On the contrary, he held the strong belief that he was a shameful failure, and he could not go on like this.

Mr L's sense of inadequacy seemed to be strongly connected with the kind of relationship he had developed with his internal objects. His parents divorced when he was a pre-adolescent, but despite that, his father maintained a strong presence in both the nuclear and the extended family while his mother was both more distant and self-effacing. Mr L's father displayed an unshakeable sense of self-worth; he would often brag about his achievements, from professional and financial success to the women he had had. At the same time, he would often make comments that were demeaning about Mr L and other members of the family. Mr L had intense and mixed feelings about his father, which involved resentment, but mainly great admiration and a powerful idealisation.

Mr L's fragile sense of self and reality was overwhelmed by the extraordinary demands of his superego that we came to call his 'internal bully'. The predominant characteristic of this kind of superego was described by Bion as 'an envious assertion of moral superiority without any morals' (Bion, 1962: 97).

The effect of the introjection of a critical and superior container seemed to have been crippling in terms of Mr L's development and his oedipal struggles, leading to the formation of an omnipotent and persecutory internal object. He developed a relentless and demoralising race against what he perceived as his shameful limitations, from which the only possible outcome was, repeatedly, a sense of defeat. Nevertheless, he did not seem to be aware of this inevitable outcome and re-punished and re-traumatized himself by bitter self-accusations, as if he thought it could be otherwise. What was remarkable was the dogmatic quality of these beliefs, which involved the omnipotent internal figure against which Mr L measured himself.

The development of a harsh and cruel superego has been studied by many authors since Freud (1923), such as Melanie Klein (1958), Bion (1959, 1962) and O'Shaughnessy (1999). The aspect I want to focus on here is that of a clear or hidden belief in the real grandiosity of an idealised figure in the patient's life. This idealisation is in the service not only of protecting both the internal and external objects from possible destructive attacks by Mr L, but also, paradoxically, of preserving hope, as will be seen later in this chapter. The attitude of the external object can powerfully stimulate these phantasies.

The dilemma experienced by the patient is that the omnipotent internal voice tells him to achieve impossible goals, despite these not being clearly defined. Moreover, whatever the achievements, the space for accusations of fault is endless. Furthermore, although these grandiose expectations oppress the patient so painfully, to maintain them nevertheless also means maintaining the idea that they, in fact, *could* be met. In other words, he could equal his idealised object one day if only he kept trying. In doing this, he does not need to let go of ambitions that are also tempting to his badly hurt narcissism. It can also be a matter of maintaining the idealisation of parents or other important figures in the patient's life.

The paradox is that, on one hand, the patient feels extremely oppressed by these glowing figures to whom he feels he cannot compare. On the other hand, however, he can indulge in the phantasy of being the son or heir, even if he is deemed undeserving so far to such extraordinary beings.

This poses specific challenges to the analyst. Interpretations, for instance, that can bring relief and be felt by the patient as liberating from the excessive and oppressive internal demands can, at the same time, be felt as depriving him of something: as if the analyst wanted to remove from him this perceived exceptionality of his internal objects. Similar feelings can be triggered if the interpretation is felt as devaluing or undermining the developing idealisation of the analyst himself.

A complex relationship develops between internal excessive and oppressive demands and the real self that cannot cope with those demands. There are different ways of managing this impossible tension, and for many patients, resorting to omnipotence means they will be able to dismiss any evidence that is in contradiction to their manic illusions. A self-denigrating patient like Mr L is not capable of following this path, which he, nevertheless, believes he should. In one session, Mr L spoke of childhood daydreams of being able to save the family from disaster, a task in which he felt he had failed. He could only build castles on the beach that were washed away, he said.

Clinical fragment

Mr L would usually be on time for his sessions but tended to arrive at the last minute, as he did for all his commitments, because he felt compelled to use all the time he had to be 'productive'. Therefore, he would leave the house or prepare for a phone or zoom meeting without time to spare. That was a source of tension since he also felt pushed to make the best possible use of his sessions and would not, therefore, forgive himself for arriving late. There seemed to be an impossible demand in his mind that he should not be late but also should not leave or prepare himself too early for his session or other commitments as well. As a result, he was always rushing, stressed, and puffing. This need to be omnipresent will be discussed further later.

To this session, unusually, Mr L was a few minutes late, having previously sent a message letting me know he would be late. He explained that he was just finishing preparing some work and wanted to have it done.

'I'm in a positive mood now, just because I finished this work. It's almost as if this isn't the real me'. It seemed to me that Mr L was elated not only for having finished the work but also because of his capacity to be rebellious and be late for a few minutes to his session without feeling too persecuted by me. This triumph, however, did not last, and after a brief pause, he went on to say: 'It must be a passing mood'. It appeared that he was placating me, concerned that I might feel angry and retaliate for his lateness, dampening his brief feeling of self-satisfaction by making a dismissive comment. This dynamic was often present in his analysis.

Even when he was feeling better, not out of manic defence but because he had worked through some difficult issue, was able to make use of an interpretation, or had had an insight, the thought that I might dismiss his good feeling would immediately come to his mind: 'Oh, this is ridiculous. Carlos will say you are being pretentious; this is not how it is'.

This seemed to be confirmed when he added something that indicated improvement in terms of his acute work-related anxiety, which he himself immediately dismissed. On one of these occasions, after voicing a thought of his own, he promptly followed it with self-denigration: 'Work is going better; it was really good yesterday. Then I think: "Oh, this is just part of the truth; I was trying to avoid self-criticism."'

I remarked that it seemed that one of us needed to feel small, less important, looked down on. This is how he imagined I felt because he left me waiting while he finished preparing his work, and I might retaliate, 'spoiling his party', looking down on him and his feeling that he was less tormented.

After a pause, he said that yesterday morning he was feeling bad, but later, after managing to do some work, he felt happy about it. 'I hate these ups and downs. I'm cautious about saying that I'm fine'. That seemed to confirm that I might not like to see him feeling 'fine' and would need to pull him down. It seemed as if 'fine' would necessarily be interpreted by me as 'up above me' or trying to compete with me. I would then duly show him his place. It seemed that I was, in the transference, an aggressively superior object, at the same time idealised and cruel.

What Mr L was calling his 'up' moments corresponded more closely to average moments of contentment. It seemed that the 'up and down' was linked to the relationship between him and me. He said he felt these 'up' moments as if they were fake.

Occasionally, Mr L would have a recollection that seemed to have been forgotten and which could interfere with the all-powerful internal image he had of his father, as when he recalled seeing him in a crisis when he went bankrupt. In the third year of his analysis, he casually mentioned that his father had always suffered from occasional bouts of depression and has been in an on-off treatment for it. Mr L also thought his own children should not know about his need for psychotherapy, of which he felt ashamed, seeing it as a weakness. As with Mr G, it was remarkable that Mr L had by no means acknowledged the contradiction between these memories and the invulnerable figure he carried inside.

Mr L's belief was split from the evidence. At the same time, whenever something was identified as not real, he turned that against himself, preserving and keeping separate his idealised internal object: 'The "up" moments, I feel as if they are fake, a façade, not real'. I said he seemed to identify feeling good about something or about himself as arrogance that would later lead to him being punished, and any good feeling would be taken from him. It seemed there was only room for one of us being potent, and paradoxically, if he felt better and was improving in his analysis, I would promptly 'put him in his place'.

On one of these occasions, he was telling me that the day before he had dealt better with a task about which he used to feel overwhelmed. He then interrupted himself with a self-critical comment. When I remarked that he seemed to be afraid of my response to his comment, he said: 'Yes, you'd say: "Don't be ridiculous, oh, okay, you're better, when only last week your world was falling apart"'.

I was struck by the kind of figure I was in his mind here: cruel, ironic, undermining, looking down on him. For Mr L, my anticipated reaction would be justified. I was an idealised and omnipotent object in the transference, and my meanness was irrelevant. Any annoyance on his part with this rivalrous and contemptuous object was projected into me and did not belong to him.

A theory repeated in Mr L's family was that success and failure alternated between generations: his father succeeded after the failure on the part of the previous generation. The implication was that Mr L belonged to the next failed generation; there was only room for his father's success in the family. This was also clear in another anecdote he recalled more than once: when he was at school, he once came home happy about an excellent grade he had received in an exam and told his father. His father's response was to the effect that Mr L should not celebrate the catch since he did not have the hunter's trophy to show yet.

Mr L's attachment to his beliefs involved, as is frequently the case in these patients, the unrealistic belief that things could one day change for the better if only he could redeem himself. If he were able to become the person he should be according to the demands of this unforgiving internal object, which were perceived as justified and justifiable, then everything would fall into place, and he would feel properly deserving of love and respect. This masochistic mechanism is described in detail by Fairbairn in connection to traumatized young patients he worked with (Fairbairn, 1943).

The perfectionist demands from this omnipotent internal object do not correspond of course to the actual qualities and characteristics of the idealised primary object. The flaws of this object, however, even if somehow vaguely perceived, were not assimilated into the patient's mental life. This could be said to resemble religious experience, an extreme version of which can be seen in sects in which disciples, under the leadership of a guru, can be led even to collective suicide, as with Jim Jones's followers in Guyana in 1978. In our own times, we can see damaging choices made by followers of populist manipulative or tyrannical leaders.

I had the opportunity to observe in Mr L's sessions hints of impossible internal demands for the two other attributes that define divine power: omniscience and omnipresence, as can be seen in the following vignettes.

On the occasion when a friend encouraged Mr L to apply for a prestigious job that was being advertised, he reacted with near panic. His anxiety involved the possibility of 'making a fool' of himself by applying and not getting it. At the same time, he would be a failure by not applying. When I pointed out to him how impossible the situation was in his mind, he answered that he *knew* he would fail. I wondered about his reluctance to apply for the job because he should only apply if he were sure he would get it, and it reminded me of the boy in a party who could only approach a girl if he knew for sure she'd be receptive, so he didn't approach any. Mr L was startled: 'How did you know that? I don't remember telling you that!'

I wondered also about the need for certainty: on one hand, he should only apply if he were completely sure that he would succeed. On the other hand, since this was not possible, he should at least be sure that he did not apply – 'I *know* I will fail' – thereby avoiding what he called the ridicule of applying and not getting it. In other words, if he could not be the best, he could at least be the worst. But then he felt that it was mediocre and unforgivable of him not to apply. The labyrinthine aspect of his thinking process here involved humiliation and a sense of defeat in the presence of uncertainty.

In another session, Mr L described his anxiety and his feeling of crushing failure in regard to what he believed would be social demands on him. He had been invited by two different friends to social events on the same date and at the same time, happening on opposite ends of the city. He was not excited about either of them but felt unable to reject either, fearing his friends would be disappointed in him, so he accepted both. His plan was to attend one of the events for half an hour and then leave to go to the other one. Out of his anxiety, he happened to arrive at the first one before his friend and felt he needed to leave; he left greetings for his friend with a common acquaintance. On his way to the other engagement, he was caught up in traffic, and by the time he arrived there, his friend had already left. Mr L told me this kind of thing happened to him regularly, leaving him feeling depressingly defeated, as if he believed that he *should* be able to be everywhere at once.

Here we come to another important aspect that can be found in these cases: a certain sense of reality which is preserved is seen as weakness. An important requirement to keep a grandiose self-regard is a strong capacity to ignore and deny any evidence that contradicts this self-image. Here, on the contrary, the patient is painfully aware of both his real and his phantasised or exaggerated limitations. His thinking disturbance is present in the belief that these limitations should not be there at all.

Mr L's conviction about the truth of his beliefs was striking. Britton mentions the cases in which this kind of conviction derives from the impossibility of developing an independent viewpoint from which to think about whether the convictions are true or untrue due to the intolerance to the oedipal situation (Britton, 2009). In cases like Mr L's, it seems that oedipal rivalry and its working through are not allowed to fully develop due to the overwhelming presence of this superior and crushing figure in the patient's mind. A huge part of the personality then capitulates to the control and domination of this infallible and intimidating superego. Thinking independently and critically is prohibited, and the patient protects himself from even more damaging punishments by belittling himself first, before this God-like figure does it.[3] The analyst can be subtly lured into this powerful position himself or into responding to an invitation to take the place of the patient's omnipotent primary internal object.

Expectations

Unreasonable expectations from an omnipotent internal figure deeply affect the development of the personality. Even if, to a lesser extent, we may all experience their impact, they can also inhibit the development of real capacities or distort the perception of achievements, which can then be seen as poor or unworthy. The gap between these and the over-ambitious hopes – to which the omnipotent phantasies deeply contribute – increases the shame and guilt around a feeling of failure. These excessive internal expectations can be powerfully stimulated by narcissistic projections from important external figures onto the patient, as with Mr L.

There are different ways in which this over-demanding internal figure can develop, gain strength, take hold and almost take charge of the personality. In Dickens's *Great Expectations* (1861), Pip's life after his parents' death is overshadowed by his sister's authoritarianism and omnipotence allied to her abusive and relentless criticism of him. This is coupled with the appearance of an initially mysterious benefactor who grants him an unexplainable opportunity in life. Pip then seems to feel he should repay this by achieving great things which he is not sure he is capable of. Furthermore, he mulls the question of whether he is really deserving of this chance. It is difficult for Pip to believe his worth since his sister's bullying has the approval of the local community, where she holds a respectable place. The only supportive adult around, his kind but naïve brother-in-law Joe, is completely incapable of protecting Pip. We can suppose that, although Pip wants to see his luck as a compensation for his misfortunes, there is something in him that prevents him from believing he deserves it: from the start, he finds a way of misusing his money, either by being over-generous with his friend Herbert or by spending it lavishly. It is almost as if he wanted to get rid of it, even before knowing where it had come from. This feeling of worthlessness also seems to be an important component of his infatuation with Estella, who treats him contemptuously from the moment they first meet.

As with Pip, this kind of guilt is observable in patients like Mr L, making them feel undeserving and unworthy. Their emotional needs, vulnerability, uncertainties and ambivalent feelings which could not find an adequate container might be perceived as unacceptable weaknesses by their infallible and unforgiving internal objects. It is against the backdrop of such rigid defences that the analytic work gradually makes room for reconciliation with reality.

Notes

1. Wittgenstein defines the function of the philosophy of language in a way I find similar to one of the functions of the analyst in the clinical situation: 'to pass from a piece of disguised nonsense to something that is perfect nonsense' (Wittgenstein, 1997: 133c).
2. The mechanism of erasing pieces of evidence that would contradict a previous belief is interestingly investigated by the philosopher Renford Bambrough (1991).
3. These are also the tactics used by Kafka's characters in many of his stories.

References

Bambrough, R. (1991). Fools and heretics. In Griffiths, A.P. (Ed.), *Wittgenstein Centenary Essays*. Cambridge: Cambridge University Press, 239–250.

Bion, W.R. (1959). Attacks on linking. *International Journal of Psychoanalysis*, 40: 308–315.

Bion, W.R. (1962). *Learning from Experience*. London: Karnac, 1991.

Bion, W.R. (1963). *Elements of Psycho-Analysis*. London: Heinemann.

Bion, W.R. (1970). *Attention and Interpretation*. London: Karnac, 1984.

Bion, W.R. (1989). *Two Papers: The Grid and Caesura*. London: Karnac Books.

Britton, R. (1998). Belief and psychic reality. In *Belief and Imagination: Explorations in Psychoanalysis*. London: Routledge, 2009.

Dickens, C. (1861). *Great Expectations*. London: Penguin Books, 2003.

Fairbairn, W.R.D. (1943). The repression and the return of bad objects (with special reference to the 'war neuroses'). *British Journal of Medical Psychology*, 19: 327–341.

Freud, S. (1923). *The Ego and the Id. S.E 19*. 3–63.

Genesis 2.18 ESV. (1957). Holy Bible. King James Version. New York: Harper Collins.

Klein, M. (1958). On the development of mental functioning. In *Envy and Gratitude and Other Works 1946–1963*, vol. 3. London: The Hogarth Press and the Institute of Psychoanalysis, 1980, 236–246.

O'Shaughnessy, E. (1999). Relating to the superego. *International Journal of Psychoanalysis*, 80 (5): 861–870.

Wittgenstein, L. (1953). *Philosophical Investigations*, 2nd ed. Oxford: Blackwell, 1997.

Chapter 11

From patients to presidents
The Grand Illusion

Frank Summers

Jane, an attractive well-dressed young woman, came for psychoanalytic therapy although she could not quite say why except for a vague explanation that others had not treated her well. In the course of the first interview, she casually mentioned that she was 'in the field.' So I assumed she was a therapist, but her history included no education or work history in the mental health field. Imagine my surprise when she indicated that she was 'in the field' because she had once been an x-ray technician.

This was the first of many experiences with Jane in which I was distressed, amazed, nonplussed, and incredulous at her avowed self-certainty in areas in which she was a novice and shamelessly self-aggrandising in the way she described herself. Not feeling her self-perception required any introspection or exploration, Jane possessed an illusion of omnipotence, a belief that she knew all and controlled all that could never be questioned. Jane is an iconic representation of patients whose personalities are organised around such an illusory belief in their omnipotence.

The purpose of this chapter is to show the unique nature of the defensive organisation of this illusion and the particular therapeutic problems to which it leads and to adumbrate an analytic approach designed for this perplexing personality organisation.

What is the illusion of omnipotence?

In the analytic literature, omnipotence is viewed primarily in two distinct but related ways: as a normal state of early infancy and as a defensive construction characteristic of severe pathology. The focus of this chapter is on omnipotence as a defence, as can be seen, for example, in Jane's deployment of the omnipotent illusion whenever she was in a situation of limited capability or knowledge. When she started a new job, she felt a vulnerability she could not tolerate, so she acted and spoke as though she were omnipotent. She adopted the posture of the experienced, knowledgeable veteran of the company who had to teach others how to do their jobs, although in reality, she was the new employee who was expected to

DOI: 10.4324/9781003185192-15

learn her job from them. This sensitivity to vulnerability and the refusal to feel it in any way is what typically activates the illusory omnipotent defense.

Literally speaking, 'omnipotent' means all powerful, the ability to do anything without limitations. Because such a state is not achievable by humans on this earth, when we say 'omnipotence' we mean the phantasy, illusion, or delusion of omnipotence, not the actual state itself. The conscious phantasy of omnipotence is perforce transparent: that is, it is known to be phantasy when it is taking place (Sartre, 1940/2010). Thus, phantasy makes no reality claim and therefore does not conflict with reality.

The pathological form we face most commonly in analytic therapy is the *illusion* of omnipotence, usually unconscious. Unlike phantasy, illusion does make a reality claim, albeit in a distorted form. The illusion of omnipotence contains the belief in extraordinary powers and therefore clashes with the reality of one's limitations. It is this illusion of omnipotence and not the phantasy that we confront in character pathology and borderline states, not conscious but active within. Any suggestion of limited capability will immediately evoke the defense, with the implicit belief that there can be no limitation on the patient's actual ability.

The delusion of omnipotence is a psychotic transformation of the very identity of the self into a delusional figure, such as Jesus Christ or Napoleon. The discussion here will confine itself to the illusion of omnipotence as found in character-disordered individuals, not psychosis.

This grand illusion means there is a belief in one's superior abilities, including the achievement of 'total control' over events in one's life without the delusional transformation of one's very identity. That is, the illusion is held while contact with reality is maintained.

Jane had some organisational skills and personality strengths, and she had once been an exceptional dancer, but on every one of the several jobs she held during her psychotherapy, she presumptively arrogated to herself the role of expert from her first weeks on the job. On one job, she said of her coworkers on her second day of her orientation, 'They do not know how to do it. They make so many mistakes. I have to show them.' This statement was remarkable only for its typicality. Jane had no interest in questioning her claim of elevated knowledge and skill in a field in which she had no previous experience or training. To the company, she was a new employee in training, but to Jane, she was the most knowledgeable person in the room. This was not simply an unrealistic assessment but a character trait that organised her way of relating to the world.

Needless to say, it was not only on the job that Jane offended people with her self-aggrandisement. She claimed to have men pursuing her constantly, and while she was attractive and undoubtedly did get some male attention, the 'pursuers' seemed to drop away rather quickly. Whenever a man ended a relationship, no matter how short lived it had been, Jane came to her next session reciting excessive praise she claimed to have received from men. She recounted a string of stories about men who wanted to date her. In a rather pathetic fashion, Jane maintained the pretense of living an expensive lifestyle by renting a tiny apartment on a prestigious street that cost her half her monthly income. Jane was an expert at 'name dropping.' If she was once in the same room with a wealthy or well-known person, she claimed a relationship. She showed no indication that she was aware of the absurdity of her claims or of how they were perceived by others.

From whence does it come?

The illusion of omnipotence mirrors the earliest stage of infancy. In the phase Winnicott (1963a) called 'absolute dependence,' needs are met without the infant signalling to the caretaker. The parent must read the child's behaviour as the expression of need and meet the need without any direct communication from the infant. The baby's perspective is that needs are met by their very existence in a state Winnicott (1960, 1962) called 'early infantile omnipotence.'

If all goes well, at about six to eight months, the child begins to be aware that his needs are met by an other outside her control (Mahler et al., 1975). To adjust to this potentially distressing reality, the child enters a *transitional phase*, in which the child tries to cope with the anxiety of not being able to meet his own needs by attaching to a transitional object, which he knows is outside himself but treats as though it is part of the self (Winnicott, 1951). With the help of this transitional phase, the child begins to accept the reality of the other and so begins to signal needs, first by gesture and later by word. Each such developmental step diminishes the belief in omnipotence and constitutes a corresponding step towards the sense of reality (Ferenczi, 1911).

If the child's efforts to communicate are futile, she is likely to be arrested in the transitional phase or even regress to the phase of early infantile omnipotence, thus impeding the infant's ability to fully accept and embrace reality and dependence on the other (Winnicott, 1962). The belief in self-sufficiency, the ability to meet all one's own needs, defends against the pain of helplessness, the futility of an unresponsive environment. The child is attempting to withdraw from dependence on the environment that has proven so painful. In lieu of movement forward towards autonomy, the illusion of omnipotence is sustained lest its faltering reveal vulnerability, helplessness, shame, and ultimately annihilation anxiety.

Inquiry into the origin of Jane's defensive omnipotence revealed a picture of a mother who was simply unable to respond to her and focused such limited maternal skill as she possessed on Jane's older sister, who was deeply attached to her mother through her adult years. The mother's neglect of Jane was so extreme she often forgot Jane's activities; sometimes she neglected to pick her up from school and seemed to know very little about her younger daughter's life. Jane was a lonely child who felt unloved, often invisible, and in so much pain that at some point in childhood, she sought refuge in becoming the child of her early infantile illusions.

Jane characteristically recounted stories of her early life in which she claimed to perform academically and otherwise at a superior level. However, in her narrative, she glossed over several incidents that blemished her assertion of a perfect academic record. For example, without seeming to notice, she mentioned that her mother had been called to school to discuss questions about her academic performance on several occasions. She also let drop a comment that she was known as the 'skinny kid with glasses' who, of course, flowered into a 'beauty' later on. In the midst of her account of exceptional social success were examples of boys losing interest in her. She seemed oblivious to the implication for her narrative of boys competing without exception for her affection.

As a growing child, she concentrated her affective life on the illusion of omnipotence. But the defence never worked fully, and her anxiety was manifest enough to be noticeable to those around her. Her self-aggrandising behaviour routinely alienated many children, and she had few friends, which she, of course, attributed to others' envy. But her self-description as the 'skinny girl with glasses' made her pseudo-explanation ring hollow.

After an erratic academic performance in high school, she avoided college application by joining a prestigious international dance troupe that travelled the world, dancing and spreading good will. Jane had always been an outstanding dancer, and she was readily accepted. She loved the experience, and it was the one time in her life she felt both cared about and proud of her actual accomplishments, rather than a chimera she constructed. But even in this group, known for its loving and caring way of relating, she managed to alienate many in the company. Unlike in all other situations, this group talked to her empathically about her disaffection from others and offered a supportive, caring environment. Jane told me all this without seeming to recognise that she was revealing how difficult she was to get along with and how problematic life had been for her. She left the dance group after her one-year stint ended, tried college, but was unable to complete the coursework, and since then, she had not been able to hold a job for any length of time.

The illusion as a self-organisation

Self-esteem is the realistic appreciation for one's talents and limitations (Kernberg, 1976). Those who can only accept few, if any, restrictions on their ability or influence have lost the narcissistic equilibrium necessary for realistic self-esteem. Once the illusion of omnipotence is deployed in this defensive manner; any potential awareness of constraints on one's power will evoke a reaction reestablishing the illusory omnipotence. Because awareness of limitation is ever present, at this point the illusion of omnipotence is crystallized as *the self-organisation.*

This self is dominated by the belief in one's omnipotence. If the defence were only applicable to a circumscribed sector of the personality, other parts of the self would be vulnerable to the awareness of any shortcoming. Since that is prohibited, once the illusion of omnipotence is deployed to protect against any imperfection, the self becomes defined by its illusory omnipotence. Real-world events that threaten to bring out awareness of a defective self must be denied or dissociated in the service of the illusion.

Ironically, such a patient requires others' recognition of his 'superior' ability to combat awareness of self-deficiencies that continually threatens to emerge into consciousness. Requiring constant fortification by the environment, the illusory omnipotent state creates the very dependence the defense is designed to avoid (Benjamin, 2018). Dependence on others is denied as the patient claims no concern for others' perceptions, even as he makes extensive efforts to win their approbation.

The illusion is invested with the emotional strength of self-definition. That is why there is more at stake in challenging the illusory omnipotent self than the awareness of painful affects or motivations. The very sense of self, of who the patient is and shall be, is threatened, thus evoking annihilation anxiety, arguably the most debilitating form of anxiety (Klein, 1946; Winnicott, 1960).

Furthermore, the patient's need for others to affirm the illusion puts the patient at risk of having the omnipotence exposed as illusory. This contradictory combination of the belief in one's total self-sufficiency and the need for affirmation from others is what makes the defence unique and so exceptionally difficult for the analyst to resolve and for the patient to relinquish.

The other major flaw in the self-organisation is that events and situations of daily life continually threaten to expose limitations to the patient's control of events. Being under a boss or other authority, making a mistake, being thwarted by the opposition or non-cooperation of others, or any of the myriad experiences that limit the power to control events are threats to the illusion. The belief in omnipotence cannot pass the test of reality, with its inevitable clashes with the stubborn nature of the world the patient cannot control.

The fact that the defence becomes a self-organisation and is dependent on others in contradiction to its very essence puts this defence in a special category. The consequences for the object relations of such patients are far reaching. Because the need for continual approbation dominates the patient's way of relating to others, those who collaborate with the illusion are 'all good' objects and sought out for friendship, love, support, colleagueship, and even business partnerships. Their flaws are easily overlooked because their affirmation of the illusion obliterates awareness of any negative traits they may possess.

Analogously, those who question or in any way cast doubt on the professed omnipotence are immediately marked as dangerous because, in fact, they do endanger the illusory omnipotent stance. They evoke annihilation anxiety and must be attacked or dismissed as lacking credibility (Winnicott, 1963b). In this way, the illusion of omnipotence introduces an extreme form of object splitting into part objects of 'all good' and 'all bad' (Klein, 1957). A clear example of the relationship between the omnipotent illusion and splitting can be found in the public domain.

Trump's Grand Illusion

The illusory omnipotence of a self-organisation resulting in primitive splitting has been writ large for all Americans and, indeed, for many around the globe to see. The immediate past president of the United States, Donald Trump, believes himself to be capable of magnificent feats. His view of himself as possessing virtually any capability, as spectacularly successful and of exceptional talents, was shown on the nightly news on an almost daily basis during the Trump presidency. He boasts claims of spectacular business and political success and claims dozens of exceptional abilities and accomplishments, only a very few of which can be listed here. His alleged abilities include 'the highest IQ,' 'not smart, but genius,' 'the best memory,' and a 'natural ability' in medical knowledge; his claimed accomplishments include 'the greatest electoral college victory in the history of the United States,' responsibility for the 'greatest economic recovery in the history of the world,' 'the largest tax cut and reform in the history of our country by far,' claiming responsibility for a law passed two years before he became president permitting veterans to see private doctors. This very small selection of Mr. Trump's claimed abilities and accomplishments demonstrates conclusively his illusory omnipotence. He never admits he made a mistake, has never apologized for anything he has done, no matter how many people may have been hurt by his behaviour, such as in his failure to act to control the COVID-19 virus spread while lying about the danger of the virus. To hear Trump tell his story, he has never failed at anything, not even had a setback on his way to exceptional success in everything, despite his having filed for bankruptcy at least five times and the fact that some of his most highly touted projects, such as the Taj Mahal casino, were miserable failures, and as a result, no American bank would lend him money.

None of Trump's claims are true (Moran, 2021), but they are asserted as inviolable facts because, to sustain his illusion of omnipotence, Mr. Trump must obliterate systematically any aspect of reality that would tarnish his self-image of perfection and omnipotence. Only claimed exceptional abilities and achievements are admitted to his self-perception, and all flaws or mistakes are denied or blamed on someone else. So we can see that Mr. Trump's self-image is organised to exclude all possible blemishes in order to sustain the illusion of omnipotence. That is to say, Mr. Trump's illusory omnipotence has become his self-organisation, his characteristic ways of being and relating.

The point for our purpose is that to sustain the illusion of omnipotence, Mr. Trump told lies about his performance and abilities. In the world of illusory omnipotence, truth is always the first casualty. It requires that he maintain a flawless image of always being victorious; always the best at everything; at the top of any ranking; and, above all, without vulnerability.

To sustain such a self-perception, he must distort reality when it confronts him with his shortcomings. The omnipotent illusion must be sustained at any cost. While for most people whose self-perception is organized in this fashion, the injuries are limited to themselves and those in their direct circle, when the president of the United States requires lies and distortions to sustain his illusion of omnipotence, the nation suffers, and the world feels the impact, the sacrifice of truth and reality to bolster Mr. Trump's self-aggrandisement. Mr. Trump is a public illustration of the way illusory omnipotence becomes a self-organisation that must be continually fed with lies and distortions of reality to sustain itself.

Furthermore, to maintain this self-organisation around the illusion of omnipotence Mr. Trump only has contact with those in his administration and now in his post-presidential life who support his lies, never oppose him, and praise him effusively. Foreign leaders curried favour with him by doing the same, and some achieved foreign policy goals with simple flattery. During his presidency, those who ventured an occasional disagreement or held an independent opinion of any type were not only fired for their 'disloyalty' but were also insulted and degraded, even if they were once close aides and allies who had been recently accorded high praise.

In the Trump administration, the same person could switch from angel to devil on a moment's notice, depending on their relationship to the illusory omnipotence. Mr. Trump's own lawyer, Michael Cohen, went from being 'a fine person, an honest, honorable lawyer' when he was paying hush money for Trump to keep porn stars silent about their affairs with Mr. Trump to 'very bad,' doing 'terrible things' when Cohen cooperated with investigators and testified before Congress. When James Mattis was Trump's secretary of defense, he was praised effusively as a 'brilliant, wonderful man,' but when Mattis broke with Trump on his Syrian policy, he became 'the world's most overrated general.' Cohen and Mattis both went from angel to devil, from an 'all good' object to an incompetent 'all bad' object, and they joined a long list of others who were once praised but then vilified when they disagreed with Trump or revealed a truth that he wanted covered up.

Those who agree with Mr. Trump fortify his illusory omnipotence, and therefore he views them as part objects who are exceptional people upon whom he heaps praise. For example, Trump refuses to concede that he lost the 2020 presidential election, and a group who believes him attempted to take over the US Capitol by force in a fight with police that left more than one hundred people injured, five dead, and offices of legislators reduced to rubble. Mr. Trump called these insurrectionists 'very fine people.' Another example involves Mr. Trump's former campaign manager, Paul Manafort, a felon, having been convicted of bank and tax fraud and foreign lobbying–related crimes. But Mr. Manafort never publicly departed from Mr. Trump in any way and so was praised by Mr. Trump, who called him 'a very good person' and eventually pardoned him. But anyone who disagrees with Mr. Trump or suggests a different view of reality than that held by him is degraded and insulted, often called incompetent. When John Bolton, Trump's former national security advisor, opposed a plan for martial law floated in the Trump administration, Mr. Trump called his former nationals security advisor 'one of the dumbest people in Washington' (thehill.com/homenews/administration/531034).

The persistent threat that his limitations might be seen casts suspicion on all those who do not overtly affirm the illusion. And the news media and unsympathetic politicians have documented his lies and his ethical breaches, so, for Mr. Trump, they are the enemy. He calls the legitimate investigation of his statements 'fake news.' So the projection of 'badness' into suspicious objects easily becomes a source of paranoia. And all objects that suggest any imperfection become suspicious. That is why Mr. Trump and his supporters lapse easily into conspiracy theories to explain any shortcoming of his that is revealed to the public, such as his losing the 2020 presidential election. That is to say, the need to defend the fragile construction of illusory omnipotence against all threats is the source of the paranoia that dominates the psyches of many with this self-organisation, which results in what appears to be a paranoid personality but is, in my view, a self-pathology based on an illusory self-organisation

So we can see that Mr. Trump embodies all the characteristics of those who maintain a self-image of omnipotent illusion. Mr. Trump has formed his illusion into a self-organisation. He denies any reality that does not fit his grandiosity; he splits people into all good and all bad part objects depending on their affirmation or objection to his views; and he is willing to lie early and often to protect his Grand Illusion, which takes precedence over all else, including truth and reality.

The psychoanalytic process

For omnipotent narcissists who are willing to enter analysis, the struggle with reality plays out in the transference-countertransference interaction. The patient seeks reaffirmation of the illusion from the analyst, who is quickly caught in the dilemma of whether to put the analytic relationship in jeopardy by asserting the truth or sacrificing truth for the sake of continuing the relationship. The patient will take advantage of every opportunity to show her presumed ability and strength and expects it to be recognized and even admired by the analyst. There is a thin line between recognising and being empathic with the patient's belief in her omnipotence and endorsing the patient's illusion.

For example, Jane routinely gave unsolicited opinions to more experienced employees on how to do their work, but it was difficult to get Jane to see that she was overstepping her bounds. When I tried to indicate that others had expertise and experience she lacked, Jane simply talked over me and recounted the mistakes she claimed others were making. As a result of such interactions, I could see that any direct confrontation with her would only lead to explosive anger and greater defensiveness on her part.

The analyst's challenge is to convey understanding of the patient's experience, especially when the patient is disturbed by a conflict, without suggesting any weakness or vulnerability on the one hand or accepting the defensive illusion as reality on the other. To perform this delicate act of analytic dexterity requires more than analytic tact; it necessitates that the analyst find a means of connecting with the patient's experience.

The opportunity lies in the patient's feeling of unjust treatment when others suggest a limitation in the patient's capacities or influence. The patient is offended and needs reassurance and fortification of her illusory omnipotence. Instead of reassurance, the analyst empathizes with the patient's sense of injury and anger at what she (or they) believes to be a slight or insult. In this way, the analyst can be empathic without suggesting the patient possesses any vulnerability. Attempting to balance on a narrow tightrope between reality and doing injury, the analyst will inevitably fall off either way at times, but the treatment hinges on the analyst's ability to sustain the analytic stance despite falls off the tightrope.

The analyst's task is to recognize and respond to the patient's pain without referring to the helplessness that is at the heart of the distress. This delicate and nuanced form of empathy is directed not to the feelings of weakness and helplessness that motivated the omnipotent illusion but to the injury that is its consequence. To the patient, the injury is an injustice perpetrated upon her, so she is able to accept empathy for the wound she feels has been unfairly inflicted. The pain can be appreciated without implying that the patient has a weakness. The patient is gratified by the empathic recognition of the injury and typically dissociates the need for help. Patients who are unable to dissociate and cannot tolerate the empathy may not be suitable for analysis.

Many patients whose selves organised around the omnipotent illusion are able to tolerate the pain when the analyst empathises with the feeling of injustice. The analyst's understanding relieves some of the sting of loneliness and holds the patient through the recognition of the injury and the frustration and anger at having to defend the very sense of self.

Winnicott (1960) called this phase 'holding' because the analyst's task is to absorb the patient's affects, anxiety, and distress in order to form and sustain a relationship that the patient regards as useful. While 'holding' may seem like therapeutic stasis, the analyst's attention to and appreciation for the patient's experience conveys a sense of value for who the patient is, not who he purports to be, a rare, perhaps unique, experience in the patient's life.

At a deep unconscious level, the patient knows the admiration he gets for his crafted image is not real. The analytic engagement is qualitatively different from the admiration he receives for his self-presentation. He may not be able to articulate the difference but he feels it and knows he is getting something unique in his experience, and that is why the patient is able to accept analytic empathy.

Jane struggled to tolerate the analyst's unwillingness to affirm her beliefs about herself. When Jane recounted incidents at work in which she was being given orders or instructions, she adopted a supercilious posture, imperiously reciting the alleged mistakes of her colleagues and acting as though she was already in possession of the knowledge being imparted to her. She conducted herself as though there was no authority above her, as though all her colleagues were beneath her grade. It would have been impossible for anyone listening to guess that she was virtually an entry-level employee. And as is common among patients who believe in their omnipotence, Jane attributed her relatively modest real-world status to others' envy of what she regarded as her superior ability. With this defence ready to hand, Jane was able to accept the analyst's empathy for her sense of injustice without any suggestion that the analyst agreement with her self-perception.

In my withholding confrontation with Jane's illusory omnipotence while acknowledging her pain, I was 'holding' her while she fought battles, even with people who were her friends. At this juncture, I was beginning to doubt I would ever find a way to contact her pain and helplessness, but things began to change. After spending her life building, fortifying, and protecting an illusory identity, cracks in the façade began to appear. The desperate effort to maintain her expensive apartment eventually failed after another of her job losses left her without income. She tried hard to convince herself that she was not moving due to financial constrictions.

Judging that I had built a good enough relationship that met her need for an emotional connection and understanding, this time I tilted towards the side of reality. I said she was in pain at having to give up an apartment she loved, but in reality, it was not currently affordable, and we needed to understand her frequent job losses. When she objected that the string of firings were due to others' mistreatment and envy, I said that we had to face the reality that her job changes happened too frequently to ignore what she was contributing to her rather unimpressive vocational trajectory. She objected, but not wholeheartedly, and I felt she was finally beginning to show grudging acceptance of the fact that she could not continue to live defending the illusion of her omnipotence.

When, in subsequent sessions, I emphasised that I knew she was suffering, but her 'solution' of impressing others with her wealth and expertise was adding to her stress, not relieving it, she concurred. It was not explicit that she had concocted false claims, but we were able to discuss her need to make an elitist impression on others. Jane felt understood in that I knew she was filled with anxiety and the tension of having to prove herself. But most importantly, in my view, she could accept that she was not at the top of every ladder in her life because the analytic attention to her emotional states gave her a nascent feeling of value.

The mode of intervention at this point was concentrated on empathy for her current pain as well as the suffering of her lonely childhood. She spoke of the shame of the loneliness and her desperate effort to hide it, and I could sense her relief at not having to protect herself from the reality of her pain and vulnerability. It was her awareness of my interest and her feeling of having some worth without impression management that allowed her to begin to relax her need to protect herself. When I repeatedly emphasised that she was still battling to prove she was not the marginalized 'skinny kid with glasses' inside, she understood not only the origins of her illusion of omnipotence and its corollary need to impress, but also the reality that her sense of inadequacy was a *feeling*, not the reality of who she was.

Jane had real talents as she recalled that she had travelled the world with a prestigious dance troupe. She had never mourned the loss of that group when the year ended, and she returned to her mundane life at home. The dance troupe had been highly supportive of her and met her rather desperate need to impress with empathy, support, and above all, assurance that they cared about her for who she was. It was clearly the best year of her life, but she had never recognized the depth of that loss and what it meant to her.

At this point, I put emphasis on the profound loss she had experienced when she left the dance troupe. With ambivalence, she accepted my interpretation that she had lost the most supportive, caring environment of her life. Nonetheless, she was reluctant to focus on the feeling of loss because she felt the pain would be too great. But when I underlined the difference in her life once she left the troupe, she broke down in tears and said she realized for the first time that her life had never been the same since that year ended. Working through that trauma was highly disruptive to Jane because the process shattered what was left of her illusions about her current life. 'Now I feel I have nothing; everything looks bleak compared to that year. You have taken away all my beliefs about myself, all myths I guess, but I lived on them. What do I live on now?' 'Reality,' I said. 'But what am I? What is real?' 'I think you know. There are people with more skill and experience than you in many areas, and you have skills and qualities many do not have, but to reach where you want to go, you will have to continue to learn and grow,' I said.

This type of intervention would have fallen on deaf ears in the first few years of our work together. She was able to hear it now because a) the hard knocks of reality had forced upon her the awareness that she was not among the elite, and b) she felt a sense of value in my sustained empathy for her actual experience that 'held' her throughout her various setbacks and losses. Because the analytic relationship had held her enough that she could feel valued and even nurtured without any pretense of fame or fortune, she found herself responding to her recent firing and the loss of her prestigious address without losing all sense of her value.

My consistent interpretive line to her was that she did not believe in herself, and I showed her why. In her lonely childhood, no one was interested in her experience. Her mother was preoccupied with her sister, and her father seemed oblivious to both girls. Feeling lost, lonely, and unloved, Jane had no sense of her own experience and no reason to rely on it. I told her that this explained why she had to believe she knew things she did not know. Without using the term, I interpreted her omnipotent illusion as a desperate childhood move to believe in herself and avoid the feeling inside that what she had to offer was just not good enough. But I showed her I believed in who she was and could be by my interest in understanding what led her to live on the illusion. I wondered who she could be without it.

Nonetheless, the illusion did not disappear. The damage to the illusion is a painful blow to the sense of self and the fear of losing it evokes the anxiety of annihilation. Patients who have lived on the illusion of omnipotence struggle to sustain a semblance of that self-perception and therefore continue to fight their human fallibility even as they come to a reluctant acceptance of it. As they are forced to accede to the limitations of their ability, however grudgingly and fitfully it occurs, the self they have always lived on slips away, and often a depression soon follows. Although the patients will often say they do not understand why they are depressed, the dysphoric state emerges as the illusion loses its grip on the personality. Under moments of confrontation with harsh reality or assaults on self-esteem, they often try but are unable to resort to their archaic omnipotent posture. The patient can become lost, almost disoriented and confused, without the moorings that have always guided them through the world.

While Jane was palpably relieved to live without having to prove herself, the relinquishing of her omnipotent illusion resulted in a threat to the only self she had known. Jane became highly anxious, and I interpreted the anxiety as the fear of losing her sense of self. The 'easier life' with reduced narcissistic tension came with new anxieties. If she was not the woman of her omnipotent illusion, who was she now?

This was a hard fall for Jane. I told her she was not alone; I was with her in our effort to discover her authentic self. At this point, when I asked her if there might be something she was doing to contribute to her string of job losses, she nodded in grudging agreement and said, 'I am not an idiot. I know I turn people off with my boasting.' When I said she had never admitted that before, the discussion turned to how difficult it was for her to accept this fact, and she said she had always known 'in some way' that she caused negative reactions in others 'with my bluster, but I had never been able to admit it to myself.' I said that this awareness constituted the recognition that she could not go on as before. She then admitted that her job losses had hurt her vocational aspirations. She was distraught but relieved to be able to say what she knew to be true.

For a time, Jane oscillated between moments of sober reality, in which she accepted herself as having limited skills and knowledge, and moments of regression to 'psychic retreats' (Steiner, 1993), in which she momentarily lapsed into states of illusory omnipotence. I said that having a prestigious address was important to her because she had been so neglected and devalued that she had difficulty believing in her very real strengths. With each such comment, she listened in agreement, but there was always the underlying tension of seeing her old self disappear. When she was able to be in a mode of accepting her limitations and strengths, the relief allowed her to face the somber reality that she had no career and would have to begin to build one from an entry-level position. This was not easy to accept, but I emphasised her real strengths in organisational skills and verbal fluency, and we kept returning to the reality that she had no choice: her efforts to leap over stepping stones had only left her lying on the stones, aching.

Jane eventually did well, working her way up the corporate ladder in the usual manner and working assiduously to avoid regressing to her former illusory self. When she left treatment, it was not clear in what direction she was headed, but she was happier than she had ever been in her life. Years later, I ran into her at a wedding I was attending, and she was the party planner: a perfect vocation for her, I thought.

References

Benjamin, J. (2018). *Beyond Doer and Done To*. London: Routledge.
Ferenczi, S. (1911). Stages in the development of the sense of reality. In *First Contributions to Psycho-Analysis*. New York: Brunner/Mazel, 1952, 213–240.

Kernberg, O. (1976). *Object Relationships and Clinical Psychoanalysis*. New York: Aronson.
Klein, M. (1946). Notes on some schizoid mechanisms. In *Envy and Gratitude and Other Works 1946–1963*. New York: Dell.
Klein, M. (1957). Envy and gratitude. In *Envy and Gratitude and Other Works 1946–1963*. London: Vintage, 1997.
Mahler, M., Bergmann, A. & Pine, F. (1975). *The Psychological Birth of the Human Infant*. New York: Basic Books.
Moran, L. (2021). Donald Trump Has Told a Truly Disturbing Number of Lies Since Taking Office. *HuffPost*. www.huffpost.com/entry/donald-trump-lies-washington-post-number-november-2020_n_5ff44826c5b61817a5398564.
Sartre, J.P. (2010). *The Imaginary: A Phenomenological Psychology of the Imagination*. London: Routledge (original work published 1940).
Steiner, J. (1993). *Psychic Retreats*. London: Karnac Books.
Winnicott, D.W. (1951). Transitional objects and transitional phenomena. In *Through Pediatrics to Psychoanalysis*. New York: Basic Books, 1975, 229–243.
Winnicott, D.W. (1960). The theory of the parent-infant relationship. In *The Maturational Processes and the Facilitating Environment: Studies in the Theory of Emotional Development*. New York: International Universities Press, 1965, 37–56.
Winnicott, D.W. (1962). Ego integration in child development. In *The Maturational Processes and the Facilitating Environment: Studies in the Theory of Emotional Development*. New York: International Universities Press, 1965, 56–64.
Winnicott, D.W. (1963a). From dependence toward independence in the development of the individual. In *The Maturational Processes and the Facilitating Environment: Studies in The Theory of Emotional Development*. New York: International Universities Press, 1965, 83–92.
Winnicott, D.W. (1963b). Psychiatric disorder in terms of infantile maturational processes. In *The Maturational Processes and the Facilitating Environment: Studies in the Theory of Emotional Development*. New York: International Universities Press, 1965, 230–241.

Why is omnipotence so difficult to give up?

Chapter 12

Overcoming obstacles in analysis

Is it possible to relinquish omnipotence and accept receptive femininity?

John Steiner

It is not uncommon to find that patients in analysis make significant progress and then become stuck in an atmosphere that feels repetitive and stultifying. Sometimes it seems as if the treatment has come up against a barrier beyond which it is impossible to proceed, and this presents a difficult situation for both the patient and the analyst. Should they tolerate the frustration to see if something new can develop, or should they accept the limitations and allow the analysis to end? On a larger scale, the same dilemma faces our theoretical approach to obstacles in analysis. Sometimes obstacles can act as a stimulus to a theoretical advance, which may lead to a better understanding and enable progress to be resumed. At other times, a better theoretical understanding can help us to accept limitations on what analysis can achieve.

Freud's pessimism: 'Thus our activities are at an end'

Freud took a pessimistic view, particularly in his late work, epitomized in *Analysis Terminable and Interminable* (1937), in which he described a bedrock beyond which progress seemed impossible. Having concluded that ultimately, 'our activities are at an end,' he attributed the limitation to two factors: namely, the operation of the *death instinct* and the *repudiation of femininity*.

Freud's views with respect to both these factors are controversial, and our contemporary approach to them differs significantly from that held eighty years ago when his book was published. In this chapter, I am going to attempt to modify rather than to dismiss his views to see if a contemporary Kleinian approach can rescue some of his basic ideas and even perhaps enable new ones to be applied to the problem of resistance.

DOI: 10.4324/9781003185192-17

An antilife instinct expressed as envy

Freud was clearly concerned to link the ultimate cause of resistance in analysis to the operation of a destructive force.

> No stronger impression arises from the resistances during the work of analysis than of there being a force that is defending itself by every possible means against recovery and which is absolutely resolved to hold on to illness and suffering. . . . These phenomena are unmistakable indications of the presence of a power in mental life which we call the instinct of aggression or of destruction according to its aims, and which we trace back to the original death instinct of living matter.
>
> (Freud, 1937: 242–243)

Klein supported Freud in his view of the primary conflict of the life and death instincts, but through her descriptions of the critical role played by envy as a destructive force, she set the scene to enable us to reconsider the nature and motive for destructive attacks. Klein (1957: 176) did not specifically link envy to the death instinct, but she did describe it as 'an oral-sadistic and anal-sadistic expression of destructive impulses, operative from the beginning of life, and that it has a constitutional basis.'

While there may be disagreement about the importance and nature of the death instinct, there does seem to be abundant evidence for a deeply ingrained resistance to change, supporting Freud's contention that something in all of us 'is defending itself by every possible means against recovery.' If we modify the views of both Klein and Freud and replace the idea of a death instinct with that of an antilife instinct expressed as envy, we can postpone an examination of the deeper meaning of these processes and concentrate on the situations that provoke and sustain envy. We can also explore the mechanisms and phantasies through which destructive attacks are mounted and examine the aftermath of destructive attacks and their effect on the individual and his or her relationships.

What provokes envy?

It seems to me possible that the persistent and habitual denigration of femininity that we see both culturally and in analysis is, in fact, based on an earlier and perhaps deeper appreciation of femininity that is valued and, indeed, temporarily overvalued and idealized. Klein (1957) argued that a good relation with the breast as a symbol of maternal value was vital if the infant was to establish good internal object relationships in order to provide the foundation for future development. She wrote:

> We find in the analysis of our patients that the breast in its good aspect is the prototype of maternal goodness, inexhaustible patience and generosity,

as well as of creativeness. It is these phantasies and instinctual needs that so enrich the primal object that it remains the foundation for hope, trust and belief in goodness.

(p. 180)

However, she also recognized that envy led to a hatred, initially focused on the mother and her breast but subsequently directed against any relationship made by the mother that threatens to intrude and disturb the perfection of the primal couple. What seemed especially likely to provoke envy were images of the mother's rich potential to relate both to external figures in the family and to her internal world. For example, 'the mother receiving the father's penis, having babies inside her, giving birth to them, and being able to feed them' (p. 183).

Envy is, then, often experienced in response to signs of the mother being an independent person, engaged with others or even with her own thoughts – her mind seemingly turned away from her infant to her internal objects, including her husband and her unborn babies. These images represent the mother as a participant in a generative couple, with her baby in the early oral relationship and with her husband in a primal scene, and they all provoke envy. Especially when we feel excluded, we envy what we most value, and here what is attacked are all those activities that symbolize growth, development, liveliness, and creativity, both in the creation of new life and in caring for it, sustaining it, and protecting it.

At a part object level, the creative symbol may involve the link between nipple and mouth and between penis and vagina, but these symbols can be extended to areas beyond the concrete level to include mental functions such as feeling and thinking. Hence, in his description of 'attacks on linking,' Bion (1959: 308) suggested that envious attacks are directed towards 'anything which is felt to have the function of linking one object with another.'

Here Bion includes the link between the analyst's verbal thought offered to the mind of the patient, where both the receptive capacity of the patient's mind and the ideas offered by the analyst can become the focus of envious attacks on the link between them. Feldman (2000) has argued that all such life-affirming activities become the focus of antilife attacks closely related to envy and that there is no need to go beyond this to postulate a death-seeking instinct.

Envy and the repudiation of femininity

Envious attacks can succeed in destroying the creative link by a focus on either the male or the female component of the couple, but it does seem that images that involve the feminine receptive component of the link are particularly valued and particularly provocative of hatred. It is not clear why this should be so or even if it only appears to be so because envy of true creative masculinity may be hidden beneath a desire for phallic omnipotence, which is perhaps itself an envious attack. Nevertheless, with her capacity for fecundity, for her role in the care and feeding of the infant, and perhaps in part because of her vulnerability, it is the woman, particularly her breast and her genital, who so often seems to bear the brunt of attacks, and in my view, it is this that leads to the repudiation of femininity in favour of a phallic masculinity. These considerations allow us to look at section VIII of *Analysis Terminable and Interminable* from a new point of view and to see Freud's observations as arising from his patients' unconscious phantasies rather than as describing normal female development.

Freud introduces the repudiation of femininity as a novel theme quite unconnected with the rest of the book, and I have found it remarkably easy for the reader, including myself, to overlook it. Thompson (1991: 175), in his detailed analysis of the paper, heads his discussion of section VIII as 'The Surprising Turn' and states, 'It seems curious that this factor, after the careful arguments about the limitations on psychoanalytic treatment that precede its introduction, is declared to be the "bedrock" of resistance to progress.'

Freud's (1937: 250) critical paragraphs read as follows:

> Both in therapeutic and in character-analyses we notice that two themes come into especial prominence and give the analyst an unusual amount of trouble. It soon becomes evident that a general principle is at work here. . . . The two corresponding themes are, in the female, an envy for the penis – a positive striving to possess a male genital – and, in the male, a struggle against his passive or feminine attitude to another male. What is common to the two themes was singled out at an early date by psycho-analytic nomenclature as an attitude towards the castration complex.

Freud believed that both these factors led to an unyielding resistance.

> The decisive thing remains that the resistance prevents any change from taking place – that everything stays as it was. We often have the impression that with the wish for a penis and the masculine protest, we have penetrated through all the psychological strata and have reached bedrock, and that thus our activities are at an end. This is probably true, since for the psychic field the biological field does play the part of the underlying bedrock. The repudiation of femininity can be nothing else than a biological fact, a part of the great riddle of sex. It would be hard to say whether and when we have succeeded in mastering this factor in an analytic treatment.
>
> (p. 252–253)

These two paragraphs, and the male superiority that they imply, today seem anachronistic and prejudiced. The idea of the woman as inferior, passive, and characterized by lack has been vigorously challenged, early on by Horney (1924, 1926), Riviere (1934), and Deutsch (1925) and more recently by a large number of writers including Chasseguet-Smirgel (1976) and Birksted-Breen (1993, 1996). These, together with an extensive feminist literature (Person and Ovesey, 1983; Dimen, 1997; Goldner, 2000; Balsam, 2013), mean that we no longer think of feminine inferiority as a fact. Britton (2003) suggested that Freud's picture of a woman who lacks everything is a defense to counter an image of the mother as the woman who has everything. In this respect, Klein's work has been a major impetus to revisions of Freud's picture of feminine inferiority, common in his time and still common in the form of sexist prejudice.

Redefining the creative link

Both the male and the female components of the creative link are misrepresented in Freud's claim that the problem arises because of 'in the female, an envy for the penis – a positive striving to possess a male genital – and, in the male, a struggle against his passive or feminine attitude to another male.'

First, I will argue that the 'positive striving to possess a male genital' in this situation is more appropriately thought of as a wish to possess omnipotent phallic superiority and is a desire prevalent in both men and women as a defense against dependency and need. Second, I will suggest that there is nothing passive or inferior about femininity and that Freud's view of a 'struggle against a passive or feminine attitude' is, in fact, a struggle against the adoption of a receptive position, which, although feminine in its imagery, is equally important for both men and women to accept. Both men and women have to be able to adopt a receptive stance, not only in relation to the breast in infancy but also in order to be receptive to the thoughts and feelings of others through a capacity to receive and contain projections. However, this should not be taken to mean that there are no differences between the way men and women react. It is rather that in the area of obstacles to progress, they have many issues in common, and all of us have to be able to accept the existence of both male and female phantasies and to tolerate the link between them.

The resistance to progress delineated by Freud can thus be thought to arise from the predilection to phallic omnipotence on the one hand and from the reluctance to adopt a receptive position on the other. Here the nipple, the penis, and the analyst's thoughts can be viewed as 'entering,' 'inserting,' or 'giving' while the mouth, the vagina, and the patient's mind are 'receiving.' However, the traffic goes both ways, and just as the mother must be open to the projections of her baby, it is essential for the analyst to be receptive to the projections of the patient if a creative relationship is to be established.

It seems to me that receptivity is a capacity that leads to some of the most important and valued qualities that we associate with femininity in both men and women. These include creativity and the capacity to engage with an internal world associated with images of pregnancy and care for others. It is an essential stance for us to be able to adopt if we wish to give and receive from others and thereby to grow and to develop both in life and in analysis.

For progress in analysis to be resumed following a setback, both the male and the female elements need to be restored to their true value so that a receptive femininity can join with a benign masculinity in a functional creative link – namely, a link in which omnipotence is relinquished and feminine receptiveness is valued and accepted. We can surely agree with Freud that this task is difficult, but the redefinition I have attempted allows us to explore each of these elements in turn and to examine if further understanding can restore progress or if it forces us, at least temporarily, to accept a bedrock.

Phallic omnipotence and narcissistic organisations

The idea that the *penis envy* referred to by Freud may more appropriately be thought of as *phallus envy* or even perhaps as *omnipotence envy* is in keeping with the views of Birksted-Breen (1996), who proposed that 'penis envy is often phallus envy, the wish to have or be the phallus which, it is believed, will keep at bay feelings of inadequacy, lack, and vulnerability'.

She contrasted phallic masculinity, which is based on omnipotence and a desire to control and dominate objects, with a masculinity that recognises relationships and values femininity, which she called "penis as link." It is the omnipotent version of masculinity that is turned to as a defense and which is often also the vehicle for destructive envious attacks against creative links.

Of course, the imagery of the phallus is masculine, but the desire for omnipotence arises in both male and female patients, and both commonly turn to such phantasies to magically solve the pains of reality. Indeed, creative links are often envied and hated precisely because they involve the capacity to tolerate the lack of omnipotence.

The most common manifestation of omnipotent phallic phantasies takes the form of narcissistic idealisations based on pathological organisations that create a powerful image of phallic superiority as a defense against dependence, vulnerability, and need (Rosenfeld, 1971; Steiner, 1993). They commonly create illusions of idealised states based on omnipotent control of ideal objects, which are sometimes believed to have existed in reality rather than in phantasy, often in the form of a blissful paradise at the breast or sometimes even in the womb. These Garden of Eden illusions underpin the omnipotent phantasies described by Akhtar (1996) that 'someday,' the bliss will be magically restored or that they might still exist 'if only' the disaster had been avoided.

When the idealisation collapses, the patient may respond with a terrible sense of disillusionment, sometimes felt as a catastrophe and often associated with feelings of having been robbed or even castrated. It was perhaps such phantasies that led Freud to his image of woman as a castrated man, even though it seems to me to be clear that such fears are based on the collapse of defensive phantasies and, of course, affect both male and female patients.

The relinquishment of omnipotence

It might be thought that giving up of omnipotence and accepting receptive femininity would yield its own rewards, but the benefits tend to be delayed and uncertain. By contrast, omnipotence works instantly and with a magical certainty and often seems to have such a hold on the personality that its relinquishment is problematic. Freud (1908: 145) claimed that it is never possible to fully give up a source of instinctual satisfaction, and it is probably never possible to fully relinquish the pleasures of omnipotence. Perhaps, as Freud suggests, the best we can do is to acknowledge its existence, to recognize the damage it can do, and to watch if its hold on the personality can weaken. To do this, we must admit the pleasure that omnipotent destructive phantasies provide so that the omnipotence can be properly missed and mourned (Segal, 1994). However, even when phallic omnipotence is to some extent replaced by the idea of a 'penis as link,' a second task confronts the patient that may be equally difficult, and this involves the acceptance of a receptive femininity in order to permit the restoration of a creative couple.

Phantasies of feminine mutilation

We then have to consider why it is that femininity is so difficult to value and accept, and it is here that unconscious phantasies of female mutilation may play a part. These phantasies lead to receptivity being associated with images of the female genital that is not only vulnerable but felt to be inferior, repellent, and even disgusting. To understand how these images arise, I believe it is necessary to recognize that some of the primitive unconscious phantasies that make up the aftermath of destructive attacks may be extremely disturbing and provoke aversion. Klein, for example, described how violent some of the unconscious phantasies can be:

> In his destructive phantasies he bites and tears up the breast, devours it, annihilates it; and he feels that the breast will attack him in the same way. As urethral and anal-sadistic impulses gain in strength, the infant in his mind attacks the breast with poisonous urine and explosive faeces, and therefore expects it to be poisonous and explosive towards him.
>
> (Klein, 1957: 63)

Sometimes the nipple is the focus of hatred when it is associated with a masculine aspect of the mother, which is seen as hostile to the infant and protecting the mother by limiting access to the breast. Biting off the nipple may give rise to an image of the breast as damaged, bleeding, and mutilated and may form the basis for phantasies of the female genital as castrated, damaged, and vulnerable to hostile intrusions. Riviere described how the sadism comes to be directed towards the mother's body:

> The desire to bite off the nipple shifts, and desires to destroy, penetrate and disembowel the mother and devour her and the contents of her body, succeed it. These contents include the father's penis, her faeces and her children – all

her possessions and love-objects, imagined as within her body. The desire to bite off the nipple is also shifted, as we know, onto the desire to castrate the father by biting off his penis. Both parents are rivals in this stage, both possess desired objects; the sadism is directed against both and the revenge of both is feared.

(Riviere, 1929: 309)

Klein describes further details of how violent, disturbing, and primitive the phantasies may become:

> The phantasied onslaughts on the mother follow two main lines: one is the predominantly oral impulse to suck dry, bite up, scoop out and rob the mother's body of its good contents. . . . The other line of attack derives from the anal and urethral impulses and implies expelling dangerous substances (excrements) out of the self and into the mother. . . . These excrements and bad parts of the self are meant not only to injure but also to control and to take possession of the object.

(Klein, 1957: 63)

Sometimes a vertical split may appear in which feelings of repulsion are directed towards the lower half of the body and especially to the female genital. We see this in Shakespeare's Lear, whose hatred for his daughters is expressed through his disgust:

> But to the girdle do the gods inherit; beneath is all the fiends'. There's hell, there's darkness, there's the sulphurous pit – burning, scalding, stench, consumption! Fie, fie, fie, pah, pah! – Give me an ounce of civet, good apothecary, to sweeten my imagination. There's money for thee.

(Act 4, Scene 6)

Freud (1930) pursued this theme when he linked the development of feelings of disgust to the time in prehistory when man assumed an erect posture. Standing upright led to an enormous expansion in the role of vision, and the development of disgust evolved in relation to smell, touch, and taste, especially towards ano-genital functions. When the female genital becomes the focus of envious anal and urethral attacks, it leaves behind a kind of battle scene of mutilated and defiled body parts, so being feminine and receptive became associated with feelings of vulnerability to phallic attacks, combined with repellent images of mutilation and contamination with faces and urine.

It seems to me that these images associated with sadistic attacks directed at receptive femininity give rise to the preference for the excitements of phallic triumph as well as to feelings of revulsion towards feminine receptivity. The images are frightening and sometimes repulsive and make the task of restoring femininity to its true value a difficult one. Since they are deeply rooted in our unconscious, they can only be partially altered by education and social change. We can, however, hope that a psychoanalytic approach might be more effective and that the analysis of the damage done through envious attacks can set a more benevolent reparative process in motion. If feelings of guilt, regret, and remorse can be tolerated, mourning the loss of omnipotence may lead to a less destructive view of masculinity and a less damaged view of receptive femininity.

Receptivity and thinking

Receptive femininity is also vital in the field of ideas where both giving and receiving are necessary in order to think creatively, and sometimes patients seem especially to repudiate female types of thinking and, in particular, fail to allow the feminine to interact with masculine thinking in a productive way. This is true of the patient I am going to discuss, whose analysis became stuck and unproductive because she seemed unable to use her considerable intelligence.

A similar problem in thinking associated with receptive femininity was described by Riviere (1929) in the analysis of a woman of ability and competence who had problems deploying her intelligence. She hid her considerable knowledge and showed deference to men by giving an impression that she was stupid while seeing through them in an apparently innocent and artless manner. She used a flirtatiousness to conceal an intense rivalry with men and could not accept a deeper view of femininity as receptive, creative, and valuable. Britton also illustrates this theme in a patient who had idealised her analyst as a source of magical power without which she was unable to think. An omnipotent phallus was felt to be a shared possession as long as the phantasy of a mutual idealisation was sustained, and exchanges between the analyst and his patient were viewed as a symbolic intercourse. However, neither his patient nor the one described by Riviere was able to sustain the illusion, and its collapse resulted in what appeared as a kind of stupidity.

> When this illusion collapses there is not a sense of loss but the phantasy of having been literally or symbolically 'castrated.' If the phallus is symbolically equated with the intellect the consequent feeling of castration is experienced as losing all mental potency, of being stupid.
> (Britton, 2003: 66)

Britton described how the loss of the belief in a secret phallic supremacy exposed his patient to the most intense experiences of envy and despair and made her feel that she had become mentally defective.

Clinical fragment

I will present a fragment from the analysis of a patient, Mrs A, who felt blocked in her life and also in her analysis. She complained of feeling trapped and disadvantaged because she was a single mother. She admired those people, especially men, who were free to exercise their power and also those women who could live a life of luxury under the protection of powerful men. She seemed to view intelligence as something masculine and powerful but dangerous and damaging both to women and to other men. This led her to repudiate her own intelligence, using it mostly to protect herself from intrusive exploitation, and in particular she felt that she needed to avoid a receptive thoughtfulness in relation to my work.

She emphasised her dissatisfactions, stressing the things she lacked, such as a professional career, a husband, and the wealth and comfort that only men could provide. It was striking that she was unable to get pleasure from the good things she did have, like her friends, her work, her children, and especially her capacity to think. She described her work as a futile place with no prospects and no future, and she saw herself as plagued by bad luck and by repeated misfortunes and betrayals. She had no serious relationship, and she used her women friends to complain about men and her analysis to reiterate her unhappiness because of the unfair hardships she had to endure.

She described similar resentments towards her father, a lay preacher who had introduced a strict and arbitrary morality into the home, which her mother and her considerably older sister accepted without protest but which she suspected was corrupt and hypocritical. The parents slept in separate rooms, and she shared her mother's bed until she was given her own room when she was eight years old. She linked many of the feelings of unfairness to this expulsion, and she seems never again to have felt loved and valued.

Unlike her sister, who did not go to university but married a successful businessman, she did well at school and earned a place at the university, where she surprised everyone when she was the top student of her year in math and physics. However, in her second year, she had a breakdown and was sent home in an acute anxiety state with depersonalisation and some persecutory thoughts. She gradually improved but could not return to college, and after two years, she took a secretarial course and worked in a large firm of solicitors, eventually rising to a senior and highly responsible position in her office.

When she began analysis, she spent many sessions in a rambling, dreamy state, describing her failures and seeming to expect them to be put right for her. She adopted a little-girl quality in her relationships, which were highly erotized and accompanied by a naïveté and apparent innocence. She dressed seductively and encouraged men to make advances in a way that tended to put them in the wrong. For example, she held hands under the table with one of the senior lawyers at an office party but expressed outrage when he offered to see her home. In the sessions, she was seductive but also easily felt misused and became indignant if I interpreted the erotized atmosphere that she created. It seemed to me that she went into a kind of dream state in which she felt close to me in a vaguely erotized way but that if this was interpreted, the spell was broken, and she felt expelled from this intimacy, as she had been from her mother's bed.

In spite of her intelligence, a striking aspect of Mrs A's behaviour was her inability to make full use of her intelligence. As with the patients of Riviere (1929) and Britton (2003) mentioned earlier, she seemed to display a pseudo-imbecility, as if thinking and curiosity had become erotised and inhibited (Mahler-Schoenberger, 1942; Hellman, 1954). She would adopt a kind of thoughtless whining and moan, 'Why don't you tell me what to do?' or 'You didn't tell me I should free associate. I have been coming all these years, and I never knew what I was supposed to do.' It was difficult to believe that this same person could have excelled in science at the university, and it was only as I got glimpses of a quite superior intelligence – for example, when she mastered complex and subtle problems at work or when she pointed out errors of thinking on my part – that I began to realise that she was not properly utilising her capacity to think. In part, she seemed to split it off and project it onto me so that she came to depend on me for the most elementary thought while watching me carefully and used her intelligence to point out my errors, both factual and ethical. She seemed to view thinking as a masculine activity of a dangerous kind that could be used to exploit and misuse the vulnerability of women. Feminine desire was also dangerous because, in her view, the link between a man and a woman was damaging and exploitative.

A fragment of a session

Here is a fragment of a session in which she began, five minutes late, by explaining that she had been delayed because she had to struggle to get away from a friend who wanted to chat. She then described a dream in which she was descending in the underground but, at the foot of the steps, found herself having to make a choice between the left-hand passage leading to town and the right-hand one leading to her home. She stood there, unable to choose, feeling terribly heavy and found that she had a gardening sickle in her hand. Her indecision made her late, and she was relieved since this meant that she did not have time to go into town and could go home and do the work that needed to be done in her garden, which was terribly overgrown and untidy. She recalled that often, when she felt she had too much work to do, she would leave it in a mess and go to town and wander round the shops. A neighbour had loaned the sickle to her some two years previously, and she discovered it a few days before while clearing out her garden shed. She felt guilty, not only because she had not returned it but also because she had never used it. She described it as a horrible sharp thing and wondered why the neighbour had not asked for it back. Perhaps he had forgotten that he had lent it to her.

I interpreted that perhaps the choice that was so heavy in her dream represented the conflict she was in between doing difficult analytic work and fleeing from it. I suggested that she saw her mind as overgrown and untidy like her garden and that there was a lot of work for us to do. Perhaps, on her way to the session, she had to choose between embarking on this work and chatting with her friend.

In response to these interpretations, she said that she felt heavy now, and she complained that my interpretations made her feel bad. If there was a lot of work to be done, she must still be very ill, and that is a horrible thing to say to a patient. As the session continued, she expressed further resentments, even though I thought that she had shown a fleeting interest in the dream and my interpretation of it.

Discussion

Mrs A seemed to me to have made some use of the analysis but then became stuck in a situation that, like her work, had become 'a futile place.' My own disappointment in my work with her led to periods of self-doubt and eventually to the idea that perhaps no further progress was possible and that we might have gone as far as we could go. Gradually, I became interested in the question of why we were so stuck, and this led me to return to Freud's formulations on the repudiation of femininity as a way of thinking about our situation. I wondered if part of the patient's failure to develop further was connected with the low opinion she had of her femininity on the one hand, together with a fear of using her intelligence on the other. Like Riviere's patient, she used her femininity to evoke desire in men, which she then felt obliged to resist because she could not value or feel safe with a receptive femininity.

In her dream, she did feel guilty that she had not used the sickle which she had borrowed, and I thought that this might point to a capacity to work and to think, which she was aware that she kept unused. It seemed to me that she did have some idea of a creative femininity but felt obliged to repudiate it, as she did not want to be seen working with me in a cooperative way. If she used her intelligence, she would be wielding a sharp and dangerous weapon, an ugly thing. This is how she described my work, which she said made her feel bad, and she seemed to visualize her own intelligence as having the same destructive dangerous quality.

However, in her first year at the university, she had been able to think and perhaps had allowed herself the freedom to be curious, to reason, and to enjoy her capacities. However, this freedom did not last, and after her breakdown, she was obliged to settle for a secretarial post that she saw as feminine and inferior. Perhaps at that time her freedom to question established assumptions was felt to be dangerous if it led her to see through the righteousness of her father's morality. Certainly in the analysis, she was quick to see through my own intellectual and ethical shortcomings and then seemed to draw back as if to protect me from a more forceful expression of her views. Sometimes she seemed to be pretending to be stupid so that she could use her intelligence to catch me out and then argue that she could not protect herself because she was a vulnerable woman at the mercy of powerful men. Phantasies of violent mutilation may well have made her expect horrible attacks with sharp sickle-like weapons and made the idea of a receptive femininity repellent and dangerous.

It seemed to me that while feminine receptivity was repudiated, so, too, was a loving and productive masculinity. This meant that she felt that she was at the mercy of a phallic superiority and had to protect herself by refusing to let me in. A creative couple in which a receptive feminine side of her could allow a caring side of me to enter became impossible to realize. She claimed that she admired successful men and envied women who did not need to work, but I think she recognized that this view was based on phantasies of phallic superiority and devalued a true feminine creativity, which remained only as a potential within her. Her intense rivalry and jealousy made her fear that if she were to allow a creative intercourse within her mind as well as within the analysis, she would become the object of violent envious attacks from others.

Conclusion

As we proceed to study obstacles to progress in development, we come up against a variety of factors, and in this chapter, I have singled out two that are derived from Freud's original observations but are also a significant departure from them. While I have supported the idea that a critical aim is to relinquish idealisation and omnipotence, I have argued that both the patient and the analyst have, in addition, to overcome their reluctance to value femininity and that difficulties arise from either or both these factors. Omnipotent phallic organisations create idealised retreats that protect the subject from both shame and guilt, and emergence from these states involves both seeing and being seen (Steiner, 2011). When the attacks are motivated by envy and directed against creative links, the damage to good objects and good relationships may give rise to unbearable feelings of shame and guilt, particularly when these are directed at receptive femininity, seen as the weaker and most damaged element of the link.

The analysis, then, has to provide a supportive structure in which shame and guilt can be examined and the question of whether they are bearable can be explored. Sometimes the patient seems able to accept the loss of phallic superiority and face the guilt of the damage it has done. Moves in this direction are possible if guilt is bearable, and when this does prove possible, reparative wishes can be mobilised to initiate a benevolent cycle in which objects become less damaged and less persecutory so that the severity of the superego is moderated (Klein, 1957).

However, even when moves towards facing these difficult aspects of reality are embarked on, a further difficulty remains if a receptive femininity cannot be accepted and valued. This further step requires the value and importance of receptivity to be acknowledged both within ourselves and in others. The vulnerability associated with opening ourselves to masculine entry requires a vigilance because we can never be sure that the masculinity is not concealing a phallic damaging and exploitative force. Feminine receptivity has to be protected by the creation of a setting in which it is valued, and the dangers associated with it are appreciated.

I have described these tasks as if they were problems the patient has to face and as if the analyst functions as a helpful benign influence. It is obvious, however, that the analyst faces precisely the same problems to do with his own omnipotence and precisely the same reluctance to accept his receptive femininity. It is clearly important that the analyst is able to examine his own contribution to the deadlock in the analysis, and it is only possible to help the patient with his omnipotence if the analyst has been able to address his own.

References

Akhtar, S. (1996). "Someday . . ." and "if only . . ." fantasies: Pathological optimism and inordinate nostalgia as related forms of idealization. *Journal of the American Psychoanalytic Association*, 44: 723–753.

Balsam, R. (2013). Freud, females, childbirth, and dissidence: Margarete Hilferding, Karen Horney, and Otto Rank. *Psychoanalytic Review*, 100: 695–716.

Bion, W.R. (1959). Attacks on linking. *International Journal of Psychoanalysis*, 40: 308–315.

Birksted-Breen, D. (Ed.). (1993). *The Gender Conundrum: Contemporary Psychoanalytic Perspectives on Femininity and Masculinity*. London: Routledge.

Birksted-Breen, D. (1996). Phallus, penis, and mental space. *International Journal of Psychoanalysis*. 61: 39–52.

Britton, R.S. (2003). The female castration complex: Freud's big mistake? In *Sex, Death, and the Super-Ego*. London: Karnac, 57–70.

Chasseguet-Smirgel, J. (1976). Freud and female sexuality: The consideration of some blind spots in the exploration of the "dark continent." *International Journal of Psychoanalysis*, 57: 275–286.

Deutsch, H. (1925). The psychology of women in relation to the functions of reproduction1. *International Journal of Psycho-Analysis*, 6: 405–418.

Dimen, M. (1997). The engagement between psychoanalysis and feminism. *Contemporary. Psychoanalysis*, 33: 527–548.

Feldman, M. (2000). Some views on the manifestation of the death instinct in clinical work. *International Journal of Psycho-Analysis*, 81: 53–65.

Freud, S. (1908). Creative writers and day-dreaming. *S. E. 9*: 143–153.

Freud, S. (1930). Civilisation and its discontents. *S. E. 21*: 59–145.

Freud, S. (1937). Analysis terminable and interminable. *S. E. 23*: 211–253.

Goldner, V. (2000). Reading and writing, talking and listening. *Studies of Gender and Sexuality*, 1: 1–7.

Hellman, I. (1954). Some observations on mothers of children with intellectual inhibitions. *Psychoanalytic Study of the Child*, 9: 259–273.

Horney, K. (1924). On the genesis of the castration complex in women. *International Journal of Psychoanalysis*, 5: 50–65.

Horney, K. (1926). The flight from womanhood: The masculinity-complex in women, as viewed by men and by women. *International Journal of Psychoanalysis*, 7: 324–339.

Klein, M. (1957). *Envy and Gratitude*. Reprinted in *The Writings of Melanie Klein*, vol. 3. London: Hogarth, 1975, 176–235.

Mahler-Schoenberger, M. (1942). Pseudoimbecility: A magic cap of invisibility. *Psychoanalytic Quarterly*, 11: 149–164.

Person, E.S. & Ovesey, L. (1983). Psychoanalytic theories of gender identity. *Journal of the American Academy of Psychoanalysis and Dynamic Psychiatry*, 11: 203–226.

Riviere, J. (1929). Womanliness as a masquerade. *International Journal of Psychoanalysis*, 10: 303–313.

Riviere, J. (1934). Review of new introductory lectures on psycho-analysis. *International Journal of Psycho-Analysis*, 15: 329–339.

Rosenfeld, H.A. (1971). A clinical approach to the psychoanalytic theory of the life and death instincts: An investigation into the aggressive aspects of narcissism. *International. Journal of Psychoanalysis*, 52: 169–178.

Segal, H. (1994). Phantasy and reality. Reprinted in *Psychoanalysis, Literature, and War: Papers 1972–1995*. London: Routledge, 1997.

Steiner, J. (1993). *Psychic Retreats: Pathological Organisations of the Personality in Psychotic, Neurotic, and Borderline Patients*. London: Routledge.

Steiner, J. (2011). *Seeing and Being Seen: Emerging from a Psychic Retreat*. London: Routledge.

Thompson, A.E. (1991). Freud's pessimism, the death instinct, and the theme of disintegration in "analysis terminable and interminable." *International Review of Psychoanalysis*, 18: 165–179.

Chapter 13

Omnipotence and the difficulty in relinquishing it

David Simpson and Jean Arundale

This two-part chapter begins with a theoretical presentation, followed by a clinical paper exemplifying the theory. The two papers were presented as a panel to the Scientific Meeting of the British Psychoanalytic Association on February 27, 2020.

Difficulties giving up a belief in omnipotence: the importance of unconscious guilt

David Simpson

I will consider why giving up a belief in omnipotence is so difficult and will focus particularly on the role that unconscious guilt dating from infancy plays in this.

To possess omnipotence and omniscience means respectively to be all powerful and all knowing, which means to be essentially godlike. Freud (1909) recognised that a belief in the omnipotence of thought was a characteristic of obsessional neurosis, in which he identified unconscious guilt as an important factor. Following Freud's (1911) paper on the two principles of mental function, Ferenczi (1913) described stages in the development of a sense of reality. He considered the omnipotence of thought seen in patients with obsessional neurosis to be a relapse to an earlier infantile state of wish fulfilment, or 'childhood megalomania', where the pleasure principle dominates. He proposed that 'the state of being in the womb' is a normal antecedent of this state, which is characterised by 'unconditional omnipotence', in which all needs and desires are provided for. He postulated that this omnipotent state of mind, which corresponds with Freud's notion of the complete domination of the pleasure principle, is achieved by maternal care. He followed Freud's view that following birth, when the infant has to face reality, this state of mind is gradually but not completely relinquished. Although the reality principle is ascendant, infantile omnipotence is retained, being manifested in certain circumstances including dreaming, hallucination, and as part of neurotic conditions where reality is resisted, and the pleasure principle continues to dominate.

What is the function of a belief in omnipotence, and how does it operate in the mind? What makes it difficult to relinquish, and what is the role of unconscious guilt in this?

Omnipotence is an aspect of phantasies which are used to bridge the gap between a need, or desire, and its satisfaction. Omnipotent phantasies of wish fulfilment can mitigate frustration and deprivation. I concur with Isaacs' (1948) view that phantasies are the mental representations of instincts. Conscious and unconscious phantasies underpin thought. Omnipotent phantasies, like the phantasy of returning to the womb, correspond with Freud's (1911) idea of a class of thinking that is split off from reality testing with real objects and is subordinate to the pleasure principle. The conscious versions of this are represented in daydreaming and children's play. Klein recognised omnipotence as an important element in her early work with children. In 'Development of a Child' (Klein, 1921), she described the struggle with reality for the very young Fritz and made an important observation that his omnipotent views, including of his parents, receded and his reality sense increased following his growing impulse for investigation. This is a crucial point that underlies the importance of the epistemophilic drive, the drive for knowledge, in the relinquishment of omnipotent phantasy.

How does the drive for knowledge contribute to a lessening of omnipotence, and what are the sources of pain that stand in the way of this?

Klein emphasised the conflict that takes place in a child's mind between its growing reality sense, determined by its search for knowledge, and its 'omnipotence feeling', determined by the pleasure principle. She pointed out that a key feature associated with the latter is the child's wish to maintain parental omnipotence alongside its own; however, when reality is subsumed, and its omnipotence fades, there is a corresponding decrease in parental power, which she viewed as an incentive to its growing sense of reality.

Segal (1994) sheds further light on this conflict in her ideas regarding phantasy and its function in the perception of reality. She agrees with Money-Kyrle's (1968) idea that alongside omnipotent phantasies, human beings possess innate unconscious phantasies of need-satisfying objects based upon their biological instinctual needs. Unlike omnipotent phantasies, these phantasies are essentially reality seeking and determined by the life drive. Like Money-Kyrle, she includes in this category an innate phantasy of a satisfying relationship between two objects: essentially a parental couple, which forms the basis of the Oedipus complex. I would view these innate phantasies as the basis of the newborn infant's search for parental sustenance and the basis for the development of supportive internal good parental objects. In Segal's view, the infant's drive for knowledge occurs by virtue of an active process of perception in which phantasy and perception of reality interact. Inborn phantasies act as primary preconceptions, in Bion's (1962) sense, which are then matched against reality in a process that continues throughout development. This is the basis of imagination which underpins creativity in all forms, including science and art.

Omnipotent phantasies under the aegis of the death drive can distort this process, altering the perception of both the internal state and the object perceived, thus interfering with reality testing. Acting in this way, omnipotent beliefs damage the perception of reality. From the beginning of life, the infant has to struggle with painful experiences that result from the perception of reality, and it uses its omnipotent beliefs to protect itself from this. Following birth, the infant needs parental care to supply its needs, and to sustain it, in the face of its desires and fears, which include its fear for its continued existence. Frustration and hostility which result from this and other sources, including envy and jealousy, are inevitable and are projected into the mother. If this is not excessive and the mother is able, the infant's feelings are contained, in Bion's terms (1962): a process that requires the mother's capacity to bring reality to bear on the phantasies and anxieties projected from her infant. Reality testing in this way is a central aspect of what Bion called alpha function; the mother's capacity for this enables the development of the infant's alpha function and its ability to tolerate anxiety. The potential for reality testing depends on the mother's symbolic coupling with the father, who represents reality, which requires the presence of a good paternal figure in the mother's mind. This coupling itself can evoke the infant's hostility. If excessive, or if the mother's capacity to tolerate this is reduced, this can damage the infant's experience of containment through omnipotent phantasies that disturb and distort the infant's innate conception of a realistic and helpful parental coupling. This can be turned in the infant's mind into a terrifying object or objects, being the essence of a primitive superego, which is usually obscured from view.

Omnipotent beliefs thus both damage and act as a defence against the perception of reality; they can engender pain, including the pain that results from the effects of the damage. This can lead to an escalation of damage. This is true in infancy and throughout life. Omnipotence is a central part of the narcissistic systems of defence against the pain engendered through object relations. If these work, they result in denial of reality at the cost of damaging the ego's capacity for perception. If they do not work, they can result in terrifying persecution.

An important consequence of the destructive aspects of narcissistic systems that depends on omnipotent phantasies is that they leave the individual subject to guilt, which is largely unconscious. Klein (1937), like Freud (1923), recognised guilt as a very important factor behind patients' difficulties in progressing in psychoanalytic treatment. She described unconscious guilt as originating in the infant's omnipotent belief that it had damaged its mother, the object of its love, through its destructive phantasies towards her, the latter being derived from its intrinsic cannibalistic and sadistic wishes intrinsically mixed with its hunger. This is the essence of what she called 'depressive anxiety', which involves concern for the object, although when experienced, it is often felt as persecutory, as in feeling blamed. Klein (1935) viewed the sense of omnipotence as the cardinal feature of the manic defence against unconscious guilt. In the manic defence, unconscious guilt is denied as part of the denial of psychic reality. Its features also include control the splitting of parental figures into ideal and bad and a belief in omnipotent reparation. The latter confers a magical capacity to repair damage to objects.

Magical omnipotence, included in reparative ability, is frequently associated with phantasies about the penis. Phallic omnipotence occurs in both sexes and is associated with distorted views of parental coupling, which is a source of guilt. Birksted-Breen (1996) distinguishes this from non-omnipotent symbolic paternal function, which she calls penis-as-link, which lends structure to the mind through recognition of the full Oedipal situation, including the parental relationship.

Omnipotent phantasies thus function as both a source of unconscious guilt, through the distortions and damage they cause, and a defence against this. Because they act as a defence, particularly through offering the phantasy of omnipotent repair, it makes them very difficult to give up. Although omnipotent reparation can never be realised, and ultimately the defence fails, it, however, perpetuates the problem.

The consequence of being unable to give up omnipotent belief systems, as part of the narcissistic level of the mind, and I include in this manic defences, is that this stands in the way of facing painful feelings of guilt and persecution that are part of the difficult negotiation of psychological separation during development. This includes both separation externally with parental figures during childhood and adolescence, and inside the mind between the self and internal parental objects. It thus prevents the working through of the depressive position and the establishment of a normal mourning process, which begins in infancy, and which needs to be repeated in the face of losses throughout life for healthy development.

During mourning, there is always a powerful struggle between the narcissistic pull from the pleasure principle, using omnipotent beliefs, to evade reality and deny loss and the impulse to face it. In the early stages of grief following the death of a loved one, it is common to hallucinate and to see the dead person as if alive. The grieving individual is frequently plagued by guilt for any hostile feelings or actions, both real and imagined, towards the deceased. If it is their parent who dies, this guilt inevitably includes guilt from an oedipal source. For a child or adolescent, this is magnified and potentially traumatic. Guilt may become attached to other unconnected events and actions and even can become an unconscious motivation for crime. In severe melancholic states, this is exaggerated. Omnipotent narcissism rules, and the individual may suffer from delusional beliefs that they have caused all manner of destructive atrocities in the wider world. They may be wracked with guilt for which they believe they deserve extreme punishment. In analytic patients, it is not uncommon to find systems of melancholic omnipotent belief with manifestations that are less extreme, subtle, and not clearly apparent. In those with chronic low-grade depression, this can present as pessimism that is rationalised as realistic, and attempts to counter this are usually resisted powerfully.

A not-infrequent example is seen in those patients who present in a midlife crisis, frustrated with their progress and productivity in their lives and careers. Although often feeling overlooked and blaming of others, they mainly blame themselves for failing to meet their own standards. They display undue concern about other peoples' needs and wishes and suffer from charging themselves with omnipotent expectations to support others including organisations. They often work in caring and public service professions. The origin of their omnipotent systems usually lies in their childhood relationship with their parents, and particularly their mothers, who are likely to have had difficulty functioning, often being depressed. Such patients are driven throughout life by an omnipotent task of repairing their parental figures and those who come to represent them. In analysis, they are reluctant to give up their omnipotence because to do so means giving up their 'magic': their belief in their omnipotent reparative capacity, even if this is clearly illusory. They correspond with Riviere's (1936) description of patients who cannot recover because of guilt that results from their belief that their parental objects can never recover. In my view, it is these patients' belief in their capacity for omnipotent reparation, driven by an omnipotent 'god', an internal object, essentially a super-ego figure, imbued with 'godlike 'power, which by acting as 'a lock' prevents the relinquishment of their omnipotent belief system. Such a patient may complain to their analyst that to give up their omnipotent system 'feels like leaving prison, but to do so fills me with dread because it is so dangerous'.

The lifelong struggle to face reality and to relinquish omnipotence, including the use of omnipotent reparation as a defence against guilt, is illustrated in the poetry of William Wordsworth (1995). Wordsworth struggled from childhood with what he called the 'abyss of idealisation', essentially omnipotent illusions in which he believed that nothing existed outside himself and that he would never die (Britton, 1998). He suffered states of high anxiety and derealisation where he had to steady himself by touching physical objects like trees. Wordsworth's mother died when he was eight years old and his father when he was thirteen years old.

The following episode from his autobiographical poem, 'The Prelude', of 1799, exemplifies his predicament, including his omnipotence and his efforts to deal with this. The episode is an example of what he called 'spots of time', and there are several in the poem, being childhood memories of a profound nature with latent future significance which correspond closely with Freud's 'Screen memories' (Freud, 1899). In the poem, he describes returning over and over again in his mind, during his life, to an event that occurred a few days before his father's death. This event took place just before the Christmas holidays, when he was waiting in excited and anxious anticipation of the arrival of horses which would take him from his boarding school to his father's home.

In the poem:

> '*Feverish, and tired, and restless*'. He goes ahead to the highest summit of the crag, and from this stormy vantage point, '*half sheltered by a naked wall*'

with a '*single sheep*' on his right and '*a whistling hawthorn*' on his left, he '*watched with eyes intensely straining, as the mist gave intermittent prospects of the wood and plain beneath*'.

Within ten days he was back at school, his father was dead, and he and his brothers had '*followed his body to the grave*'. He described the event: '*with all the sorrow that it brought, appeared a chastisement, and when I called to mind that day so lately passed, when from the crag I looked in such anxiety of hope, with trite reflections of morality, yet with the deepest passion, I bowed low to God who thus corrected my desires*'.

He goes on to describe how '*the spectacles and sounds*' he experienced looking out in anticipation from the windswept crag would return to him in later life. '*I often would repair, and thence would drink as at a fountain. And I do not doubt that in this later time, when storm and rain beat on my roof at midnight, or by day when I am in the woods, unknown to me the workings of my spirit thence brought*'.

I think by returning to this image, in the 'spot of time' which occurs just before the death of his father, he uses omnipotent illusion in an attempt to deny his father's death, and at the same time, he breaks this illusion and feels the reality of his death and the pain this evokes. I suspect he also relives the painful experience of his mother's death. This pain includes guilt, and he vividly describes it like a chastisement for his excited passion. I think this shows that the early adolescent Wordsworth was in touch with oedipal guilt at a deep a level, and I suspect this follows his illusory oedipal wish for an exclusive relationship with a parental figure. At an unconscious level, I think he feared retribution for this wish, and the hostility intrinsic to it, which he believed was omnipotent and was concretised by the death of his father.

As with other 'spots of time,' his original experience was disturbing, tinged with dread. However, through reliving this experience and in his poetic description, he was able to see himself as a child experiencing the trauma surrounding his parents' deaths, the omnipotent phantasies, and the illusions he used to defend himself from this, and the guilt and dread that he feared when these defences failed. He was then able to see himself with an adult eye, and through evoking parental concern for himself, like the infant who can '*gather passion from his mother's eye*', to use his own words from 'The Prelude'; thus, he was able to begin to relinquish his reliance on omnipotent illusions and to tolerate his pain and guilt and mourn his parents. In this way, working through his depressive anxieties, which was a lifelong task, he could establish his parents as a couple symbolically in his mind. This gave him strength in his life. It allowed him to develop as a man and provided the impulse and medium for his creative work: namely, his imagination.

Wordsworth's poetry is essentially a form of reparative self-healing, which is non-omnipotent in that the reparation is done through love, which allows acceptance of the limitations of reality. I think this helped him in his continued struggle with relinquishing his tendency to omnipotence. We as readers are invited to join him in this struggle.

This illustrates how the ever-present tension between omnipotent illusion and its relinquishment, this facing reality, and particularly the realities involved in mourning *loss*, is at the very heart of the creative process. It shows how the difficulty of facing guilt, including particularly the guilt which results from omnipotent wishes and beliefs, including their failure, is central. This difficulty is magnified when we are over-reliant on omnipotence as a defence against guilt, which we are then reluctant to relinquish and which perpetuates the problem, rather than, like Wordsworth, in being able to work at engaging with reality and finding within us parental figures who foster our capacity to see our human predicament with compassion.

References

Bion, W.R. (1962). *Learning from Experience*. London: Tavistock.
Birksted-Breen, D. (1996). Phallus, penis and mental space. *The International Journal of Psychoanalysis*, 77: 649–657.
Britton, R. (1998). *Belief and Imagination*. London and New York: Routledge.
Ferenczi, S. (1913). Development stages of the sense of reality. *The International Journal of Psychoanalysis*, 1 (2): 124–138.
Freud, S. (1899). *Screen Memories. S.E.* 3: 301–322.
Freud, S. (1909). *Notes Upon a Case of Obsessional Neurosis. S.E.* 10. 153–329.
Freud, S. (1911). *Formulations on the Two Principles of Mental Functioning. S.E.* 12: 218–226.
Freud, S. (1923). *The Ego and the ID. S.E.* 19. 3–68.
Isaacs, S. (1948). On the nature and function of phantasy. *The International Journal of Psychoanalysis*, 29: 58–59.
Klein, M. (1921). The development of a child. In *The Writings of Melanie Klein, Vol. 1*. London: Hogarth Press, 1–53.
Klein, M. (1935). A contribution to the psychogenesis of manic-depressive states. In *The Writings of Melanie Klein, Vol. 1*. London: Hogarth Press, 262–289.
Klein, M. (1937). Love, guilt and reparation. In *The Writings of Melanie Klein, Vol. 1*. London: Hogarth Press, 306–343.
Money-Kyrle, R. (1968). Cognitive development. *The International Journal of Psychoanalysis*, 49: 691–698.
Riviere, J. (1936). A contribution to the analysis of the negative therapeutic reaction. *The International Journal of Psychoanalysis*, 17: 304–320.
Segal, H. (1994). Phantasy and reality. *The International Journal of Psychoanalysis*, 75: 359–401.
Wordsworth, W. (1995). In Wordsworth, J. (Ed.), *The Prelude. The Four Texts 1798, 1799, 1805, 1850*. London: Penguin Books.

* * *

The trouble with omnipotence: Clinical material

Jean Arundale

As Dr Simpson has so eloquently described, the basis of infantile omnipotence lies in omnipotent aggressive phantasies, which produce guilt, a manic drive to repair, and the inability to mourn. In the following clinical material, I will describe a patient who exemplifies this complex situation and the difficulty in giving up omnipotent phantasy.

B had been given my name several years before contacting me but, believing psychoanalysis to be rubbish, did not get in touch until he found himself in a serious depressive crisis, overcome by the belief that everything he had done in his life was wrong, and he was a complete failure. For confidentiality reasons I have not described his background, except to say that in B's professional life he was highly competent and dominant, while in his personal emotional life he was submissive and self-sacrificing; he has had a number of girlfriends, but, in spite of enjoying sex and wanting a child, all his relationships have gone wrong.

Clinical material

Early into analysis, B told me in his articulate way that he suddenly saw that he had become a spectator to his own life, not a participant. He was shocked to become aware that he had no idea who he was or what he felt or wanted, that he felt at a distance from himself.

Free association started the process of his self-discovery. As we began to see how he projected his needs into others, caring for them while neglecting himself, B began to be more sociable with friends he hadn't seen in years; he had two medical procedures for painful conditions that he had been putting off; and he renovated and decorated his house. Claiming that he wanted to lead his own life and spend less time under the direction of his mother, I could see nevertheless that his improvements at this time were due to compliance with what he thought I wanted, the so-called transference cure, not reaching deep structures. I began to see his separation anxiety was not of the ordinary garden-variety kind.

In the first years of work with Mr B, there was an idealised omnipotent fusion with me that replicated his relationship with his mother, in which he played back to me what I said or what he thought I wanted to hear, usually in a disguised form. I was made into his dominating and controlling, idealised mother, which meant he could then sink into being the compliant son, not having to think or be responsible, safe in a merged state with me, the same state he attempted to create with his girlfriends. I took up this desire to merge with me repeatedly, reaching to find his cut-off emotional life, attempting to bring into focus his authentic feelings and thoughts and moments when he felt separate or different from me.

B told me his strongest desire all his life had been to unite his battling parents. He told me of the excruciating experience of sitting on the stairs as a little boy, listening to his parents' fight. 'I couldn't sleep when I heard them arguing, I listened to everything, every twist and turn, every long terrifying argument. They tore each other to pieces. It was character assassination, but worse, lots of shouting "I hate you". Then she would threaten to walk out, to leave. I was terrified that she would'.

This brought to light the extent of B's terror of separation and provided better understanding of his constant and habitual pattern of merging with his objects in identification, eliminating himself, which precipitated a significant period of work in the transference. There was a frightened little boy in him – indeed, a forsaken baby, as it was later revealed – who was afraid of abandonment: indeed, afraid here with me that if he didn't please or comply, I would walk out or reject him.

On one such occasion when I made a transference link, B responded by saying, 'Yes, that could happen; you could end this'. He immediately moved to his father: 'He was the only one who didn't expect me to do things for him; he didn't judge me'. Speaking again of his mother, he said he was so afraid of being close to a woman who is high maintenance; he would have to be her slave, like he was with his mother. I took this up in the transference and said that he felt anxious that being close to me made him feel he would have to be my slave and that I was trying to take him over. Avoiding my comment, he said: 'Every fibre of me wants to go to stay with my parents. I'm so keen to go live with them. I'm embedded in my parent's relationship'. It was clear there were two systems in competition for his involvement and that the psychoanalytic relationship did not feel much of an improvement on his family. I took the cue from his language: 'Yes', I said, 'embedded, you want to be right there in the bed between them, in the bedroom, the place of intercourse, sex, conception, right in the middle of what you believe is an exciting, violent place of battle'.

'The war zone', he said. 'I lived with turmoil. I'm a cauldron with the lid on; things never got better. I don't think I'm fixable. I feel such terror when a woman begins feeling she wants to move in with me'. I said, 'You and I have moved in together here.' B responded, 'It's odd that I trust you. I really must cultivate a relationship. It shouldn't be so difficult. I literally could not allow myself to have anything I wanted until I began analysis. Now I've bought a car, an expensive camera. and the TV I wanted, so why not this? Something *big* is holding me back. Others can take the risk; why can't I? I know I've talked about this *ad infinitum* – it is deeply ingrained. I can't have control over my life'.

I talked with him about how he stays on the edge of relationships, always late, always covertly in control, holding back emotionally, terrified he will repeat his parent's relationship, as he is with me: not here 100%, speaking from his intellect, not allowing himself be close or to feel anything.

B continued the recitation of his past relationships with women – how he tried to fuse with them, what went wrong – stories I had heard many times. Unable to use his own mind and to think for himself, he gets others to think for him: his mother, his girlfriends, and me. This was a striking example of the way in which he could not take back his projective identifications; he was not able to bear separation, relinquishing his object even a little bit, to experience loss and mourning; thus, owning his own mind, the act of thinking and feeling for himself, could not take place. His thinking apparatus was projected, lodged in the other, stuck there, and he served the object, the thinking mind of the other, that told him what to do. I was beginning to conceptualise this as an infant confusional/ fusional state with mother, as discussed by Rosenfeld, which if he were to break out of there would be catastrophic loss (Rosenfeld, 1999: 273). At a deep level, his baby self was so entwined with mother, with no bridge to his adult self, that it was inconceivable for him to think he could survive without his links with her. My interpretations began to be addressed to his baby self and his fear for his survival.

More interested in saving others than in saving his own vulnerable self, B began going over and over his failed relationships with women, consistently chosen because they needed rescuing. He told me, 'With my girlfriends, I always think I can change them if I try hard enough', and indeed, he described in detail his efforts, while knowing at the same time that telling them what to do had no effect. The omnipotent narcissistic belief that was evident here, that he could change, control, and repair his objects. was apparent throughout his analysis, the phantasy that he could make his family members and girlfriends do what he wanted for their own good, even though they showed no interest in changing and fought him off, often engaging in shouting matches. In the face of this, he launched a vigorous campaign to repair his mother and sister, who lived in the family home two hours away. His silent father he allowed to be, although B was worried about his health. Manifesting a compulsive need to visit his family in person, 'to make sure they are breathing', as he put it, he badgered his mother and sister relentlessly, insisting that they exercise, go on diets, see friends, buy things to make life easier or healthier. He shouted at them when they didn't listen, refusing to follow his lead. B was determined to fix them, an impossible task in view of their intransigence, in a cycle of endless manic reparation. Repeatedly, he would go to his parent's house, tell them what to do, fail to be effective or listened to, get angry, leave, kill them off in his mind in fury, feel guilty, then go back again to repair them the next weekend. He told me he couldn't begin his life until his family were well. His manic reparation, driven by a cruel superego, blocked mourning and the acceptance of their reality, the people they were, the depressive position. He was terrified of another depressive breakdown were he to lose his omnipotent belief he could make them better, the fear of collapsing into a useless, hopeless, chaotic, fragmented baby self, the opposite of omnipotence. This patient's terrifying vulnerabilities were masked by this omnipotent defence. He used manic reparation to keep hope alive while hope was actually dead in him. These things were interpreted, then lost and interpreted again over intervals in our work.

As Mr B went over and over his failed relationships with women, it was difficult not to believe, judging from the way he treated his girlfriends, that there was a substantial amount of hidden hostility towards them: in his leading them on and then not being able to commit, making them wait, wasting their time as the clock was ticking. These were acts of revenge against his mother, represented by the girlfriends, as I saw it. I interpreted in the transference that he kept me waiting like a girlfriend, compliant, seeming to use the analytic relationship for his benefit, but covertly going his own way, not fully committed, cruelly making me watch his fruitless self-destruction and refusal to take anything in.

Often in the countertransference I felt sidelined and unwanted, a repetition of how he felt as a child in his family. He spoke of his 15-hour day, with not enough space for other things, and I pointed out that he felt there wasn't even space for *him* in his busy life, a space to be. I said that he talks on and on in a new defensive maneuver, not giving me any space to be, leaving me out, interrupting and ignoring me, pushing away what I say. I said I felt this was a recreation of the situation in his childhood when he experienced his mother as not having any space for him. I said he turns it around with me, treating me as the neglected child. I'm left out, and he plays the mother who doesn't let me/him in.

After saying this and similar things, I experienced B as leaving more space for me in the session, being more open and, not filling the room with a barrage of words. Occasionally, there was more contact, if only for seconds, more space and light, even play. But he soon returned to the repetitive mantras used to forestall his anger and prevent him from slipping into the dark depths of helplessness and melancholia. I began to see that underneath the shield of words, there was a primitive tie with his mother that he was terrified to break, and that, together with manic reparation and an intellectualised network of words, he held himself together, unable to trust and experience a nurturing maternal transference to me for fear that I, too, would imprison him, an alternate system of slavery. These notions I put to him.

Glimpses of anger, depression, and mourning

After some time, there appeared more rifts in B's armour, some glimpses of anger, depression, and mourning. He complained that the work here felt so hard, that he usually found everything easy, but this was hard. I responded, 'I think it frightens you here; you feel terrified to be in touch with your deep feelings of turmoil inside, not connected with anyone or anything, afraid of falling apart, breaking down.' To my surprise, he said, 'I'm very angry. I'm angry with everyone', then he was silent. I said he was frightened by his anger. He replied, 'Mainly I'm angry with my mother, my family. I'm very angry with a client right now, angry with all of them. I'm bad, toxic, how about that, huh? My family is so cruel, so difficult; how has it happened we are so unlucky? We are so dysfunctional. I'm furious with my brother; he treated me badly for no reason. I've felt so shackled to my sister all my life, afraid I would make her feel bad every time I passed an exam and she didn't. When I was accepted at university, I thought, I always thought, "How will this make her feel?" I've carried her like a monkey on my back'.

Another moment appeared when his anger could not be denied. Mr B was given a prestigious award, and instead of praising him, his mother absentmindedly said, 'Oh, that's nice dear', and turned to something else. B was furious, speaking of his wasted time, effort, and emotion trying to please her and failing. 'She just doesn't love me like she does the others. It's not a figment of my imagination. I'm not any more going to sacrifice myself to her. All she has to do is click her fingers and I go running. I'm profoundly sad today, it's as if I'm in mourning for the mother I thought I had. But actually, I never had her at all'. I felt moved by his sadness and spoke of his profound disappointment.

Discussion

Hanna Segal writes of manic reparation as a desire to repair the object that is believed to be damaged by the patient, in order to relieve depression, anxiety, and guilt. Mr B's phantasy of destructive omnipotence, the belief he was the cause of all his family's considerable problems by being born, induced manic omnipotent reparation, desperate, frantic, and compulsive. Segal points out that manic reparation seeks omnipotent control of the object, often driven more by a need to relieve persecutory guilt than by love and concern (Segal, 2008: 147–158). I felt Mr B's hyperbolic guilt also stemmed from oedipal guilt, when in phantasy he stepped into his father's shoes to argue with his mother, and sibling guilt for taking his brother's place as the favourite child, the golden boy, both of which he denied. In any case, as long as he kept alive the phantasy that he could 'fix' his family (the 'altruistic defence', Riviere, 1936), there was no mourning for the state they were in, no recognition or acceptance of their reality, and no separation and individuation for himself. Only when mourning, its working through, and a relinquishment of the external object take place can a 'true internalisation of the object' be achieved (Steiner, 1993: 9). He worked to keep alive the delusional phantasy of an ideal family, merged into one and deathless, in which he could live as a loved and protected baby.

I often interpreted his sadistic treatment of girlfriends; having begun with denial, he is beginning to think this might be true. When I commented on his addiction to the excitement of going to his mother's and rowing with her, he responded, 'Yes, it's perverse'. I felt B was beginning to touch on his underlying destructive narcissism, Rosenfeld's notion of a vengeful rejection of object relationships, hiding within a psychic withdrawal (Rosenfeld, 2008: 119). This is what B meant, I believe, by his toxic core, intuiting the existence of cruelty and perversion in him, further confirming his belief that he is dangerous and damages his objects. John Steiner, in discussing pathological defensive organisations, thinks there can be an addiction to this destructive mental state, involving a perverse gratification and thus no remorse and movement towards the depressive position (Steiner, 1993: 12–13).

This seemed the case with Mr B: defended against intimacy, absorbed in his objects by both idealised identification and sadomasochism, driven by accumulated anger and revenge, he unconsciously acted out. He bullied his mother and sister; withheld a grandchild from his mother; led his girlfriends down the garden path, never intending to marry, using them for sex, then leaving them without a baby; and he cruelly deprived and denigrated himself. In the transference, I, too, was deprived of emotional contact and satisfaction in my work.

B's dilemma was tragic. He was without the internal foundation to be stable on his own; in his internal world, he existed in a pre-symbolic, concrete state of fusion with the mother imago, a defence against chaos and fragmentation. Deprived of his mother soon after his birth and turned over to his maternal grandmother who disliked both physical and emotional contact, with only custodial care, a good real maternal object was not available. Instead, he created a fused state of projective identification with his object, which became idealised, and he did not develop symbols to make the transition to objects that substitute for mother, the comforting link to a blanket, soft toys, games, books, friends, etc., that could act as surrogates and symbols to take him into the external world. Rosenfeld described the confusional/fusional state in early infancy in which love and hate, good and bad, self and other exist in chaos, are so confused that the infant cannot tell whether an object is good or bad. This is an overwhelming and impossible situation for a developing infant and interferes with normal splitting of experience into groups of good and bad, providing organisation and clarity in the infant's internal world and allowing the infant to believe in the existence of a good object that can be internalised (Rosenfeld, 1999: 273; Steiner, 2008: 62).

Many have written about how the failure of containment in infancy can result in aggressive superego attacks on the self. Mr B attempted to evade his harsh superego by means of narcissistic collusion and massive projective identification into his idealised mother. 'I have always lived in my mother's house in my mind', he told me. Rosenfeld's description of narcissism could be of my patient. He says, '[H]idden in the omnipotent structure there exists a very primitive superego which belittles and attacks the patient's capacities, observations and particularly his attempt to accept his need for real objects' (Rosenfeld, 2008: 87–88). Rosenfeld suggests this powerful supreme superego figure is disguised as a seductive and persuasive ideal figure, promising a guilt-free land of plenty, if only he could repair the objects he has damaged.

As Mr B's attempts went on to erase his guilt by the omnipotent manic defence, so did the pathological projective identification that was constantly active between the patient and his mother, confirming the idealised fusional/confusional state between them. B's manic reparation held at bay the terror that lay beneath, his fear of losing the state of identification with his mother and being left with nothing, a terror bordering on the schizo/paranoid – violent, nameless, and primitive – thus, the need to retain his omnipotent phantasies. He feared being destroyed by falling into catastrophic fragmentation and chaos. As Steiner puts it, at this primitive level, separation from the object on whom one believes survival depends, is indistinguishable from death (Steiner, 1993: 63).

In view of the intensity of his schizo/paranoid terror, it is understandable that he strongly resists giving up his omnipotent defences. On this point, Segal has noted there is an 'infantile need to annihilate any thought that would conflict with his own omnipotence'. The work of analysis, Segal suggests, is treating omnipotence as a hypothesis to be tested. She says it is the process of thinking with the patient, 'comparing and matching and judging', that integrates the phantasy with reality (Segal, 1986: 222, 226). She recognises this can be hard going as omnipotent patients are partly functioning on a primitive level and hate thinking (1986: 222).

In his theoretical discussion, Dr Simpson mentions the epistemophilic drive and urge towards investigation as factors that bring omnipotent phantasies into scrutiny under the reality principle. These factors operate, but rationality is slow in making inroads into my patient's existential terror and infantile need to merge with his object. I rely on the analytic process to eventually reduce his anxiety around separation, together with a further experiential process in analysis that may help my patient relinquish the omnipotent phantasy that he is completely self-sufficient, that nothing exists outside himself: that is, the lived experience that I exist not as a part of him in the fused transference but outside his narcissistic structures and his control. This experience unsettles him, and yet each contact with me means a tiny moment of trust in otherness outside himself, the development of a sense that a safety net might be available, that he need not fear a catastrophic leap into the abyss.

References

Rosenfeld, H. (1999). *Impasse* and *Interpretation*. New Library of Psychoanalysis. London and New York: Routledge.

Rosenfeld, H. (2008). *Rosenfeld in Retrospect*. Ed. J. Steiner. London and New York: Routledge.

Riviere, J. (1936). A contribution to the analysis of the negative therapeutic reaction. *International Journal of Psychoanalysis*, 17: 304–320.

Segal, H. (1986). Manic reparation. In *The Work of Hanna Segal*. London: Free Association Books & Maresfield Library, 147–158.

Segal, H. (2008). Discussion of Ron Britton's paper. In Rosenfeld, H. & Steiner, J. (Eds.), *Rosenfeld in Retrospect*. London and New York: Routledge.

Steiner, J. (1993). *Psychic Retreats*. London: Karnac Books.

Steiner, R. (2008). Some notes on A.H Rosenfeld's contributions to psychoanalysis. In Steiner, J. (Ed.), *Rosenfeld in Retrospect*. London and New York: Routledge.

The desire for power
in culture and society . . .

Chapter 14

Omnipotence and the paradoxes of insight

A Darwinian look

Jorge L. Ahumada

By 1883 Freud had read and annotated seven Darwin books (Ritvo, 1990); his biological blow to human narcissism showing that man 'is of animal descent' (Freud, 1917: 141) opened the way to the psychological blow, whereby *'the ego is not master in its own house'* (Freud, 1917: 143, emphasis in original). Darwinism shines in his late writing: the id-ego-superego psychical apparatus 'may be supposed to apply as well to the higher animals which resemble man mentally' (Freud, 1940: 147); however, evolutionism receives scant psychoanalytic attention. To Darwin 'most of the more complex emotions are common to the higher animals and ourselves' (1879: 92), the main difference being moral conscience: self-recognition, a key requisite for insight, though, arises mostly late in evolution.

Psychoanalysis started as a study of the neuroses, built around ego-dystonic symptoms. It relied on accomplished individuation and was spelt mainly in terms of intrapsychic dynamics, all of which applied less and less as the twentieth century unfolded. Omnipotence opposes notionally the evolved adult, conscious, discriminating and discriminated, 'civilised' frames of mind met in normality and in the main in the neuroses: it is an elusive, hard-to-delimit notion. With no expectation to exhaust the issue, let me mention:

1. Omnipotence in the initial psychic stages, at best partly outgrown along each child's path to adulthood and maturity. As Ferenczi (1909) posited in *Introjection and Transference*, to the newborn infant, everything appears monistic. Later, he distinguishes from his ego the malicious things in the outer world that do not obey his will. Such unconditional omnipotence – which, to Ferenczi (1913), was the grounds for the almost incurable megalomania of mankind – was described by his disciple Alice Balint (1939) as an archaic, reality-less egotistic love for the mother. Akin is Freud's assertion that in the beginning 'The breast is a part of me, I am the breast'. Only later did it become: ' "I have it" – that is, "I am not it" ' (1941: 299), recognising that the primal object as separate comes later than identity with it.
2. Omnipotent mass psychology enactments at the level of Bion's 'basic assumptions' (1961), Gaddini's 'identity' (1984) and Matte-Blanco's (1988) notion that the unconscious acknowledges only classes, not individuals. Impersonal

DOI: 10.4324/9781003185192-20

mass enactments, unleashed in ideological, social and political frays, usually entail idolising identification with, and submission to, messianic leaders under populist guises.
3. Omnipotence of the self, overtly enacted or masked. The conceptual contrast of omnipotence versus normalcy is currently under high tension due to the rift between the modern and postmodern worldviews about, among other topics, the wilfull self-remoulding of sexual identities: the LGBTQ issue. Is self-engendering one's sexual identity a pathology, as Freud (1910) thought, or an inalienable human right?
4. Omnipotence of the objects, internal and/or external, entailing impotence of the self – illustrated by the vignette to be presented.
5. Last but not least, omnipotent denial of self and reality – an omnipotence of negativistic passivity: massive in shell-type infantile autism, it fuels the 'epidemic of autism' and a global autistoid turn of psychopathologies, locally called the *ni-ni* (neither-nor) who do not study or work or want to do anything about this.

Omnipotence in primitive man and in the origins of Western civilisation

The term 'omnipotence' first turns up in Freud's paper ' "Civilised" sexual morality and modern nervous illness' concerning a basic conflict between instincts and civilised life:

> Generally speaking, our civilisation is built up on the suppression of instincts. Each individual has surrendered some part of his possessions – some part of the sense of omnipotence or of the aggressive or vindictive inclinations of his personality. From these contributions has grown civilisation's common possession of material and ideal property.
>
> (1908: 186)

Thus, civilisation and a civilised mind are built upon renouncing omnipotence, aggression and vindictiveness.

While in the Rat Man (Freud, 1909) – and in neuroses generally – 'omnipotence of wishes' was a symptom, mainly ego-dystonic, that did not configure his personal identity, to primitive man, omnipotence had no limits. It entailed both a personal omnipotence of the rulers and a mass psychology attribution apt to be reversed whenever it failed. In *Totem and Taboo*, omnipotence rules the primitive stages of mankind, rulers being endowed with sacred and dangerous magical powers; savages ascribe their king's power over rain and sunshine, wind and weather, and then depose them or kill them because nature disappoints their hopes of a successful hunt or a rich harvest (Freud, 1913: 50). The child's attitude to his father, assigned well-nigh excessive powers, is of distrust as well as admiration. Shortly before, though, in *Leonardo* (Freud, 1910), a similar ambivalence characterised the early bond to the mother, at once supremely enticing and sinister; thus, ambivalent omnipotence marks the initial link to both parents.

Intense emotional attachment to a given person, concealing unconscious hostility behind the tender love, is the prototype of the ambivalence of human emotions. Savages, argues Freud (1913: 57), are afraid of a dead person's ghost; his soul has become a hostile demon seeking to drag the living in its train. Death being the gravest misfortune, the dead are deemed to envy the living. Taboos on the dead fall upon their mourning relations, widowers and widows, leading to prohibitions and ceremonies. Prohibition against uttering their names is severely enforced; savages treat words in every sense as things – the same, he says, as our own children.

By way of projection, unconscious hostility, of which the survivors know nothing and want to know nothing, is ejected into someone else; hence, the dead become demons, their nearest and dearest having most to fear. But projection also occurs where there is no conflict, playing a very large part in determining the form taken by our external world. Attention, states Freud (1913: 64), was originally directed to the external world, and only after a language of abstract thought was developed were internal processes gradually to be perceived; as concerns magic, primitive man had an immense belief in the power of his wishes, as do children. Nowadays the primitive belief in omnipotence partly survives, Freud says, especially in the 'magic of art' and the view of the artist as magician (1913: 90), but later on, he far extends this view, deeming present-day man a prosthetic god (Freud, 1930).

Darwin conjectured in *The Descent of Man* (1879) a primitive horde led by a single, powerfully dominant male retaining all the females – the model for the primal horde; Freud's core addition was, after the murder of the primal father, the role of the sons' guilt and grief in setting a new social structure, the totemic brother-clan. Though we descend from the multi-male chimpanzee line, one marvels at the core psychic dynamics disclosed in *Totem and Taboo*: the ever-present and limitless ambivalence, heightened in close personal links; the role of grief and guilt in mitigating ambivalence and in gaining a moral conscience; the primordial equation of words and events, to mention a few.

A crucial achievement in the prehistory of civilisation, the unity of personality, is shaky and recent. Close to our time, in ancient Greece, says the historian E. R. Dodds in *The Greeks and the Irrational* (1951), we discern a process of individuation from Homer's prehistorical times to the properly historical classical times. Homeric man lacks a unified concept of 'soul' or 'personality'; his universe is an accretion of concrete events that it would be erroneous to deem private. His actions do not have an 'ego' as their start, responding to other people's actions, the events themselves or the intervention of the gods. His *thymós* – vehicing his impulses – came as an independent inner voice not acknowledged as part of his own psyche: in Homeric sagas, *até* is a passing partial madness attributed to an external or demoniac agent. Dreams are 'objective' for the dreamer who 'sees' them coming and going; violent fury and sudden impulses, coming from the gods, are not personal events. The arrival of classical times put an end to such oneiric primacy of images, allowing further individuation. Socratic argument, by weighing the evidence and delimiting the contexts, made it possible to learn from experience, giving rise to a 'civilised' mind.

Mind as inferential from its start

Freud's (1913: 64) idea that attention was originally directed to the external world is prescient for what a succinct history of mind teaches us. Sketching what was detailed recently – to which I refer the reader – (Ahumada, in press), let me argue that mind is coeval with animal life starting at sea in the Cambric explosion 500 million years ago: a geologically short time span engendering myriad species, from arthropods and cephalopods to vertebrates such as fish. In the context of mutual predation – search, hunting and defence – each species' evolution changed the habitat, forcing the other species to evolve, leading to an 'armament race': in those times evolved eyes, antennae and claws, as well as nervous systems (Godfrey-Smith, 2017).

Species evolution being a war of each against all, tactical grasp – a must for survival – requires inferences. Octopuses' mimicry involves inferential responses on two sides: to predators' presence and to the visual qualities of whatever they lie upon in order to disappear visually; mimesis may also involve adopting another species' garb – toxic, venomous or otherwise fearsome. Instinctual endowment is acutely context-dependent; throughout biology, alertness to context defines mind or psyche.

Darwin saw instincts as processes of discharge: this sounds mechanistic, but *The Descent of Man* counters that 'Only a few persons now dispute that animals possess some power of reasoning' (1879: 96). Freud did refer to instincts as processes of discharge, conspicuously so in his 1915 metapsychological papers in which instincts, a demand for work upon the psychic apparatus, are external to it; later, though, he avowed that id and ego are originally one (Freud, 1937: 240), there being no clear line between them. Phyllogenetically, aggression long antecedes evidence of loving affect, advening with mammals in the Pleistocene 60 million years ago. Herd, pack, group and community bonding mitigate intragroup aggression in those species, chimpanzees included, where such groupings are the unit of survival; however, in chimpanzees, the unremitting territorial strife between communities direly threatens their survival.

Darwin remarked that 'Monkeys are born in almost as helpless a condition as our own infants' (1879: 25). In the first year of life, baby apes contact mother's body night and day, held in arms or hanging from her; instinctual unfolding demands mind-to-mind co-evolution of instinct, object and emerging self, mother soon entering into reciprocal games with the baby and regulating his social contacts with other infants. At about age four, mother starts a highly adversarial weaning, opposed by an infant feeding by himself but bent on retaining possession of the breast: ambivalence as rivalrous possessiveness has an early start. Co-evolution of instinct is social from infancy on: infant play evinces once and again the most varied aggressions as well as sexuality, with penetration of co-evals and of female adults, who lend themselves to it as an infant game. The family is matrilineal, with no identifiable father. After weaning, the mother reassumes sexual life: when males mount her, the youngest infant jumps on her back, slapping on the face the offender, who rests undisturbed at this 'primal scene' reaction. Should an older infant act similarly, he gets ousted by a backhand blow by the adult male without damage; it is just a disciplinary clue.

To Jane Goodall (1989) the mark of the chimpanzee is a strong instinct of dominance, giving firm support to Freud's *Bemächtigungstrieb*, soon subsumed under his wide-ranging *Todestrieb*, the death instinct. Social structure displays two status hierarchies: a supra-ordinated male one and a female one; dominance quarrels for status being unending, so are alliances and hostilities. Status has a strong sexual bent, the dominant alpha male seeking, though hardly securing, monopoly of females. When, as often happens, the alpha male runs across a couple in coitus, the female disappears, and the male covers his erect penis with both hands, voicing vigorous submission calls which the alpha male usually accepts, abstaining from reprisals. Submission is counterpart to dominance.

Intragroup aggression normally causes no serious damage while intergroup fighting may at any time lead to the extermination of a community, females and infants not excepted; females secretly mate with males of rival communities when their own are enfeebled. A male chimpanzee rarely leaves his community's territory alone because, on crossing an alien group, he risks being killed; there is nothing personal in that kill, it just diminishes the power of the victim's community. What is felt individually is the killers' mighty enthusiasm: going for the kill, and barbarism generally, are intensely euphoria inducing. Is this the original sin of our species?

Aggressive rivalry, traceable to the origins of mind, proceeds all along evolution. That the sexual instinct requires co-evolution is shown by numberless experiments of infancy affect-deprivation: deprived male monkeys exhibit sexual arousal but bite or try to mount experienced females by the armpit, instead of penetrating them.

As said, in the evolutionary context of unremitting predation, tactical grasp is a must for survival: instinct and situational tactical moves go together. Tactics refer to manoeuvers on contacting prey or predators; ages later, higher animals – the lion, the wolf, the killer whale, the apes – show strategic thought prior to contact with prey or predator and involving a group acting consensually. At these levels, it would be moot to try to sort out what is omnipotent and what is not.

The long road to reflective thought

A crucial issue is *reflective thought*, having thought of itself as its own object: recognition of oneself as individual, an extremely late evolutionary feat, appears to be its prerequisite. The first chimpanzee bred in deaf-mute gestural sign language,

Washoe, brought the pioneering evidence of self-recognition; asked in front of a mirror 'Who that?' she responded, 'Me, Washoe' (Goodall, 1986: 35). Apes, but not monkeys, show self-recognition in a mirror; the lion does not, despite high strategic intelligence in group hunting. Relevantly, not all chimpanzees attain it; it weakens as they age, and, centrally, emotionally deprived infants do not attain it. Self-recognition requires sustained loving throughout unavoidable ambivalent infant-mother co-evolution. Sign-bred chimpanzees readily evince reflective thought; they have private sign talks with themselves, bearing no intromission; when intruded upon, Washoe went up a tree to gain privacy.

Most sign-language gestural interchanges refer to their social interactions – conflict, appeasement and reconciliation – evincing the richness of interpersonal affect and conflicts in chimpanzee life. Their referential abilities concern present objects and also absent ones, and they create new signs to denote new situations (Fouts and Fouts, 1993). Co-evolution of the baby-mother link relies on intersubjectivity – inferences on the other's mind, called mind-reading by primatologists – as do all chimpanzee social, sexual, status and power interactions. It evidences the inventiveness in chimpanzee cultures that many communities employ diverse types of tools, including sticks and stones used as weapons. From early on, infants in the Bossou community are patiently taught by their mothers to crack oil palm nuts using two stones as hammer and anvil, an ability taking years to master; they shape up their stone tools for better use showing awareness of their function (Matsuzawa, 1994). Feeding, thus, is both instinctual and a cultural ability unique to a community: gestural communication much previous to verbalized languages conveys elaborate intellectual grasp.

Moreover, how to unravel instinct and reason in Jane Goodall's report of Mike's power coup? Low ranking but ambitious, he stole 15-liter kerosene cans from Goodall's camp, banging them in his charging displays at other males; in the course of four months, with no need for making direct attacks, he attained alpha-male status by way of fright in the 14-male community (Goodall, 1986: 426). Such an instinct-propelled eureka process of discovery, unknown to the species, required inferences based on his previous acquaintance with the noise of the cans as well as an anticipation of the other chimpanzees' emotion – their fear – at the clamorous noise. Instincts in higher animals cannot be thought of as mechanistic: the omnipotence sought and put to act is both social and personal. Now, power is not happiness. Though meeting no direct threats to his dominance, Mike was tense and overreactive for some two years, after which he became a satisfied alpha male, which signals the inherent instability of omnipotence, much stressed by Freud in *Totem and Taboo* (1913).

As the Anglo-German psychoanalyst Kristin White (2010) notes, translations to English as 'instinct for mastery' and to French as '*emprise*' omit the eventual cruelty to objects the German term *Bemächtigungstrieb* conveys. The key Freudian term *Trieb*, deriving from the verbal form *Treiben*, strongly connotes being driven or pulled as happens to a piece of wood in a stream or to an adrift vessel pushed by wind and waves. Instinctual impulses, then, unknowingly push or pull us: they are, insists Freud (1920), the most important and the most obscure part of psychoanalysis – and of the human mind.

Tracing the continuities with our animal condition, Darwin recognised in 1873 that visible and vocal gestures are signifying, able to express basically adjectival meanings like 'good' and 'bad', adverbial approval and disapproval and much else based on emotional states (Armstrong et al., 1995: 189). Our ancestors' affect-laden communications, pro and con, took place as 'conversations in gestures': along primate evolution, *'language in the form of visible as well as vocal gesture provides the mechanism for the emergence of mind and self'* (Armstrong et al., 1995: 154, emphasis in original). Social communication by gesture and vocalisation in our prehistory is hardly refutable: human languages are some 100,000 years old while hominisation took millions of years! While we do not grasp chimp conversations in gestures occurring in the wild, the fact that, when raised in deaf-mute sign language, they proficiently adopt it and invent new signs when needed hugely expands Freud's (1913: 64) avowal that only after a language of abstract thought was developed were internal processes gradually able to be perceived. Conversations in gestures, sustaining complex interactions, illustrate that Freudian *terra incognita*, unconscious thing presentations which, referring primarily to organisms' relation with each other, I would rather call *relationship presentations* as they convey impulses and affects (Ahumada, 2005). In the clinical situation, they present that most difficult task, accessing the nonrepresented unconscious. Conversations in gestures raise to interpersonal levels Freud's (1923) basic notion of the ego as first and foremost a bodily ego.

Indeed, what is 'a language of abstract thought'? Not 'logic' in the formal sense because, as put by the eminent logician Hans Reichenbach (1947), in person-to-person interchanges, pragmatic impact overrides the semantic content and logic as such. A whole scale of levels of awareness of meaning going from iconicism to symbol formation in others and in oneself takes place prior to verbal languages, which will later gain conscious centre stage: Freud's avowal that 'everyone possesses in his unconscious mental activity an apparatus which enables him to interpret other people's reactions' (Freud, 1913: 159) readily applies to gestural languages anteceding verbal languages, as does his stating that 'in the beginning was the Deed' (Freud, 1913: 161).

Totem and Taboo's argument that attention was originally directed to the external world was reinforced in a private 1929 letter to Albert Einstein. Freud said:

> All our attention is directed to the outside, whence dangers threaten and satisfactions beckon. From the inside, we want only to be left in peace. So if someone tries to turn our awareness inward, in effect turning its neck round, then our whole organization resists – just as, for example, the oesophagus and the urethra resist any attempt to reverse their normal direction of passage.
>
> (Grubrich-Simitis, 1995: 117)

While resistance is an initial theme in psychoanalysis, Freud's emphasis here underlines the built-in paradoxes met by our analytic attempts at tempering instinct through insight (Ahumada, 2011): that mind deploys diverse levels accounts for the paradoxicalities of insight.

Traversing the paradoxes: A clinical vignette

When I opened the door on Mrs. L.'s first interview, I found nobody there. Turning to my right, I saw her, a middle-aged woman hunched at a shadowy corner (Ahumada, 2005). Once in, she stated she feared a breakdown, that she would stop functioning, her thoughts deserting her when most needed and choosing wrongly where it most mattered. Two previous analyses provided support but little knowledge; she interrupted her last, a Lacanian one, running from the couch after an unbearably traumatic interpretation. Then she kept off treatment for years. She came to see me after long observing how two patients of mine evolved. I was, she said, her only hope. Though surprised when I mentioned her collapse at the door, which she had not noticed, but said it fitted with what she knew about her collapses. At the end of the interview, I said that because of her link to my two patients, I wasn't sure about the requisite space for treatment and asked her to evaluate this. She was late for a second interview, having felt my doubt as a cataclysmic rejection: she came back, she said, because for the first time in her analyses, she had felt she associated freely. She felt nonetheless entitled to a grudge. Based on her cataclysmic feelings of rejection, I suggested face-to-face work initially; much relieved, she said that on the couch, she fell into unsurmountable silences. It took her months to get to the couch.

From infancy, she experienced blighted expectations, including several divorces, leading to 'falling into a hole'. After collapsing, she stayed for hours in the bathtub and then for days in bed to recover, only to again collapse upon new mishaps. When on trips abroad, she was vital and resilient but had no idea why; on returning, this lasted some three weeks, and then she collapsed again, attributing it to work, but we learnt in due course that motherly gestures – a kind email from a friend – often helped her out of her collapsed state. Weekend breaks were proof of my aloofness and lack of interest, and small incidents in session, such as my telling her 'until Thursday' – instead of until Wednesday – after a Tuesday session, were felt as devastating. This happened despite her consciously recognising this error as minor.

What precedes illustrates what Freud described as the omnipotent ambivalence marking core emotional links. While it can be said that Mrs. L. is dealing with her internal world projected on an analyst who *represents* her internal objects, it fits better to say that in her psychic reality the analyst *is*, concretely, her internal objects, endowed with the omnipotence of such objects. The term *represents* sets the issue at the level of symbol formation rather than that of enactment: what we find here are iconic equations (Ahumada, 2005) to sizeable failures of symbolisation. Part of the patient's mind – the part that can consciously symbolize – keeps out of such concreteness, making treatment possible. The situation is strictly paradoxical: the analyst is/is not the archaic object, an ongoing pragmatic paradox that requires solving through a renouncement of omnipotence in an emotion-laden process of learning from experience.

Having no awareness of her anger, she then exploded on minor issues: when a friend towards whom she had an undetected gripe dropped a piece of cake on her rug, she went into a boundless fury, saying things she had not thought before and did not intend to say. Analytic work allowed her some contact with her split-off furies as distinct from her all-too-available collapses, but, as her furies were felt as insoluble, insights were felt as useless.

Exploring her frozen hates opened the way to a frozen infancy and a frozen mother, who often said that children were just a bother. Dolls were their only toys, and, as her sisters were blond and she was dark haired, they got fair dolls while she got black ones; her main play was being mother to her younger siblings. She saw herself as a withdrawn and sad child, having no happy memories about home, just about school and her grandparents' home nearby. Her mother, she says, lived in houses full of mirrors, fascinated by her own image; their only tender contact involved a reversal of roles, combing mother's hair which the mother much enjoyed. Later on, in adolescence, her mother used to tell her that no man would love her because of her dark nipples. She still felt her mother, although now aged, was undaunted and immortal, with neither wrinkles nor feelings ('I never saw her cry'); she envied her invulnerability, seeing herself as beaten down by affects and by mother's critique. Similarly, she feared in session that I might eject her arbitrarily or that she might feel expelled through some error of mine. The first alternative rested on my incarnating the omnipotently rejecting frozen mother, the second one on her relentless, furies-driven demand for a flawless, omnipotently all-satisfying object. So treatment stood on a thin line. Anyway, analytic work brought, to her surprise, memories of loving people in infancy and later childhood; with one of them she spoke fluent French, but now, when she tries to speak it, she loses her voice. Also, she came to put some limits to her adolescent son, which much relieved her.

A memory from age five, when her mother's adored brother died in an accident close to Christmas time, after which Christmas was never again celebrated at home, helped a change in perspective, coming to see her mother not just as devastating but also as devastated, mitigating her felt invulnerability and omnipotence, as well as her fear of her. Eventually, she came to see her family of origin not only as unjust and cruel but also as disturbed in themselves and in their monetary mishandlings, which, in turn, allowed her to deal with entangled inheritance themes.

Though Mrs. L. appreciates my unobtrusiveness and puts this to words, the negative transference shines through in her coming late, in her feeling that analysis and the need for thinking things through are part and parcel of the injustices of life, in hugely resenting my fees, and in a depressed mood in session due to her rancour at my not alleviating her pain as fully as she felt I should. Her unremitting unconscious demand for a mother alleviating all malaise was enacted outside, as the enthusiastic mother of her adolescent son and her grandchildren, but there again, she collapsed whenever her loved ones did not fully respond. Omnipotence and impotence were two sides of the same coin. Gradually, she grasped that her costly maternal crusades attempted to provide for others what unconsciously she desperately demanded for herself, whereby she became better able to receive affect, first from a little granddaughter and, later, from friends. But the tenderer the affect, the worse the ensuing separations.

On coming to a session, she became furious with a man walking by stiffly, in a way she thought characteristic of locals, while foreigners she found more natural, free and relaxed: this led to why she felt badly in the city and imagined herself doing and feeling well only when away. The infuriating starchy stiffness she traced to her mother's artifice and coldness in relating, sarcastically adding it was good that I am not short in height as her mother is. In what Matte-Blanco (1988) called a *symmetrisation of classes*, the city was concretely equated to a frozen/freezing mother embodied in its starchy inhabitants, the analyst included – the omnipotently enacted, ever-present maternal imago.

Being a teacher, she connected her incapacity to be openly angry at me with what she had read about deprived children who, when angry, bite and lacerate themselves instead of getting angry at their parents. Then she recalled a dream at age five in which she furiously stuck knitting needles into a breast; on recounting the dream, she had felt vivid wishes to stick needles into me. Though she no longer smoked, she lighted cigarettes in session, saying 'better to smoke than to kill you'. At about that time, furious at the fact that her son's father had not deposited the agreed money, she went to his office armed with a huge can of paint, which she splattered all over the furniture and whatever documents she came across. It then came to her attention that after one of her divorces – at times involving physical violence – she had avoided her empty depression, keeping active and able to successfully work and study, and entered a defiant political movement against the then-ruling military regime, dressed up in a sort of Maoist uniform – despite not being Maoist. She felt happy and sure of herself in her rebel uniform, which she used at all times, night outings included, until it fell apart. An example of our battling primate inheritance, militant omnipotence is uplifting indeed!

By that time, she had been relieved of constipation requiring strong laxatives from infancy on; she dreamt of a baby with a dirty nappy, whom she recognized as herself. Then she had a kind phone call from her gym teacher whose group she had been missing; she had gone there but had not entered, feeling she would not be recognized. She noted the gap between the warm telephone call and her own inability to keep receptive attitudes alive and that this happened all the time with her absent children and grandchildren. The kind call got her out of her 'hole', and she reflected calmly on the damage ensuing from her inability to retain a viable memory of her affects. While these insights made her feel better, they also heightened her felt anger towards me, given that she felt nothing could improve because whatever was treasured turned unpredictable and then collapsed: thus, analytic insights and progresses again and again evoked the traumas of the swindle she linked to her feeling of being cheated from infancy on, such as the numberless times she had left the pleasurable enclave of her grandparents' house in order to return to the encapsulated coldness of her home and mother.

Let me finish this clinical narrative on omnipotent ambivalence with a triumphant revengeful association. Mrs. L. recalled the final images of a Swedish film seen two decades earlier, in which the protagonist, falling into schizophrenic annihilation, wilfully contemplated how her children, her husband and her analyst, whom she had invited for dinner, ate the poisoned grapes she had served at the table. But despite the revengeful, spiteful tone, this was an association, a thought skirting the murderous Deed: she was struggling to digest the paradoxes.

Omnipotence in postmodernity and postmodernism

Our phyllogenetic psychic prehistory illustrates the vicissitudes of oral and phallic sexuality – anal and urethral dynamics being, as Fairbairn (1952) thought, subsidiary. Only by contrast does it illuminate genital sexuality: i.e., *psychosexuality*, a recent, uniquely human cultural achievement ensuing from mature, civilised, well-accomplished co-evolution in which renouncements of omnipotence mitigate the ambivalences of instinct, allowing fully individuated affective attachments. In Kleinian terms, genital sexuality is post-depressive: it requires traversing, once and again, the 'growing pains' attending the depressive position: i.e., the relinquishment of omnipotence and the acceptance of realities. This is no easy affair: as Joan Riviere pointed out, the patient guards himself and us from the depressive position because, in his psychic reality, the worst disasters have already taken place and will again turn real through the analysis (1936: 312). This issue gets added relevance in the postmodern context where, under the aegis of the purified pleasure principle, the unavoidable 'growing pains' attending psychic development are too readily felt as victimisations.

Postmodernity – the time we live in – and postmodernism – the ideology deriving from Romanticism currently sweeping academia – are vast themes and can only be sketched here, so I refer the reader to earlier papers (Ahumada, 1997, 2001, 2005, 2011, 2016a, 2016b, in press). Romanticism anticipates key postmodernist features: the abrogation of the notion of truth, the primacy of the pleasure principle and the fight against the tyranny of any given identity. To Novalis, at the start of Romanticism, *the world must be as I want it to be*; it must conform to my will: in his magical realism, the world, through poetry, turns into a redemptive dream (Béguin, 1939). The search for a poetic oneiric paradise veered in late Romanticism, after Fichte's dictum *I am only my own creation*, to the political scene, turning from Nietzsche onward to defiance and transgression as the royal road to self-redemption.

The long primate prehistory of the mind is witness to the utter lateness and frailties of self-recognition: thereafter, in ancient Greece, the passage from the oneirism of Homeric times to argumentative classical times brought further steps in individuation; later on, print culture opened to a wide public access to thoughtful, discerning civilized individual minds. What happens in postmodernity?

Early alarms were rung by Aldous Huxley in *Brave New World* (1932) and by Roger Collingwood (1937), who warned that the 'make-believe' of amusement had built a watertight bulkhead between its world and everyday affairs, bifurcating experience into a 'real' part and a hedonistic 'make-believe' part whereby practical life, on which civilisation depends, becomes emotionally bankrupt: we can call the end result the Age of Image, the Age of Media, the Society of the Spectacle, the Age of Void or the Autistoid Age. Marshall McLuhan (1964), who brought the Media Age to public attention, highlighted that in a perpetual present under the dominance of visual media, society turns tribal again, as the anonymity of postmodern media culture lifts the restrictions set by civilisation. Postmodernity, argues Fredric Jameson (1981), adopts the mediatic model of the spectacle: the infinitisation of the present and a forgetfulness of historical time leads to an incapacity to elaborate personal experiences. We have lost, he says (1983), the ability to retain the past, living in a perpetual present and a perpetual change. Information media become agents of the amnesia of history, turning reality into images and fragmenting time into a perpetual series of presents: postmodern euphoria rests on an orgy of novelty, omnipotently enthroning a transgressive apotheosis of the new.

As Jürgen Habermas put it 'Postmodernity definitely presents itself as Antimodernity' (1981: 3); its anticipation of an undefined future and the cult of the new mean it is prompted by the anarchistic intention of blowing up the continuum of history. Its overarching principles, unlimited self-expression and self-realisation beget myriad 'idols' in the arts, sports, the academy, politics, business and fashion.

Though they are at odds with each other, psychoanalytic ambiances, mainly but not only academic ones, are presently prone to fall under postmodernist spells where self-expression substitutes evidential enquiry. However, Didier Eribon (2005), Foucault's companion and biographer, upholds as a sovereign right a subjectivation in terms of self-invention instead of a 'naturalistic' search for truth, battling all previous evidence and all given norms in order to invent a new culture – which, he rightly insists, is incompatible with psychoanalysis. To Strenger (2002), postmodernist ideology strives to combine a lack of significant emotional attachments with seemingly unlimited possibilities, avoiding historisation at all costs because it sows the seeds of guilt. In our post-truth, post-guilt times, fashionable self-remouldings enact limitless, defying, euphoric self-empowerments.

A young colleague was consulted by an upper-middle-class girl in her late teens who, in a fit of what is now called filio-parental violence, broke all links to her family after finishing high school and went to live alone – supporting herself as a 'sex worker'; she sought consultation on doubts about seeking surgeries to turn transsexual. Such desperate flight from herself, clutching for techno-assisted omnipotence in order to redeem herself, reinventing her life into the other sex, is at opposite poles from insight. It is a fair example of what Castoriadis (1997) called the *amorphous disorientation* (emphasis in the original) of younger generations:

in view of the crisis of the family having gone on for a century, nobody knows, he said, what is to be a woman or a man. Already Rene Spitz (1964) had noted a sharp increase in sadistic juvenile delinquency; widespread, concealed homosexuality; severe neuroses and psychoses; strange social groupings [and ever-more-inappropriate child rearing practices – babies' and infants' exposure to electronic screens among them (Busch de Ahumada and Ahumada, 2017). Looking around, one too often notices parents paying close, sustained attention to what comes up in their notebooks or their cellphones at the expense of responding to their children's affections.

The family is the great void in the postmodernist ideology: increasingly, also in postmodern culture. As we learnt from our close relative the chimp, self-recognition as the prelude to insight depends on sustained, close, loving (if perforce ambivalent) co-evolution in the link to the primary object. Given the ongoing trend to a lack of significant emotional attachments, how can reliable-enough, amorous personal relationships leading to stable, loving family units, allowing the next generation the emotional grounds required to be sanely bred, be attained?

References

Ahumada, J.L. (1997). The crisis of culture and the crisis of psychoanalysis. In *The Logics of the Mind. A Clinical View*. London: Karnac, 2001, 1–13.

Ahumada, J.L. (2001). The return of the idols. The Freudian unconscious and the Nietzchean unconscious. *International Journal of Psychoanalysis*, 82: 219–234.

Ahumada, J.L. (2005). The double work on the clinical evidence, and the nature and limits of symbolisation. In *Insight. Essays on Psychoanalytic Knowing*. London: Routledge, 2011, 163–180.

Ahumada, J.L. (2011). *Insight. Essays on Psychoanalytic Knowing*. London: Routledge.

Ahumada, J.L. (2016a). Insight under siege. Psychoanalysis in the Autistoid age. *International Journal of Psychoanalysis*, 97: 839–851.

Ahumada, J.L. (2016b). Response to Robert A. Paul. *International Journal of Psychoanalysis*, 97: 853–863.

Ahumada, J.L. (in press). Unbridled! Thoughts on times of self-begetting and violence. *American Journal of Psychoanalysis*.

Armstrong, D.F., Stokoe, W.C. y Wilcox, S.E. (1995). *Gesture and the Nature of Language*. Cambridge: Cambridge University Press.

Balint, A. (1939). Love for the mother and mother-love. *International Journal of Psychoanalysis*, 30: 251–259, 1949.

Béguin, A. (1939). *L'âme romantique et le rêve. Essai sur le Romantisme allemand et la Poésie française*. [The Romantic soul and the dream. Essay on German Romanticism and French poetry]. Paris: Corti.

Bion, W.R. (1961). *Experiences in Groups*. London: Tavistock.

Busch de Ahumada, L.C. & Ahumada, J.L. (2017). *Contacting the Autistic Child. Five Successful Early Psychoanalytic Interventions*. London: Routledge.

Castoriadis, C. (1997). *La montée de l'insignifiance*. [The rise of insignificance]. Paris: Seuil.

Collingwood, R.G. (1937). *The Principles of Art*. London: Oxford University Press, 1958.

Darwin, C. (1873). *The Expression of the Emotions in Man and Animals*. New York: Appleton.
Darwin, C. (1879). *The Descent of Man, and Selection in Relation to Sex*, 2nd ed. London: Penguin, 2004.
Dodds, E.R. (1951). *The Greeks and the Irrational*. Berkeley: University of California Press.
Eribon, D. (2005). *Échapper à la psychanalyse*. [To escape from psychoanalysis]. Paris: Léo Scheer.
Fairbairn, W.R.D. (1952). *Psychoanalytic Studies of the Personality*. London: Tavistock.
Ferenczi, S. (1909). Introjection and transference. In *First Contributions to Psychoanalysis*. London, Hogarth, 1952, 35–93.
Ferenczi, S. (1913). Stages in the development of the sense of reality. In *First Contributions to Psychoanalysis*. London: Hogarth, 1952, 213–239.
Fouts, R.S. & Fouts, D.H. (1993). Chimpanzee's use of sign language. In Cavalieri, P. & Singer, P. (Eds.), *The Great Ape Project*. New York: St. Martin's Griffin, 28–41.
Freud, S. (1908). 'Civilised' sexual morality and modern nervous illness. *S. E. 9*.
Freud, S. (1909). Notes upon a case of obsessional neurosis. *S. E. 10*.
Freud, S. (1910). Leonardo da Vinci and a memory of his childhood. *S. E. 11*.
Freud, S. (1913). Totem and taboo. *S. E. 13*.
Freud, S. (1917). A difficulty in the path of psychoanalysis. *S. E. 17*.
Freud, S. (1920). Beyond the pleasure principle. *S. E. 18*.
Freud, S. (1923). The ego and the id. *S. E. 19*.
Freud, S. (1930). Civilisation and its discontents. *S. E. 21*.
Freud, S. (1937). Analysis terminable and interminable. *S. E. 23*.
Freud, S. (1940). An outline of psychoanalysis. *S. E. 23*.
Freud, S. (1941). Findings, ideas, problems. *S. E. 23*.
Gaddini, E. (1984). Changes in psychoanalytic patients up to the present day. In *A Psychoanalytic Theory of Infant Experience*. London: Brunner-Routledge, 1992, 186–203.
Godfrey-Smith, P. (2017). *Other Minds. The Octopus and the Evolution of Intelligent Life*. London: William Collins.
Goodall, J. (1986). *The Chimpanzees of Gombe. Patterns of Behavior*. Cambridge, MA: Belknap/Harvard University Press.
Goodall, J. (1989). Gombe: Highlights and current research. In Heltne, P.G. & Marquardt, L.A. (Eds.), *Understanding Chimpanzees*. Cambridge MA, Harvard University Press, 2–21.
Grubrich-Simitis, I. (1995). 'No greater, richer, more mysterious subject [. . .] than the life of the mind'. An early exchange of letters between Freud and Einstein. *International Journal of Psychoanalysis*, 76: 115–122.
Habermas, J. (1981). Modernity – an incomplete project. In Foster, H. (Ed.), *The Anti-Aesthetic. Essays on Postmodern Culture*. New York: The New Press, 1988, 3–15.
Huxley, A. (1932). *Brave New World*. New York: Harper, 1946.
Jameson, F. (1981). *The Political Unconscious. Narrative as a Socially Symbolic Act*. Ithaca, NY: Cornell University Press.
Jameson, F. (1983). Postmodernism and consumer society. In Foster, H. (Ed.), *The Anti-Aesthetic. Essays on Postmodern Culture*. New York: New Press, 111–125.
Matte-Blanco, I. (1988). *Thinking, Feeling and Being*. London: Routledge.
Matsuzawa, T. (1994). Field experiments on the use of stone tools in the wild. In Wrangham, R.W., McGrew, W.C., de Waal, F.B.M. & Heltne, P.G. (Eds.), *Chimpanzee Cultures*. Cambridge, MA: Harvard University Press, 351–370.

McLuhan, M. (1964). *Understanding Media. The Extensions of Man.* London: Routledge, 2004.
Reichenbach, H. (1947). *Elements of Symbolic Logic.* New York: Macmillan.
Ritvo, L.B. (1990). *Darwin's Influence on Freud. A Tale of Two Sciences.* New Haven, CT: Harvard University Press.
Riviere, J. (1936). A contribution to the analysis of the negative therapeutic reaction. *International Journal of Psychoanalysis*, 17: 304–320.
Spitz, R. (1964). The derailment of dialogue. Stimulus overload action cycles, and the completion gradient. *Journal of the American Psychoanalytic Association*, 12: 752–775.
Strenger, C. (2002). *The Quest for Voice in Contemporary Psychoanalysis.* Madison, CT: International Universities Press.
White, K. (2010). Notes on *Bemächtigungstrieb* and Strachey's translation as instinct for mastery. *International Journal of Psychoanalysis*, 91: 811–820.

Chapter 15

Lear, Kane and the workings of omnipotence

Noel Hess

In this chapter, I plan to discuss the dynamics of omnipotence through an exploration of two fictional characters, Shakespeare's King Lear and Orson Welles's Charles Foster Kane. The scholarship on both these great works of art is considerable, and I will not attempt a comprehensive review of it. My interest is in how these two works of the creative imagination illuminate omnipotence within the context of object relations, with a particular focus on how and why omnipotence fails and whether this presents an opportunity for it to be relinquished. My contention in this chapter is that a fundamental way omnipotence fails is when the object presents a demand for separateness. It is usually necessary for this to be demanded because omnipotence forcefully and powerfully opposes separateness, insisting on control of the object.

I understand omnipotence to be a universal infantile unconscious phantasy containing the belief of limitless power, resources and capacities residing within the self, including the capacity to control one's objects; its main function is to defend against intolerable anxieties aroused by an awareness of helplessness and dependence. 'With integration and a growing sense of reality, omnipotence is bound to be lessened', Klein wrote in her last paper (1963: 304), and her choice of the word 'lessened' is important, for she argues that omnipotence, like idealisation 'is never fully given up' (p 305). This echoes Freud's (1908: 145) position:

> But whoever understands the human mind knows that hardly anything is harder for a man than to give up a pleasure which he has once experienced. Actually, we can never give anything up; we only exchange one thing for another.

This is addressed again ten years later, but with a significant change of emphasis:

> It is a matter of general observation that people *never willingly* abandon a libidinal position, not even, indeed, when a substitute is readily beckoning to them.
>
> (Freud, 1917: 244, emphasis added)

The difference between these two statements is that in the later one, relinquishment becomes a possibility, albeit in the face of considerable opposition. The question of what we might call the fate of omnipotence when faced with the demands of reality will be explored in relation to Lear and Kane. Clearly for both Freud and Klein, omnipotence is viewed as a durable feature of the unconscious mind.

Omnipotence and narcissism are terms that are inclined to be used synonymously in clinical discussions or coupled in descriptive terms such as 'omnipotent narcissistic personality', but I think it is important to differentiate them. Steiner (2020a: 60) writes:

> Generally speaking omnipotence, with its magical solutions to realistic problems, is considered an obstacle to development and is often the driving force behind narcissistic phantasies that underlie pathological organisations. These organisations create obstacles to progress in analysis and it is generally understood that for development to proceed they must be relinquished in accord with the dictates of reality.

This statement clarifies that omnipotent beliefs underpin narcissistic processes which can coalesce in the organisation of the personality, sometimes ossified as a pathological organisation. The interplay between omnipotence and narcissism will be central to the exploration of Lear and Kane.

Lear

The play begins with what appears to be an act of relinquishment by Lear, the division of his kingdom between his three daughters:

> Know you that we have divided
> In three our kingdom, and 'tis our fast intent
> To shake all cares and business from our age
> Conferring them on younger strengths, while we
> Unburthen'd crawl towards death.
>   Shakespeare (1605–1606) I, i, 36–40

The insincerity of Lear's words becomes clear as he cruelly demands of his daughters to tell him 'which of you shall we say doth love us most?' As Kermode (2000: 185) states, the imperiousness of Lear's speech makes clear that the act of giving away his kingdom is a selfish one, driven by narcissism. That Lear intends to give up nothing is made apparent later in the scene, when he states, 'Only we shall retain/The name and all th'addition to a king' (I,i,134–135), which Hanly (1986: 216) calls being 'regal, without responsibility'.

Lear's narcissism has been much discussed (Hanly, 1986; Hess, 1987; Schafer, 2010) and is indeed a central theme of the play and much in evidence in this first scene, but what I want to focus on is the omnipotence underlying what this father is doing, publicly, to his daughters. It is a narcissistic act of self-aggrandisement foundered on an omnipotent belief, or phantasy, that his objects will behave in accordance with the phantasy. However, when Cordelia says, 'I love your Majesty/According to my bond; no more nor less' (I,i,91–92), she is conveying that she is not the daughter her father wants her to be but the daughter *she* wants to be. Fisher (2000) argues that Lear wants to control the fate of his endowment, demanding obedience and gratitude from his objects, in line with the phantasy of omnipotent control. When Cordelia demands her separateness, insists on being viewed as an object separate and distinct from her father's control, the omnipotent phantasy is challenged, resulting in rage, devaluation and banishment.

Lear's ascribing of Cordelia's actions to pride ('Let pride, which she calls plainness, marry her' [I,i,128]) could be seen as a projection of his narcissistic pride; Brenman (2006: 4) posits a continuum such that 'where normal pride ends and omnipotence begins may be difficult to discern'.

The issue of the devaluation of the object is worth highlighting because it is an important feature of omnipotence. When Lear directs his rage and contempt at Cordelia, telling one of her suitors, Burgundy, 'now her price is fallen' (I,i,196), it illustrates how the overvaluation of the self within omnipotence is intrinsically connected to the devaluation of the object. This is vividly and poetically conveyed in *Richard II*, when Bolingbroke comes to claim the crown. Richard says:

> Here, cousin,
> On this side my hand, and on that side thine.
> Now is this golden crown like a deep well
> That owes two buckets, filling one another,
> The emptier ever dancing in the air,
> The other down, unseen, and full of water.
> That bucket down and full of tears am I,
> Drinking my griefs, whilst you mount up on high.
> 			Shakespeare (1595) IV,i,182–189)

The image is of two buckets at a well, one high and the other low; in giving away the crown, Richard becomes the 'down' bucket and allows Bolingbroke to 'mount up on high', acquiring the manic ('dancing in the air') omnipotence that has been surrendered. For Richard, as for Lear, relinquishing omnipotence is experienced as a devaluation of the self and an aggrandisement of the object. 'Nothing' is a recurring verbal motif in the play (Wilbern, 1980), and one important reason it echoes throughout the text is as an indication of what Lear fears becoming if his omnipotence is surrendered: nothing.

It is worth noting also that Richard pictures himself as a bucket 'full of tears', which conveys some idea of the emotional pain resulting from a lessening of omnipotence, accepting dependence and allowing one's object to occupy a more valued position. Whether Lear is able to arrive at such a position in the course of the play is a question I will return to.

When frustrated by his daughters not allowing him to exercise his omnipotent control over them, Lear equates the consequent experience of pain and humiliation with a despised femininity:

> [T]ouch me with noble anger
> And let not women's weapons water-drops
> Stain my man's cheeks!
> (II, iv, 274–276)

Earlier, he cries '*Hysterica passio!* down thy climbing sorrow!' (II, 14, 57). This leads to the vicious attacks on their femininity and fecundity. In contrast, feminine images are employed in the Gloucester/Edgar subplot to convey the value and importance of emotional receptivity and the capacity to feel pain. When the blinded Gloucester asks the disguised Edgar who he is, he replies:

> A most poor man, made tame to Fortune's blows,
> Who, by the art of known and feeling sorrows,
> Am pregnant to good pity.
> (IV,vi, 218–220)

And later, when asked by Albany, 'How have you known the miseries of your father?' Edgar replies simply, 'By nursing them my lord.' (V,iii, 178–9). Pregnancy and nursing, essentially feminine capacities.

Steiner (2020b: 92) argues that phallic omnipotence contains an envious denigration of femininity and that a move away from the position of phallic superiority necessitates a valuing and acceptance of emotional receptivity, equated with femininity.

Lear, I would argue, is never able to do this. After the storm, which is an externalisation of his rage ('this tempest in my mind' [III,iv, 13]) but then becomes subsumed by his omnipotent control as though he is orchestrating it ('Blow, winds, and crack your cheeks! rage! blow!' [III,ii, 1]), his passionate fury quells, and there is a moment, in the scene at Dover with Gloucester, when he says:

> They flattered me like a dog. . . . when the rain came to
> wet me once and the wind to make me chatter,
> when the thunder would not peace at my bidding,
> there I found 'em, there I smelt 'em out. Go to, they
> are not men o' their words: they told me I was every
> thing; 'tis a lie, I am not ague-proof.
> (IV, iv, 96–105)

Lear's 'they' seems to refer to his court, or perhaps to his daughters. At a deeper level, 'they' refers to the part of his mind which contains the belief that he is invulnerable, immune to fever (ague) and illness. There is also, in my reading of this speech, a note of complaint, that he 'found 'em' and 'smelt 'em out', exposed those who deceived him into believing he had the power to 'peace the thunder at my bidding'. We could say that this moment of apparent lucidity and sanity also has a slightly paranoid flavour, which is less present shortly after when he tells Gloucester that he, Lear, 'smells of mortality' (IV,vi, 132). Here, in Klein's words, omnipotence seems to have lessened, and Lear is more in touch with the reality of ordinary human limitation.

That this awareness is unaccompanied by the pain of loss and disillusionment makes us wonder how deeply it is felt. It is also significant that Lear is also asserting to Gloucester in this scene that he is 'every inch a king./When I do stare see how the subject quakes' (IV,vi, 108–109) and, later in the scene, 'I am a king, masters, know you that?' (IV,vi, 197).

This same fluctuating state of awareness, between an acknowledgment of ordinary humanity and a retreat back into omnipotence, is present in the scene of Lear's reunion with Cordelia. He says:

> Pray do not mock me:
> I am a very foolish fond old man,
> Fourscore and upward, not an hour more or less;
> And, to deal plainly,
> I fear I am not in my perfect mind.
> Methinks I should know you and know this man;
> Yet I am doubtful: for I am mainly ignorant
> What place this is, and all the skill I have
> Remembers not these garments; nor I know not
> Where I did lodge last night. Do not laugh at me;
> For, as I am a man, I think this lady
> To be my child Cordelia.
> (IV, vii, 59–69)

His words contain a humility, hesitancy and uncertainty we have hitherto been unaccustomed to hearing; he can be ignorant, doubtful, 'remember not', and want to 'deal plainly' rather than grandly. But in the next scene, he is proposing to Cordelia that they 'away to prison/We two shall sing like birds i' th' cage' (V, iii, 8–9). As benign as this sounds, Adelman (1992: 121) sees in it a phantasy of a return to a state of undifferentiated union, and it is the Cordelia of Lear's phantasy he is speaking to, not the Cordelia who, in the opening scene, insisted on being seen as a separate object.

Hanly's (1986: 220) rather harsh-sounding assessment of the trajectory of Lear's character through the course of the play – 'that so much suffering could result in so little insight' – is borne out, I think, by the account I have given;

moments, important and moving moments, of humility and humanity, before a retreat to the security of omnipotence. Insight may be only fleetingly available to Lear, but it is abundant to the audience.

Kane

Orson Welles's film *Citizen Kane* has the structure of an investigation: Who was this man Charles Foster Kane,[1] a former media magnate and now a recluse surrounded by wealth and possessions, and why was his dying word 'Rosebud'? It takes the form of a series of interviews with people who knew and worked with Kane and with his second wife, Susan, who left him.

It is somewhat surprising that this most famous and celebrated of films has attracted little interest from the psychoanalytic community. Commentaries on the film often quote Welles's remark about it being 'dollar book Freud' as though he disparaged the psychoanalytic perspective the film takes in its enquiry into the nature of Kane and the meaning of Rosebud. In fact, as Mulvay (1998: 246) makes clear, Welles's actual quote was 'it may be dollar book Freud but that's the way I understand the film', referring to his earlier statement that 'in his subconscious Rosebud stood for his mother's love'. This makes manifest that, while Welles may have been pre-empting accusations of a somewhat simplistic 'Freudian' explanation, he was also confirming his adherence to this approach of the film.

The title is clearly ironic. Citizenship is a rather modest status and implies a certain levelling – we are all citizens. It also conveys a sense of membership of a social body, whereas, as Jed Leland remarks, 'He never believed in anything except Charlie Kane'.

The structure is gendered (Mulvay, 2012: 51), in that the men interviewed (Jed Leland apart) tell of Kane's power and rise to fame, while the women – notably Susan, but also his first wife, Emily – of his disgrace, infidelity, failure and eventual social withdrawal. It is interesting that it is the men who largely admire Kane's omnipotence and the women who feel controlled and tyrannised by it. This might be seen to reflect the dynamic, discussed in relation to Lear, of phallic omnipotence and its implicit denigration of femininity.

Despite this male/female split in the narrative, there is one occasion when a man attempts to address Kane's omnipotence (rather as Kent does to Lear in the opening scene). This is the drunken speech his old friend Jed Leland makes to Kane when he fails in his bid to run for political office, which is the first time he has been faced with the experience of failure:

> You talk about the people as though you own them, as though they belong to you. You talk about giving people their rights, like making a present to them. . . . You won't like it when the working man expects something as his right, not as your gift. . . . You don't care about anything but you. . . . You want to persuade people that you love them so much that they ought to love

you back. Only, you want love on your own terms – something to be played your way, according to your rules.

It is ambiguous how Kane receives this and how much he is able to be disturbed by it. Mostly, it appears he is able to pass it off as a product of Jed's drunkenness, but there is a brief moment, when Jed tells him he thinks 'they ought to love you back', when we see Kane turn and look sharply at Jed as though he had heard a painful truth. The moment quickly passes, and Kane's impregnable self-assurance is restored.

The similarity with Lear's apparent act of giving will be recognisable in what Leland is describing – narcissistic giving, controlling the fate of the gift and promoting an image of the giver as generous and therefore loveable. Earlier, Jed says, 'He never gave anything away, just left you a tip'. Kane's imperiousness is well captured in this comment.

Having previously commented that *Citizen Kane* has attracted little interest from psychoanalysts, there is one famous exception: Melanie Klein wrote unpublished notes after seeing the film, which exist in the Klein Wellcome archives (Mason, 1998; Phillips and Stonebridge, 1998). She clearly thought the film offered considerable psychoanalytic insight of greater value than 'dollar book Freud' and was impressed that Welles 'seemed to know a great deal of the unconscious processes underlying and influencing Kane's development and life'.

As well as her focus on Kane's manic defences, the problem he has in loving was an aspect of particular interest to her:

> [Kane] has no love to give. He ties people to him only because he wants them to love him. . . . [T]he more his capacity for love proves a failure, the more the manic mechanisms increase.
> (Phillips and Stonebridge, 1998: 252–254)

Citizen Kane was released in England in early 1942, which is when Klein would have seen it. Two years before, she published her seminal paper ('Mourning and Its Relation to Manic-Depressive States') on the depressive position, on the particular set of anxieties it evokes and on the defences, especially manic and omnipotent, against this developmental movement. It is not surprising, then, that she should respond with interest to Welles's exploration of the vicissitudes of grandiosity and omnipotence in Kane's character and how this results in his inability to love.

It is, however, in his marriage to Susan that Kane's omnipotence is most challenged. When he tries to fashion her into an opera singer, for which she clearly does not possess the necessary talent, he refuses to accept that she does not want this: 'Nonsense. We're going to be a great opera star. I don't propose to be made ridiculous'. This demonstrates the narcissistic investment ('we') he has in the project, entirely for his own aggrandisement. What is striking is his utter refusal to accept the reality of Susan's limited musical ability as it would threaten with failure his omnipotent phantasies and face him with the hated reality of limitation.

This has to be accepted when Susan, after being held captive and controlled in Kane's mansion, Xanadu, finally demands her freedom. His control of her contains an implicit devaluation: that she has become another object to collect. When she tells him she is leaving him, he says, 'You can't do this to me'. She replies: 'I see. It's you this is being done to. Not me at all. Not what it means to me. I can't do this to you? Oh yes I can.'

Earlier in the film she says, 'Everything was his idea, except me leaving him'. Susan is doing to Kane what Cordelia did to Lear: wrestling her separateness away from his omnipotent control. He erupts in rage, smashing up her bedroom, like Lear in the storm.

Where Kane differs from Lear is that we have evidence of an early trauma, which makes Susan leaving Kane more than just a demand for separateness, but evocative of the loss in childhood of his mother. (And there is evidence in the scene of his first meeting with Susan that he was thinking about his mother in the famous scene, told in flashback, of the young Charlie Kane playing in the snow with his 'Rosebud' sled while his mother inside the cabin signs papers that make Thatcher his legal guardian, in return for the deeds to a copper mine.) Kolker (2017: 52) has examined the scene in detail, famous for its deep-focus cinematography, with particular reference to its use of space within the frame. The groupings of Kane's mother and father and Thatcher are arranged in this interior shot in the foreground such that the viewer never loses sight of young Charlie playing outside the window in deep and sharp focus in the very centre of the frame. As the adults move around inside in the foreground, the boy outside becomes the still focal point for the viewer. He sings about 'the Union forever' as the union between him and his mother is being dissolved. Kane's middle name, Foster, functions like a constant subliminal reminder to the viewer of the importance of this early childhood trauma, as well as it being literally part of his identity.

As quoted earlier, Welles wrote that Rosebud 'stood for his mother's love, which Kane never lost'. What Welles perhaps means is that it was never mourned. Brenman (2006: 4) makes the point that 'deprivation of the experience of being considered significant is one element in *intensifying* omnipotence' (emphasis added). Not causing, but strengthening.

Kane spends his later years amassing art works and treasured antiquaries from around the globe to fill the cavernous spaces of Xanadu but actually amassed to fill his own inner emptiness. Borges (quoted in McBride, 1972: 33) called *Citizen Kane* a 'labyrinth without a centre', but his observation is as applicable to the title character as to the film. Corel (1998: 158) points out that the opera house he builds for Susan is also a grandiose structure with a void at the centre, for she does not recognise herself or her ambitions in the project Kane imposes on her.

This echoes Lear's repeated questions:

'[D]ost thou know me, fellow?' (I,iv, 26)
'Who am I, sir?' (I,iv, 77)
'Does anyone here know me?' (I,iv, 223)
'Who is it can tell me who I am?' (I,iv, 227)

To the last question, the Fool answers, 'Lear's shadow', an image of his emptiness. Klein, in her notes on the film, refers to Xanadu as 'a mausoleum' (p. 252) and also comments on Kane's 'incapacity to keep things alive inside' (p. 253). For Lear and Kane, then, omnipotence functions as a defence against an inner emptiness, resulting, for Kane, from an early object loss. Klein interpreted Rosebud as standing for the loss of the breast, his mother's love and his special position in relation to her, the manic omnipotent defences functioning to keep the pain of this loss at bay and covering over a sense of inner emptiness at the core of his narcissistic organisation.

Discussion

In pairing these two characters, Lear and Kane, there are obvious similarities but also key differences. *Citizen Kane* is an account of a man's life, albeit related in a fragmentary, impressionistic and highly subjective manner. We are required to piece together the fragments rather like the jigsaws with which Susan is occupied during her captivity in Xanadu. Lear shows us a man at the end of his life, from which we have to infer how he got there and how his character came to be as it is.

Beverley Houston's (1982: 2) description of the principal character in several of Welles's film, including *Kane*, is:

> A central male figure who is extremely powerful in certain ways, who can charm, force or frighten others into doing what he wants, but the desire for control is haunted by everything that evades it.

This description applies equally well to Lear. She terms this character 'the power baby', which captures the infantile origins of this omnipotent object relating. It is when their loved objects – Cordelia and Susan – demand their freedom that the omnipotence is in danger of being experienced as a failing defence. This then becomes an opportunity for it to have a lessening hold on the self and to facilitate a movement in the direction of a more integrated and balanced internal world. As I've suggested, Lear experiences moments when this is possible, but they cannot be sustained; Kane never has to face the terrifying idea that he is not ague-proof. Both men die miserably: Lear over the body of the murdered Cordelia, Kane alone in Xanadu, yearning for his lost Rosebud.[2] Segal (1986: 181) describes the death (post-analysis) of an elderly patient, which involved a need to know, as he was dying, that his objects were placed 'in reality', outside his omnipotent control. Neither Lear nor Kane achieve this degree of psychological maturity.

Having said that Leland functions in a not-dissimilar way to how Kent does to Lear, challenging the omnipotent control of Kane, Leland as an old man has some things in common with Gloucester, at least in terms of his relation to old age and death. His rueful, ironic remark to Thompson – 'old age is the one disease you don't look forward to being cured of' – conveys an acceptance of this painful inevitability, not unlike Edgar's report of Gloucester's death: '[H]is flaw'd heart . . .

twixt two extremes of passion, joy and grief/burst smilingly' (V, iii, 195–198). How different this is from the persecutory torment of Lear and the loneliness of Kane. It seems that Shakespeare and Welles are offering us another way in which life can be lived and death envisaged, without a preponderance of omnipotence.

To balance the picture of omnipotence presented here as a negative force in the personality, Steiner (2020a: 70) argues that 'before we can relinquish omnipotence, we have to recognise how much pleasure it gives us' and also that omnipotence is a necessary component of rebellion against conventional constraints, which is part of development. This is well conveyed in *Citizen Kane*, where we richly enjoy Kane as an ambitious young man railing against the limitations his elders put on him. The manic exuberance of his youthful omnipotence is infectious. It is also conveyed in the camerawork, such as the celebrated, apparently continuous crane shot down through the neon sign on the roof, then through the skylight into Susan's nightclub. The camera moves omnipotently, defying the limitations of physical barriers, and the graceful trajectory of the camera in this scene, as in others in the film, is undeniably pleasurable.

And yet, as ever, experience presents the problematic reality of limitation. Such a reality is an opportunity for relinquishing omnipotence, but what does that mean? The quotes from Freud earlier clearly indicate grave doubts as to the degree to which he thought this possible. Although Steiner (2020a: 60) states that 'omnipotence must be initially embraced and subsequently relinquished', elsewhere, he argues that: 'The best we can do is acknowledge its existence, recognise the damage it can do, and watch to see if its hold on the personality can weaken' (p. 93).

This seems to me in line with Klein's notion of omnipotence being lessened rather than given up, and the advice to 'watch to see' describes a more limited and modest view of how much we can influence the workings of omnipotence analytically. It is also in line with Brenman's (2006: 4) warning of the danger of presenting ourselves to our patients as perfect containers rather than merely limited ones, for we are no less immune to omnipotence than are our patients.

Notes

1 The prescience of Welles's portrait of this omnipotent figure is remarkable in relation to recent American politics. Kane's newspaper, *The Inquirer*, quite clearly trades in 'fake news', and when Kane loses in the election, the paper runs the headline 'Fraud at Polls'.
2 One of the narrative enigmas of this film is that if, as we are shown, Kane dies alone, who hears his dying word? We, the viewers, hear it, and this perhaps creates a privileged bond between us and Charles Foster Kane, which may make it more difficult to be aware of his cruelty, control and omnipotence. Schafer (2010) makes a similar point in terms of the audience's experience of the first scene in *King Lear*.

References

Adelman, J. (1992). Suffocating mothers in *King Lear*. In *Suffocating Mothers*. New York: Routledge, 103–129.

Brenman, E. (2006). The narcissism of the analyst: Its effect in clinical practice. In *Recovery of the Lost Good Object*. London: Routledge. The New Library of Psychoanalysis, 1–10.
Corel, A. (1998). Language and time in *Citizen Kane*. *Psychoanalytic Inquiry*, 18 (2): 154–160.
Fisher, J. (2000). A father's abdication: Lear's retreat from 'aesthetic conflict'. *International Journal of Psychoanalysis*, 81: 963–982.
Freud, S. (1908). Creative writing and day-dreaming. *S.E. 9*: 143–153.
Freud, S. (1917). Mourning and melancholia. *S.E. 14*: 243–258.
Hanly, C. (1986). Lear and his daughters. *International Review of Psychoanalysis*, 13: 211–220.
Hess, N. (1987). *King Lear* and some anxieties of old age. *British Journal of Medical Psychology*, 60: 209–215.
Houston, B. (1982). Power and disintegration in the films of Orson Welles. *Film Quarterly*, 35 (4): 1–12.
Kermode, F. (2000). King Lear. In *Shakespeare's Language*. New York: Farrar, Straus and Giroux, 183–200.
Klein, M. (1963). On the sense of loneliness. In *Envy and Gratitude and Other Works*. London: Hogarth Press, 1975, 300–317.
Kolker, R.P. (2017). *The Extraordinary Image*. New Brunswick, NJ: Rutgers University Press.
Mason, A. (1998). Melanie Klein's notes on *Citizen Kane* with a commentary. *Psychoanalytic Inquiry*, 18 (2): 147–153.
McBride, J. (1972). *Orson Welles*. London: Secker & Warburg.
Mulvay, L. (1998). Introduction to Melanie Klein's notes on *Citizen Kane*. In Phillips, J. & Stonebridge, L. (Eds.), *Reading Melanie Klein*. London: Routledge, 245–250.
Mulvay, L. (2012). *Citizen Kane*, 2nd ed. London: Palgrave Macmillan/BFI.
Phillips, J. & Stonebridge, L. (Eds.). (1998). *Reading Melanie Klein*. London: Routledge.
Schafer, R. (2010). Curse and consequence: King Lear's destructive narcissism. *International Journal of Psychoanalysis*, 91: 1503–1521.
Segal, H. (1986). Fear of death: Notes on the analysis of an old man. In *The Work of Hanna Segal*. London: Free Association, 173–184.
Shakespeare, W. (circa 1595). *Richard II*. Ed. P. Ure. London: The Arden Shakespeare/Methuen, 1974.
Shakespeare, W. (circa 1605–1606). *King Lear*. Ed. K. Muir. London: The Arden Shakespeare/Methuen, 1975.
Steiner, J. (2020a). The use and abuse of omnipotence in the journey of the hero. In *Illusion, Disillusion and Irony in Psychoanalysis*. London: Routledge, 60–71.
Steiner, J. (2020b). The unbearability of being feminine. In *Illusion, Disillusion and Irony in Psychoanalysis*. London: Routledge, 84–100.
Wilbern, D. (1980). Shakespeare's nothing. In Schwartz, M. & Kahn, C. (Eds.), *Representing Shakespeare. New Psychoanalytic Essays*. Baltimore, MD: Johns Hopkins University Press, 244–262.

Chapter 16

Applying my theory of psychosis to the Nazi phenomenon

Herbert Rosenfeld

To introduce this chapter, it originated as part of a lecture Rosenfeld gave to the German psychoanalytic society, the DPV, in 1984, in which he discussed the Nazi phenomenon as it reflected his theories of psychosis. In the lecture Rosenfeld described the striking similarity between a psychotic patient's delusional personality structure and the organisation of the Third Reich in Germany under the domination of the *Führer*, the omnipotent ruler merged with the omnipotent state in the grip of primitive destructiveness. This is a compelling view of the hypnotic, psychotic power that Hitler commanded over Germany, pictured by Rosenfeld as enforced by a terrifying mafia-like gang.

This short article was not published until it appeared in a German book edited by Karin Johanna Zienert-Eilts in 2020, a comprehensive book on Rosenfeld's life and work (Zienert-Eilts et al., 2020).

The following, a footnote to Rosenfeld's text, explains the context of the paper:

> This text is printed in English for the first time. It is a section from Herbert Rosenfeld's lecture at the DPV conference in Wiesbaden in 1984. Rosenfeld hesitated to publish this text in English until his death (for more detailed information, see Zienert-Eilts, 2020, 'Zur Biografie Herbert Rosenfelds', in K.J. Zienert-Eilts, W. Hegener & J.G. Reicheneder (Hrsg.), *Herbert Rosenfeld und seine Bedeutung für die Psychoanalyse. Leben – Werk – Wirkung*. Gießen: Psychosozial-Verlag.). To fill this gap and because of the importance of this text, the editors K. J. Zienert-Eilts, W. Hegener and J.G. Reicheneder have decided to publish it in the English version.

Now I would like to direct your attention to the close relationship between a patient's narcissistic psychotic structures and political organisations which often dominate an entire nation. I am well aware that my comparison of a psychotic structure with the Third Reich is not new to you, since Dr. Federn has dealt with the same issue in his papers (Federn, 1969).

The striking resemblance between a patient's psychotic-delusional structure and a nation dominated by a dictator centres upon the existence of a *Führer* or a leader in the patient's psychotic delusion. This *Führer*, for example, conducts

DOI: 10.4324/9781003185192-22

experiments in the case of the patient who is convinced by his delusion of being experimented upon. The patient complains often of having been sold by his parents for just a few German marks to the leader of such experiments. This leader is always very omnipotent but not clearly sadistic at first sight. The patient greatly admires this leader for his power, which is mostly described as a strong hypnotic influence. There are also reports that he is using provocative propaganda to lure more and more of the healthy parts of the personality into the psychotic world, promising that there won't be anything painful in this psychotic world and that everyone there is entitled to follow their sadistic tendencies completely.

When you take a closer look at this psychotic world or at the leader or *Führer*, it becomes clear that this *Führer* is sadistic, omnipotent, completely lacking compassion and demanding an absolute obedience from all parts of the self. Only slowly does one realize that the patient is under the constant threat of death if he should dare to make the slightest attempt to defend himself against this psychotic regime.

The patient I have described here was being pulled into a similar psychotic situation. In his hallucinations, the patient heard the threatening voice of the leader demanding that the patient commit destructive and self-destructive acts in order to prove his allegiance to the omnipotent leader.

Following my description so far, it is easy to depict Hitler as the *Führer* of the psychotic world. But instead of just a few parts of the patient's self, millions of people were hypnotized by the propaganda speeches of Hitler, speeches promising the Arian Germans superiority over all other races, especially the Jews. Just as the *Führer* of the psychotic dream world, he allowed his supporters to sadistically attack, to rob and to kill other races without mercy. He even praised his sadistic followers for all these murders.

The impartial observer realises that danger lies both in the patient's psychotic delusional world and in the psychotic omnipotent system that can dominate a nation as it did Germany. There are distortions and deformations of facts and reality which lead to cruelty and the murder of millions in the concentration camps which are then somehow justified.

In the psychotic patient, the deep sense of inferiority and murderous envy of all other people, whose ability to think and to succeed seem so superior to him and so out of his reach, is altered in a secret manner in the delusional world to a situation in which the patient, in his megalomania, is given a strong sense of self. Here a patient comes to my mind who believed himself to be Napoleon, a delusion that implied that he stood head and shoulders above all others and that he could defeat and kill all his imagined enemies – who were most likely to be people who he secretly admired and who, vis-à-vis, he felt incredibly small.

In the German nation's psychosis, the destructive, hypnotic, omnipotent power of the *Führer* succeeded in transforming people who belonged to a race that had contributed considerably to the culture of the German people into dangerous enemies of the German nation though the provocation of monstrous grudging distortions. In fact, this race that was looked upon as dirty vermin in Hitler's Germany and that needed to be destroyed at all costs had heightened the importance of the German people as one of the most foremost in the world through their contributions to German literature, music and science; to medical science; and especially to psychology and whose economic assets and skills in trade had made an enormous contribution to German wealth. To me, this tragic distortion seems identical to the distortion resulting from the envy of the delusional patient, who reacts with persecutory anxieties and murderous feelings to those whom he admired and even idealised before. There are many other similarities between the psychotic individual and a nation that is being dominated by a dictator like Hitler. Interestingly, the Nazi gang and the Mafia play central roles in the delusional world of our patients since the delusion of a gang boosts the power of omnipotent and destructive narcissism and produces a specific anxiety and threat in those patients who are starting to gain some insight into their illness and therefore beginning to doubt the value of the *Führer*'s promises of dominating the delusional world. In this situation, the patient needs a lot of help from his analyst to stand up for the healthy parts of his personality, in order to bear the constant fear, mostly of being killed by the omnipotent gang. Similarly, the threat of being murdered was too much for many Germans, although there were many who dared to defy the Nazi propaganda. It is certainly very difficult to know how many there were, but I knew quite a number of German friends who proved their courage despite great danger to themselves.

Whenever a nation is overwhelmed by psychotic-omnipotent structures, it is very difficult to understand and acknowledge this as madness. Maybe it is possible only now to study the deeper psychological details that overpowered the German nation more than fifty years ago. Complete cure of this dangerous malady, I'm afraid, will need a lot more time and active support.

References

Federn, E. (1969). Einige klinische Bemerkungen zur Psychopathologie des Völkermords. *Psyche*, 23 (8): 629–639.

Zienert-Eilts, K., et al. (Ed.). (2020). *Herbert Rosenfeld und seine Bedeutung für die Psychoanalyse* (Stefanie Sedlacek, Trans.). Psychosozial-Verlag: Gießen, 265–267.

Chapter 17

The destructiveness of omnipotence and 'perverted containing'

Psychoanalytic reflections on the dynamic between Donald Trump and his supporters

Karin Johanna Zienert-Eilts

Introduction[1]

The strengthening of anti-liberal, anti-democratic, hateful, and covertly racist and neo-Nazi developments is worldwide, including in the liberal democratic societies in Europe and the USA. Their populist or autocratic leaders – though democratically elected – confront us with significant challenges in understanding and handling these phenomena.[2] Using the example of Donald Trump – a prime example of a destructive narcissistic populist who offers omnipotence as salvation – a model of 'perverted containing' (Zienert-Eilts, 2020) will be described here to explain escalating destructive social processes rooted in phantasies of omnipotence and nourished by unconscious fears of annihilation.

Destructive narcissism: The example of Donald Trump and his supporters – a symbiotic relationship dynamic driven by omnipotent phantasies

General populism, characterised by positive goals, hopefulness, and calming people's fears, can be distinguished from 'destructive populism' as a form of 'destructive narcissism' (Rosenfeld, 1971, 2020) and 'malicious narcissism' (Kernberg, 2019), which stimulate destructive affects and agitation. It stirs up negative affects such as deep-seated fears, feelings of deprivation and persecution, envy, and primitive aggression, as well as polarisation and splitting of both the mental state of individuals and society as a whole. In the course of this dynamic, negative affects are fuelled and 'destructive narcissism', omnipotence, and brutality are idealised. Destructive populists purposefully attack the independent and power-limiting institutions: i.e., democracy-stabilising structures and institutions anchored in democracies and their constitutions, first and foremost the free press

DOI: 10.4324/9781003185192-23

and the independent judiciary. They distort them by exaggerating their threatening and aggressive intentions, which leads to an increase in the already-existing fears and aggressions, as well as in the longing for omnipotent help in corresponding individuals and population groups.

The core elements of this short description can be vividly illustrated in Donald Trump and his appeal to certain people and groups in the population, as well as in the phenomena following his lost election. Trump, a prime example of a destructive narcissistic populist, based his 2016 election campaign from the outset on attacks against the seemingly powerful 'establishment' and against independent democratic institutions. He deliberately stoked people's fears of relegation and devaluation to a lower status, as well as their desire for destructive aggression and revenge. He styled himself – e.g., by claiming that he was 'the only one' capable of redeeming the 'disconnected' – as an omnipotent saviour and even as Messiah, 'God's anointed one'. He boasted of his destructive ideas, the phantasm of his invulnerability, and that he was above all: 'I could shoot someone in the open street and still not lose any voters' (Donald Trump documentary, 2016). How he deliberately incited the cheering, jeering masses to aggression, which thereby excited and satisfied him: i.e., 'redeemed' him – showing how the symbiotic dynamic between him and the masses functioned in a mutually ecstatic, escalating way – can be impressively traced during his campaign appearances (cf. Zienert-Eilts, 2020) in an impressive scene: Trump begins: 'Nobody knows the system better than me'. The crowd reacts in surprised disbelief, remains silent, waits; some individuals applaud. Trump smiles and nods to them; people slowly start laughing; he repeats his nod and continues: 'That's why I alone can fix it!' – and the crowd cheers ('Donald Trump – the way to power', 2017). The demonstration of omnipotence and strength was supported by rising poll ratings. This, in turn, confirmed and fuelled Trump's methods. Trump began to believe that he could afford anything and was above the law – so he shouted at an election campaign appearance: 'We'll just run the illegals over' (Donald Trump documentary, 2016).

He operated by mocking political opponents and, increasingly, by perverting reality through unproven claims and lies. The more successful he was with his methods, the more he increased them.

As is well known, Trump's tools are a primitive and brutal language with a vocabulary of extremes ('completely', 'total', 'absolutely', 'grandiose', 'great'), bizarre omnipotent statements, three-word sentences, permanent repetition of his slogans and his Twitter messages. Through the latter, their frequency and the time of day (in the early morning), he gives the millions of users in his target group the impression that he is busy with them day and night, cares for them personally and has a 'real' relationship with them. With this form of communication, he satisfies their need for personal contact and further binds his supporters to him emotionally.

Trump not only instinctively recognised and consciously exploited the longings of many people for an emotionally receptive, caring, one might say 'parental' figure, as well as exploiting the emotional threat and the manifold existential fears of many Americans, but he also shares with his convinced voters, probably unconsciously, the fear of loss of status and importance – i.e., fear of internal annihilation of his inflated self-image – that drives fanatical people and is defended against with omnipotent phantasies.

Particularly vulnerable to Trump's destructive omnipotent strategy are especially fearful people: members of authoritarian subgroups, conservative fundamentalist religious groups, and other intolerant systems where they find a secure sense of worth, as well as people who are isolated or live a solitary life. All these groups feel secure and vindicated in the omnipotent system which Trump offers them, where they can then give vent to their aggressions and projections.

In this respect, it was not primarily economic reasons but above all conscious and unconscious fearful phantasies that made so many people vote for Trump as a 'saviour' (Khazan, 2018). In the regression process towards the paranoid-schizoid mode, the phantasies were transformed into fanatical beliefs.[3] Trump followers became convinced that because of changing racial and gender norms, they had become less valued in the society; they believed the previously 'high-ranking' groups, such as men, Christians, and whites in particular, were discriminated against and that as members of those groups, they would lose their social supremacy to women, foreigners, and non-whites – reinforced by the presidency of Barack Obama, the first black president. This released the unconscious fear of existential annihilation as well as fear of retaliation – namely, of being oppressed, despised, humiliated, and even murdered by non-whites, foreigners, and women, just as they themselves had treated or wanted to treat them (cf. the open hatred of Hillary Clinton with the call to 'Kill her!' and 'We want blood!'). Their threatened status must therefore be defended at all costs.

The dynamic and function of 'perverted containing'

To explain such destructive-populist societal processes, I propose a model from a psychoanalytical perspective, which I define as 'perverted containing' (Zienert-Eilts, 2020). It is based on Sigmund Freud's fundamental discoveries of psychoanalysis and Melanie Klein's further developments, especially the 'paranoid-schizoid position' (Klein, 1946), which I link with Herbert Rosenfeld's 'destructive narcissism' (Rosenfeld, 1971, 2020) and Wilfred Bion's 'container/contained' (Bion, 1962, 2018).

Rosenfeld's concept of destructive narcissism describes a perverse inner structure at the level of the paranoid-schizoid position as a pathological super-powerful omnipotent organisation with an idealised totalitarian leader – enforced by a group similar to a Mafia gang. In an archaic, pre-oedipal, primitive inner world, this leader promises superiority, quick ideal solutions to conflicts, unlimited power without fear, the elimination of humiliation and powerlessness, and the legitimisation of sadistic gratification against weaker people without feelings of guilt.

Good and evil are reversed (i.e., perverted): good, constructive, and compassionate traits are marked as weak and despicable; destructive, cruel, ruthless, and autocratic-narcissistic traits are idealised and valued as admirable and healthy. Furthermore, this kind of destructive narcissistic leader threatens retribution if the followers turn away from him, which mobilises their unconscious fears of annihilation. According to the idealisation of destructiveness and megalomania in the pathological inner world of the individual, accompanied by paranoid perceptions, delusional distortion of reality, and unbridled acting out of sadistic impulses without responsibility and without feeling guilty, the collective processes in destructive groups or masses can be understood.

Bion formulated the concept of containing as a basic pattern of relationships between individuals, paradigmatically conceptualised on the basis of the relationship between mother and baby (Bion, 1962, 2018): in order to cope with the storms of affects and for further psychic development, babies are dependent on the maternal or caring person and their capacity to take in, understand, and mitigate these affects. When the disturbing processes in the baby/child do not find reception in a maternal figure, when they bounce off a hard, inaccessible 'maternal container', the baby/child becomes desperate, hopeless, and aggressive. At the same time, however, the longing for a good maternal container unconsciously becomes stronger and stronger. This ominous dynamic escalates further and further, oscillating between exciting phantasies of omnipotence and of annihilation.

Applied to social processes, this dynamic can be imagined in the following way: in times of social crisis – driven by changes due to globalisation, technological advance, and climate change, causing in many people feelings of confusion, exclusion, and disconnection – the growing despair of people, their existential fears, powerlessness, envy, primitive aggression, and hatred cannot be heard, and their search for helpful objects in the political spectrum has not been understood or met, the negative affect becomes more and more urgent. If a personality appears in the public arena in these times who, like the disappointed, regressed people, operates in a paranoid-schizoid mode – he actually speaks the 'language' of these people, is able to 'hear' them in this sense, and shares his hatred of the 'establishment' – a destructive populist fit ensues. Such a leader reverses the isolation and the experience of being lost, redirects the people's rage of disappointment and destructive aggression towards the 'enemies' (the establishment, foreigners, etc.), and concentrates the hopes for salvation onto his person. Moreover, he bundles the isolated, regressed people and brings them together in a mass movement, in which all can experience themselves as powerful and even omnipotent. This leader promises to free his followers from feelings of powerlessness and despair by omnipotence and to allow and justify. Fatally, in the eyes of the desperate, violent, rebellious people, the longed-for omnipotent 'motherly-fatherly container' is finally found, pretending to understand and to protect. Quick satisfaction and salvation through omnipotent strength are promised to all those – and only those – who support this leader. Therefore, he is celebrated like a saviour.

In this process, however, the deep-seated unconscious fears and feelings of disadvantage, envy, and aggression are only allegedly contained; the affects are precisely not processed, transformed, or alleviated but, on the contrary, fuelled. This means that the actual function of a truly helpful, healing containing is perverted. Instead of being modified, destructive elements are stereotypically confirmed and thus escalate further and further. The original deep longing for symbiosis with a good, helpful object that takes in and softens one's own fundamental desperate affects and thus leads to a calming of the inner storms of affects, as well as the longing to be freed from one's own inner destructive impulses and from external destructive experiences, is paradoxically the breeding ground for this disastrously perverted dynamic.[4]

In a group or mass movement, this dynamic is accelerated in mutual processes of boundarylessness, the flooding of affects, and the perversion of values, and a rush of omnipotence develops between the leader and the masses. Whenever people join a group, a process of regression regularly commences (Freud, 1921c; Bion, 1961; Kernberg, 1998), with increasing levels of early fears – including archaic fears of disintegrating and being psychically destroyed – primitive aggressions, and early longings for symbiosis; the capacity for individual thinking is weakened. By identifying with the other group members as well as with the leader, each individual gains a feeling of power and security. The group as such then functions as a kind of 'maternal container'. However, the more the group members regress towards primitive fears, aggressions, and longings, and the more powerful the leader seems to be through destructive methods – such as ruthlessness, contempt for weakness, shamelessness, hatred of those who are different – the more an ecstatic feeling of omnipotence develops in each individual and the closer the connection between leader and followers becomes, reaching a kind of shared 'symbiotic omnipotent fanatic operating system'. Seen in this light, Trump offers his supporters omnipotence as perverted containing.

Now, to look further into who is psychologically responsive to this dynamic and why. We can assume that especially people with multiple traumatic experiences of failed containment in early childhood; with feelings of powerlessness, hopelessness, and humiliation; and with intense unconscious fears, annihilation, a longing for omnipotence, and a tendency towards violence are ones who choose leaders who are schizoid, destructive-narcissistic, internally chaotic and/or particularly brutal personalities (Kernberg, 1998). This results in a symbiosis between group and leader on an archaic level without the developmental possibility supplied by triangulation; triangulation means separation from the symbiosis with an object because of the presence of a third. On an archaic level, this is experienced as being thrown out of the symbiosis, which means a threat of annihilation; this, in turn, fuels the desire for omnipotence – a vicious circle in the dynamic between individuals as well as in groups.

Trump embodies omnipotence as a person; therefore, he appears convincing, so people can easily believe in him – especially those who, on an early level of intensive anxieties, feelings of persecution, and longing for symbiosis, prefer to attach themselves to one person (not to a party, a group, an issue, etc.). Thus, Trump accommodates their desires to identify and bond symbiotically with one person in total consensus – without triangulation, without doubting and space to develop individual perception and judgment. This is the base for the dynamic of extreme identification and for bonding in groups and masses (Freud, 1921c; Bion, 1961), driven by the dynamic of perverted containing which Trump, as a destructive narcissistic populist, offers.

Where the inner world of the group members as well as that of the leader are structured very similarly, so mutual identifications, based on idealised primitive-aggressive phantasies of omnipotence, are intertwined with mutual spurring. If this dynamic is deliberately fuelled by a leader, the primitive affects released in the group process escalate incessantly, resulting in an ever stronger destructive-symbiotic connection between leader and group or mass. Trump and his supporters are a vivid example of this dynamic.

Such a development is inevitably built on a powerful distortion of reality amounting to a loss of reality – sometimes even the creation of an 'alternative reality'. However, when this special world is confronted with *real* threats, the omnipotent system threatens to collapse, leading to intense fears of annihilation in the leader and his followers and thus to ever-more-bizarre increases in omnipotent phantasies and acts.

Facing real threats

In Trump's case, it is very easy to see how his destructive-omnipotent strategy drove the people's unconscious existential fears of psychic, social, or economic obliteration through phantasised threats (enemies from outside, left-wing radicals, enemies of the people, Venezuelan conditions, etc.), but this strategy no longer functioned adequately in the face of real threats, such as climate change or the COVID pandemic.

Trump understood well the importance of these real threats as an obvious limitation of his omnipotence and reacted very early with ridicule ('Climate change is an invention of the Chinese'), belittlement ('COVID is a mild flu'), and devaluation of the scientists ('Fauci is an idiot'). He acted like a liar who knows he is lying but has to keep lying to maintain his myth of omnipotence.

In the 2020 COVID-19 crisis, Trump first used his usual means: distortion and denial of reality, self-praise and directing accusations towards the usual 'enemies' (other states, the press, the Democrats, and the WHO). His omnipotent message was: I am stronger than reality; I free you from the threat. Very quickly, however, Trump's destructive populist propaganda was contradicted by real facts; the USA, due to his mismanagement, had the highest infection and mortality rate in the world in mid-August 2020 and an unprecedented impoverishment of large parts of the population, with millions upon millions of unemployed and homeless and even starving citizens.[5] In the face of these *real* consequences of the unhindered spread of the epidemic (it quickly became clear that more Americans died from

COVID-19 in one year of the pandemic than in World War I, World War II, and the Vietnam War combined and that there was currently no end in sight), more and more American citizens began to doubt Trump, to restore a grip on reality, and to protest increasingly publicly. To the extent that many citizens began to turn away from him, Trump became more radical in his moves. It now became clear that with the impending – and eventually actual – collapse of the narcissistic-omnipotent world (Trump's dreaded electoral defeat), the mechanisms of destructive narcissism had inevitably to escalate in both the leader and his supporters. They turned to targeted attacks on the Constitution and, eventually, to violent and criminal acts – always fuelled by Trump's conspiracy narrative of electoral fraud and his support for radical right-wing groups ('stand back and stand by', 'you are special people; we love you').

Trump's radical reaction was evident not only in his speeches, his denial of the election results, and his persistent claim that he had won the election, but also in his actions and his symbols: whereas he had previously shown himself before his supporters with the victory sign, the symbol of the victor, after losing the election in 2020, he then appeared showing the symbol of radical groups, the clenched fist.

For him and his supporters, his electoral defeat meant the unmasking of his alleged omnipotence and thus the annihilation of his myth, as well as the annihilation of his own feelings of self-worth – exactly what he unconsciously always feared. Losers are despicable people to Trump, so he must not be a loser and must claim over and over again that the election was not lost at all, but stolen. With this lie, he protected himself from a collapse of his personal megalomania and, at the same time, prevented his fanatical supporters from abandoning him by acknowledging reality. Moreover, by permanently repeating the conspiracy narrative of the stolen election, he created a victim phantasm, thereby indirectly asking his supporters to protect him. Thus, he inflamed them further and bound them ever closer to him due to the increase in the level of excitement, which did not provide any space for thoughtful reflection. So Trump had to invent and incessantly continue to spread the lie of electoral fraud. Only in this way can he protect himself and his supporters from a collapse of the omnipotence phantasies.

This development culminated in the storming of the Capitol on January 6, 2021, with destructive, antidemocratic, and partially murderous intentions ('Take the Capitol', 'Storm the Capitol', 'Fight for Trump', 'Hang Mike Pence'), resulting in five dead people. This outburst I see as a logical consequence of confronting the unwelcome reality of electoral defeat and, driven by Trump, the ensuing insurgency that may have opened the eyes of many conservative voters – if not Trump's fanatical core supporters, who will not be able to disentangle themselves from their symbiotic identification with him. Recognising the storming of the Capitol, with all its terrifying details, as an inevitable consequence of the destructive populist policies of Trump and his supporters is an opportunity to free the temporarily regressed citizens from the seductive pull of omnipotence phantasies.

Concluding remarks

The conspiracy narrative of the stolen election, which Trump raised long before his electoral defeat in 2020 – first as early as 2016,[6] when he, in his anticipation of a possible electoral defeat at the time, claimed that the Democrats could only win the election against him through fraud (cf. also Douglas, 2020: 7) – is a logical, systemic development of the destructive omnipotent dynamic between Trump and his voters: Trump offers a 'perverted containing' in the sense of Rosenfeld's destructive narcissistic structure. In order to be able to continue to offer himself to his supporters as the 'only saviour' and 'only victor', and thus maintain both his own inner structure of omnipotent phantasies and those of his supporters, he had to declare himself the winner of the election and invent and stereotype the lie of the stolen election. The tragedy is that Trump knows he is lying, but most of his supporters do not.

Trump's pressure to have to be an omnipotent winner, feeding his destructive narcissistic stereotypically repeated conspiracy narrative and his multiple actions to undermine the election results[7] up to the shocking storming of the Capitol that Trump later justified ('These are the things and events that happen when a sacred landslide election victory is so unceremoniously & viciously stripped away from great patriots who have been badly & unfairly treated for so long'), even lead to an organised strategy on multiple societal platforms – looking like the attempt of a kind of coup d'état; this highlights Trump's targeted force guiding these destructive processes in order to avoid the breakdown of the omnipotence phantasm, which for him – and his supporters – means annihilation.

The politicians of the Republican Party could or should be supporting the independent democratic institutions such as the judiciary and the press, with their power-limiting and thus triangulating function, the essential, corrective, stabilising elements in a democracy. The fact that the overwhelming majority supported Trump through tacit[8] or tactical or even active[9] support, and that they are therefore given a share of the responsibility for the entire development up to the storming of the Capitol, ought to be discussed in more detail. Trump's acquittal in the impeachment proceedings in February 2021, with decisive support from the majority of Republicans, no doubt restored Trump's sense of omnipotence, along with that of the majority of Republican voters and politicians, thus encouraging him to continue his destructive acts.

President Joe Biden is a very different leader to the Trumpian destructive narcissistic container of the people's hopes and fears. Fed by his own painful life experience, his losses, and the ability to grieve, he authentically represents opposite values: admitting limitations instead of omnipotence; acknowledging reality instead of denying and perverting it; taking pride in the power to overcome failure instead of contempt for 'losers'; humility instead of arrogance; compassion instead of ignorant harshness; focusing on cohesion, pacification, and healing of society instead of splitting and aggressive intensification. Biden displays a willingness to compromise instead of ruthless assertion of self-interest, a consideration of the needs of all citizens instead of only those of his own supporters, and the state of the world instead of always 'America First'.

Based on these considerations, the willingness of the current government to confront the real and devastating consequences of the pandemic, the deeply poisoned political culture as well as the need for economic support for the impoverished parts of the population, will be decisive in recovering from Trump's destructiveness – psychoanalytically formulated, by taking up the unconscious original longing for a real and sustainable calming through offering a genuine, healing containing.

The further development will span between, on the one hand, the hopeful perspective that after the experience of the COVID pandemic and the storming of the Capitol as a devastating consequence of the destructive symbiotic system of omnipotence, people can get back in touch with reality, and, on the other hand, the more sceptical perspective of Freud; the latter left no doubt about the effort and time required to develop a healing containment after the unleashing of destructive forces in a society. In 1932, he illustrated this in 'Why War?' using a picture: 'An unpleasant picture comes to one's mind of mills that grind so slowly that people may starve before they get their flour' (Freud, 1933b: 2013).

Notes

1 This contribution is based on my work from 2020 (Zienert-Eilts, 2020).
2 Other authors have also dealt with the phenomenon of Donald Trump and his voters from a psychoanalytical or group-analytical perspective, such as Rudden and Brandt, 2018; Levine, 2018; Chrzanowski, 2019; Kernberg, 2019.
3 I have tried to show elsewhere how the transformation of unconscious phantasies into conscious beliefs, the perversion of reality into an 'alternative reality', and the inner-psychic development of a readiness to phanaticise through failed containing can be imagined in early somatopsychic processes (Zienert-Eilts, 2021).
4 Another form of containment is described by Britton as 'malignant containment' (Britton, 1998).
5 www.deutschlandfunkkultur.de/hunger-und-armut-in-den-usa-jeder-achte-amerikaner-hat.2165.de.html?dram:article_id=489081
6 Similarly, Trump had stated his basic attitude to election results in October 2016: 'I will fully accept the outcome of this great and historic election – if I win'. Obama immediately warned: 'This is not funny. This is dangerous. It undermines our democracy'.
7 Such as his incitement of mass street protests ('stop the vote', 'stop the steal'), his questionably unconstitutional actions (for example, attempting to pressure Georgia's Republican election supervisor Gabriel Sterling into false vote counts), his pressure on Mike Pence to thwart Biden's election in Congress (Trump's Twitter: 'Do it Mike – these times need extreme courage').
8 These politicians are mostly intimidated by their fears of annihilation, which Trump deliberately stokes by publicly branding them as 'traitors' and 'enemies' and threatening to destroy their political careers.
9 These politicians are almost symbiotically identified with Trump at a deeper inner level, with a shared 'fanatical operating system' of beliefs of victim phantasm and threat scenarios, based on the inner-psychic dynamics described.

References

Bion, W.R. (1961). *Experiences in Groups and Other Papers*. London: Tavistock.
Bion, W.R. (1962). *Learning from Experience*. London: Heinemann. Reprinted London: Karnac, 1984.
Bion, W.R. (2018). *Los Angeles Seminars and Supervision*. London: Routledge.
Britton, R. (1998). *Belief and Imagination. Explorations in Psychoanalysis*. London and New York: Routledge.
Chrzanowski, C.S. (2019). The group's vulnerability to disaster: Basic assumption and work group mentalities underlying Trump's 2016 election. *The International Journal of Psychoanalysis*, 100: 711–731.
'Donald Trump – der Weg an die Macht', Dokumentation 2017, ZDFinfo/YouTube.
Donald Trump documentary: 'Macht, Geld und Lügen – Clinton gegen Trump'. Dokumentation 4.11.2016. ZeitgeschichteDE YouTube.
Douglas, L. (2020). *Will He Go? Trump and the Looming Election Meltdown in 2020*. New York and Boston: Twelve.
Freud, S. (1921c). Group psychology and the analysis of the ego. *S.E. XVIII*: 69–143.
Freud, S. (1933b). Why war? Letter to Albert Einstein, September 1932. *S.E. XXII*: 199–215.
Kernberg, O.F. (1998). *Ideology, Conflict and Leadership in Groups and Organizations*. New Haven, CT: Yale University Press.
Kernberg, O.F. (2019). 'Es ist immer gefährlich, sich als alles zu sehen'. Ein Interview mit Otto F. Kernberg. taz am wochenende, 10–11 August 2019.
Khazan, O. (2018). *People Voted for Trump Because They Were Anxious, Not Poor*. A new study finds that Trump voters weren't losing income or jobs. Instead, they were concerned about their place in the world. www.theatlantic.com/science/archive/2018/04/existential-anxiety-not-poverty-motivates-trump-support/558674/.
Klein, M. (1946). Notes on Some Schizoid Mechanisms. In Klein, M. (Ed.), *Envy and Gratitude and Other Works, 1946–1963*. London: Karnac, 1993, 1–24.
Levine, R. (2018). Die Perspektive einer Gruppenanalytikerin auf die Trump-Clinton-Wahl und ihre Folgen. *Gruppenpsychother. Gruppendynamik*, 54: 311–336.
Rosenfeld, H.A. (1971). A clinical approach to the psychoanalytic theory of the life and death instincts: An investigation into the aggressive aspects of narcissism. *International Journal of Psychoanalysis*, 52: 169–178.
Rosenfeld, H.A. (2020). Applying my theory of psychosis to the Nazi phenomenon. In Zienert-Eilts, K.J., Hegener, W. & Reicheneder, J.G. (Hrsg.), *Herbert Rosenfeld und seine Bedeutung für die Psychoanalyse. Leben – Werk – Wirkung*. Gießen: Psychosozial-Verlag, 265–267.
Rudden, M. & Brandt, S. (2018). Donald Trump as leader. Psychoanalytic perspectives. *International Journal of Applied Psychoanalytic Studies*, 15 (1): 43–51.
Zienert-Eilts, K.J. (2020). Destructive populism as 'perverted containing': A psychoanalytical look at the attraction of Donald Trump. *International Journal of Psychoanalysis*, 101: 971–991.
Zienert-Eilts, K.J. (2021). 'Niemals tut man so gut und so vollständig das Böse, als wenn man es guten Gewissens tut.' Psychoanalytische Überlegungen zu fanatischen Überzeugungen, Vernichtungsdynamik und Radikalisierungsprozessen. *Jb Psychoanal*, 83.

Chapter 18

Notes toward a model for omnipotence

Jean Arundale

What can be said in summary of the ideas in this book that might constitute a contemporary model of omnipotence useful for our time? It is clear that omnipotence exists in every stage throughout life, from the earliest stages of infancy, where its formation is defensive against infantile helplessness, impotence, and lack of containment, proceeding to its manifestation in the magical thinking of childhood, creating utopias, heroes, supermen and women. The phallic stage of boys and girls remains in the unconscious through life, creating a tendency to identify with powerful figures, gods and heroes of legend and mythology, fostering adolescent dreams of glory, morphing all too frequently into problematic omnipotent adult characters.

In its positive form, omnipotence is useful in order to overcome trepidation and fear of failure, but there can be a powerful pull toward adherence to an omnipotent state of mind, fearing to be plunged into helplessness, abandonment and self-blame.

This ubiquity of omnipotence suggests a model that places omnipotence on a spectrum ranging from in utero through childhood and adolescence to all of adulthood, conspiring with the pleasure principle in a harmonious mix-up to encourage and counterbalance our fundamental fragility. As Kernberg summarises, 'The concept of omnipotence therefore, refers to a primitive phantasy, a mechanism of defence and a pathological psychic structure' (Kernberg, 1995).

Thoughts about treatment. The task of mitigating omnipotence when it interferes negatively with the personality needs to be taken up in psychoanalysis. A vital constituent is considering and accepting the 'facts of life' as discussed by Roger Money-Kyrle (1968), the facts to do with differences: between generations, between the sexes, and the reality of changes in the passage of time. These are so difficult for us to accept because they provoke envy and threaten omnipotence; we hate them and deny them to avoid having to face our mortality, the impossibility of oedipal love, and our dependence on others.

Identification plays a large part in the state of mind of omnipotence, identifying with idealised or perfect objects. This means that in psychoanalytic treatment, work on reducing omnipotence requires work on de-idealising, on accepting separation and separateness from objects, and achieving self-identification. To this end, there must be a capacity for mourning, for suffering loss, which means not only a relinquishment of possessiveness and control over the object but also toleration of the loss of the merged state with the ideal. Where there is trauma, the

DOI: 10.4324/9781003185192-24

illusion of the ideal can be ever more entrancing. To give up the narcissistic illusion – I am the breast, and the breast is me, or I am the phallus and the phallus is me – can be further traumatising.

As John Steiner formulates, the work requires a relinquishment of the omnipotent phallic identification and acceptance and valuing of the feminine position of receptivity, linking and learning, accepting the need for others. Omnipotent phallic personality organisations create idealised retreats that protect the subject from both shame and guilt, and emergence from these states involves both seeing and being seen (Steiner, 2015). Oscar Wilde's tale of the Selfish Giant warns of the temptations of an omnipotent withdrawal into one's castle of selfhood, building walls to exclude others, in charge and in control, that ends with the Giant alone and unhappy in a perpetual cold winter, with no spring or summertime to be shared with happy children.

Many patients need to idealise their analysts for a period of time, so de-idealisation should not take place too early in the analysis, which has to provide a supportive structure in which shame, guilt, envy and vulnerability can be examined and the question of whether they are bearable can be explored. When the patient seems able to accept some measure of the loss of phallic superiority and face guilt in regard to damage it has done, reparative wishes may be mobilised to initiate more benevolent relationships if the severity of the superego can be moderated.

Klein goes on to say:

> In analysis we should make our way slowly and gradually towards the painful insight into the divisions in the patient's self. . . . . As a result, the feeling of responsibility becomes stronger, and guilt and depression are more fully experienced. When this happens, the ego is strengthened, omnipotence of destructive impulses is diminished, together with envy, and the capacity for love and gratitude . . . is released.
>
> (Klein, 1957)

Finding the libidinal, dependent self along with analysing the omnipotent structure as it comes into collision with reality is vital to the treatment.

Yet there are limits, as suggested by Riccardo Steiner:

> To totally eliminate omnipotence is an omnipotent idealisation of psychoanalysis related to the denial of its inevitable limitations. The same can be said about narcissism, as Rosenfeld claimed. Nevertheless, there can be very substantial improvements in dealing with infantile omnipotence, such as in the case of thick-skinned narcissistic patients.
>
> (R. Steiner, 2021)

In the end, we all have to accept being a faulty person in an imperfect world and to learn to relate with love and not control. Levine concludes: 'The truth is more satisfying and solid than omnipotent phantasy. Living in the real world more powerful and ultimately more satisfying and truthful.' (2011: 188).

Epilogue

In William Shakespeare's play *The Tempest*, the sorcerer, Prospero and Ariel, a spirit whom he has conjured up, live together on an island where they practice magic. Whether or not Shakespeare intended it, the island and its inhabitants can be viewed as representing the dilemma of the isolated narcissistic person who turns to an internal world of phantasies and 'secret studies.' Keeping his capacity to love (as represented by Miranda) undeveloped, and his primitive unconscious emotions and appetites under strict control (Caliban), Prospero lives in splendid isolation as master of all, conjuring up 'insubstantial pageants' and then dissolving them without trace.

After a storm and shipwreck, his enemies arrive on the island, and he intends to kill them in revenge for his exile. However, by the end of the play, Prospero has a change of heart. He feels compassion, apparently linked to the exquisite beauty of Miranda's love for and wedding to his nephew Ferdinand – a real spontaneous passion uncreated by his own will. In this reading of the play, it is suggested that Shakespeare intuits the inner workings of our primitive unconscious, an enclosed part of the mind that requires a wild tempest, a powerful conflict or encounter with the outside, to free it from isolation and self-love. With a degree of self-knowledge, ('We are such things as dreams are made of'), Prospero forgives his enemies, breaks his staff and drowns his book, releases Ariel, and gives up his 'rough magic', his omnipotence. In a moving recognition of the transforming power of love, he is joined up once again to the ordinary world, leaving his island to return to Milan to his work and to contemplate his life and death. In this late play, Shakespeare condenses his experiences of a lifetime to speak of the universal struggle to give up omnipotence that is required in order to be truly human, to be with others and to live in the world.

References

Kernberg, O. (1995). Omnipotence in the transference and in the countertransference. *Scandinavian Psychoanalytic Review*, 18: 2–21.

Klein, M. (1957). Envy and gratitude. In *Envy and Gratitude and Other Works 1946–1963*. London: Vintage. 1997. 176–235.

Levine, H. (2011). In Mawson, C. (Ed.), *Bion Today*. Hove: Routledge. p. 188.

Money-Kyrle, R. E. (1968). Cognitive development. *International Journal of Psychoanalysis*, 49: 691–698.

Steiner, R. (2021). Personal communication.

Index

Note: Page numbers in *italic* indicate a figure and page numbers with n indicate a note on the corresponding page.

Abraham, Karl 10, 122
Adam and Eve, and phantasy of omnipotence 110, 113
adolescence, omnipotence in 3–4, 53–67; eating disorders and paranoid mother 54–61; pubertal scene 53–54; violence as defence 61–66
adolescent experimentation, omnipotentiality, and bodily enhancement 74–77
adults, omnipotence in 4–5
aggression, and evolution 194–195
Ahumada, Jorge x, 6, 191
Almond, R. 69
alpha function 176
alpha male chimpanzee 195, 196
amorphous disorientation 202–203
Analysis Terminable and Interminable (Freud) 159, 162
anger 199–201, 209
annihilation, fears of 220, 222–227, 228n8
annihilation anxiety 146, 148, 154, 155
anorexia 57
antilife instinct 160
anti-psychotic drugs 116
anxiety: in adolescence 54; annihilation 146, 148, 154, 155; depressive 176; infantile 109, 146; separation 181–183, 187
appeal of omnipotence 4, 108–114
Arundale, Jean x, 1; model for omnipotence 7, 230; relinquishing omnipotence 6, 174, 181
Aulagnier, Piera 49

autism 192
autonomy, as ethics of, in psychoanalysis 79–81
Awakenings (Sacks) 4, 115

Balint, Alice 191
Balint, Michael 14
Barrie, James Matthew 44–45
basic fault 14
Biblical stories: Adam and Eve, and phantasy of omnipotence 110, 113; Jesus and casting the first stone 95–97
Bick, Esther 3, 23, 25, 27–28
Biden, Joe 227–228
Bion, Wilfred 14–15; container/contained and destructive narcissism 222–224; dreaming/thinking 85, 98, 105n2; relinquishing omnipotence 176; superego development 135, 137
Birksted-Breen, D. 164, 177
blinkered vision 26
bodily enhancement and customisation 4, 68–81; and adaptation to trauma 77–79; adolescent experimentation and omnipotentiality 74–77; phantasies, perfect match and self-made 69–74; psychoanalysis as ethics of autonomy 79–81
Bolton, John 150
Botox injections 70–73
brain reward system 116
Brave New World (Huxley) 202
Brenman, E. 208, 213, 215
Britton, Ronald 17, 135
bulimic eating disorders 54–61

Castoriadis, C. 202
child development, omnipotence in 1–2, 33, 146, 175
childhood, omnipotence in 3, 43–50; immigration effects 45–49; maturational process 43–45; Peter Pan phantasy 44–45, 46–47; see also infantile omnipotence
Citizen Kane (Welles) 206, 211–215
civilisation, origins of 192–194, 202
Civilisation and Its Discontents (Freud) 9
Clinical Diary (Ferenczi) 48
cocaine 116
cognisant adaptation 78
Cohen, Michael 150
Collingwood, Roger 202
'Confusion of Tongues between Children and Adults' (Ferenczi) 48
containing, perverted, in destructive narcissism 220, 222–225, 227
cosmetic surgery *see* bodily enhancement and customisation
COVID-19 pandemic: and Trump's destructive narcissistic populism 225–226, 228; and Trump's Grand Illusion 149
creative links in receptive femininity 161, 163–164, 170–171
cultures, legends of omnipotent figure(s) 110–111

Darwin, Charles 191, 193, 194, 197
death instinct 159, 160, 195
Death in Venice (Mann) 113
delusional system 110
democracy, and destructive narcissism 220–221, 227
depressive anxiety 176
Descent of Man, The (Darwin) 193, 194
destructive narcissism *see* Rosenfeld, Herbert; Trump, Donald, as destructive narcissistic populist 226–299
destructive omnipotence 9
"Development of a Child, The" (Klein) 11, 175
devotion, of parents 70–73
Dickens, C. 142
Dodds, E. R. 193
dogmas in religious belief systems 135–136, 140
dopamine neurotransmitter 116–119

Dr. Faustus (Marlow) 111
dream thinking 86, 92–95, 104–105

eating disorders, and omnipotence in adolescence 54–61
Einstein, Albert 197
elections, conspiracy narrative of fraud 215n1, 226, 227, 228n6
empathy, in illusion of omnipotence 152–154
envy: and magical thinking 87; and omnipotence 108, 111, 164, 230; and psychosis 218–219
envy, and receptive femininity: antilife instinct 160; and repudiation of femininity 161–163; what provokes envy 160–161; see also Klein, Melanie
Eribon, Didier 202
ethics of autonomy, psychoanalysis as 79–81

Fairbairn, Ronald 13–14, 98, 140
fake news 151, 215n1
Feldman, Michael x–xi, 4, 108
female mutilation 165–167
feminine inferiority 162–163
femininity: denigration of, by phallic omnipotence 209, 211; repudiation of 159, 161–163, 170; see also receptive femininity, and obstacles in analysis
Ferenczi, Sandor 9–10; childhood omnipotence 43–44, 48; paradoxes of insight 191; unconscious guilt 174
fictional characters, omnipotence of 6–7; *Citizen Kane* 206, 211–215; *King Lear* 166, 206, 207–211, 213–215
Flanders, Sara xi, 3–4, 53
Flaubert, Gustave 113
Fort Da (fort-da) 11, 46
Freud, Anna 10, 64
Freud, Sigmund 8–9; appeal of omnipotence 108–109, 112; on capacity to love 33, 40; on evolution and Darwin 191–195, 197–198; on forms of thinking 97, 105n1; on negation 44; and neuropsychodynamics 115–116, 117–118; on omnipotence 206; psychoanalysis and destructive narcissism 222, 228; and receptive femininity 159, 160, 162–163, 165, 170; superego development 137; on unconscious guilt 174–175, 176

Garden of Eden phantasy 33, 35, 40
gender fluidity in adolescents 74–77
Germany, national psychosis and Nazis 7, 217–219
gestural sign-language 195–197
Gilgamesh, Babylonian epic 111
Goodall, Jane 195, 196
good enough father 54
good-enough mother 12–13
Grand Illusion *see* illusion of omnipotence
Great Expectations (Dickens) 142
Greece, ancient 193, 201–202
Greeks and the Irrational, The (Dodds) 193
Green, Andre 17
grief after death of loved one 177, 179–180
Guadagnino, Luca 74–77
guilt: in analysis 231; and capacity to love 40–41; and omnipotent internal object 142; and perverted containing 222–223; and postmodernist ideology 202; and relinquishing omnipotence 167, 170, 171; separation anxiety and manic reparation 181–187; in traumatised patient 122, 123, 125, 128, 131–132; unconscious, and relinquishing omnipotence 6, 174–180
Gutton, Phillip 53, 56

Habermas, Jürgen 202
hallucination: of infantile omnipotence 111–112; transformative thinking 99, 101–102
Hanly, C. 207, 210
Heaney, Seamus 96
Heimann, Paula 31
Hess, Noel xi, 6–7, 206
Hitler, Adolf 7, 217–219
holding phase in psychoanalysis 152–154
hopelessness and helplessness 118
Houston, Beverley 214
Huxley, Aldous 202
hypnotic power of Hitler and Nazis 7, 217–219

idealisation: narcissistic 164, 171; omnipotent 113
Illusion, Disillusion, and Irony in Psychoanalysis (Steiner) 18
illusion of omnipotence 5, 144–156; described 144–147; origins of 146–147; psychoanalytic process 151–155; as self-organisation 147–148; Trump's Grand Illusion 148–151
immigration, childhood 45–49
immortality 110–111
infantile anxiety 109, 146
infantile autism 26
infantile omnipotence 108–109, 111–113, 146, 174–175, 181; *see also* childhood, omnipotence in
infants and mothers, and dream thinking 93–94
instinct, and evolution 194–196
insurrection at U.S. Capitol 150, 226, 227, 228
intelligence, and receptive femininity 167–170
internal object *see* omnipotent internal object, damaging effect of
Introjection and Transference (Ferenczi) 191
Isaacs, Susan 10–11

Jameson, Fredric 202
Jesus, on casting the first stone 96–97
Jones, Jim 140

Kane, Charles Foster *(Citizen Kane)* 206, 211–215
Kelley-Lainé, Kathleen xi, 3, 43
kindness 102
King Lear (Shakespeare) 166, 206, 207–211, 213–215
Klein, Melanie 10–12; appeal of omnipotence 108, 109; on *Citizen Kane* 212, 214; ego and primal splitting 31, 33; lessening of omnipotence 206, 215; and neuropsychodynamics 115; paranoid-schizoid position and destructive narcissism 222; and receptive femininity 160, 165; on relinquishment of omnipotence 122, 132, 175, 176; superego development 137; transformation in thinking 97–98; on treatment of omnipotence 231
knowledge, drive for 175
Kohut, Heinz 14

language of exile 45–46
Lear, in *King Lear* 166, 206, 207–211, 213–215

legends of omnipotent figure(s) across cultures 110–111
Lemma, Alessandra xi, 4, 68
Leonardo (Freud) 192
Levine, H. 231
loss, acceptance of 119, 230
love, capacity for 3, 31–42

Madam Bovary (Flaubert) 113
mafia-like gangs 122, 217, 219, 222
magic 8–9
magical omnipotence 177
magical thinking 86, 87–92, 104
Manafort, Paul 150
mania: and magical thinking 87; from stimulant drugs 115
manic defence 12
"Manic Defence, The" (Winnicott) 12
manic reparation 183–187
Mann, Thomas 113
Marlow, C. 111
Matte-Blanco, I. 200
Mattis, James 150
maturational process of childhood 43–45
McLuhan, Marshall 202
Media Age 202
melancholic depression 40
Meltzer, Donald 122
metaphors in immigrant child 48–49
Milton, J. 110, 113
mind and instinct 194–195
mockery 28–30
Money-Kyrle, Roger E. 110, 132, 175, 230
'Mourning and Its Relation to Manic-Depressive States' (Klein) 212
mourning loss of loved one 177, 179–180

Napoleon, delusion as 218
narcissism, link with omnipotence 2–3, 207
narcissistic character 16
narcissistic idealisations, and phallic omnipotence 164, 171
narcissistic systems, and unconscious guilt 176
Nazi phenomenon, theory of psychosis applied to 7, 217–219
'Negation' (Freud) 44
negative narcissism 17
neuropsychoanalytic view of omnipotence 4–5, 115–121
nightmares 94

Obama, Barack 222, 228n6
object splitting 148
obsessional neurosis 8, 174
obstacles in analysis *see* receptive femininity, and obstacles in analysis
odor, and repulsive body 100
Oedipus at Colonus (Steiner) 109
Oedipus myth 33, 109–110
Ogden, Thomas xi–xii, 4, 85
omnipotence: appeal of 4, 108–114; defined 69, 145; embodiment in Trump *see* Trump, Donald, as destructive narcissistic populist; illusion of *see* illusion of omnipotence; model for 7, 230–231; notions of, and paradoxes of insight 191–192; personality traits 2; psychoanalytic perspective 2–3; relinquishment of *see* relinquishment of omnipotence; spectrum through human life 230; study of 1
omnipotence envy 164
omnipotence of thought 10, 87, 174
omnipotentiality, experimentation, and bodily enhancement in adolescence 74–77
omnipotent internal object, damaging effect of 10, 135–143; dogmas in religious belief systems 135–136, 140; impossible tensions 136–141; unreasonable expectations 142
'On Termination' (Klein) 132
O'Shaughnessy, E. 137

Panksepp, Jaak 116
Paradise Lost (Milton) 110, 113
paradoxes of insight 6, 191–205; anger and collapse 198–201; Darwin and evolution 191, 193, 194–197; mind and instinct 194–195; notions of omnipotence 191–192; origins of civilisation 192–194; postmodernity and postmodernism 201–203; reflective thought 195–198
paranoid mother 56–60
Parkinsonian patients 115, 120
pathological organisations *see* relinquishment of omnipotence in traumatised patient
Pence, Mike 228n7
penis as link 164, 165, 177
penis envy 162, 164
perfect match phantasy 69, 73

perversion of values 223, 224
perverted containing, in destructive narcissism 220, 222–225, 227
pessimism 118
Peter Pan phantasy 44–45, 46–47
phallic omnipotence: and denigration of femininity 209, 211; and narcissistic idealisations 164, 171; relinquishment of, and valuing of femininity 231
phallus envy 164
phantasy(ies): of feminine mutilation 165–167; illusion compared with 145; omnipotent, and unconscious guilt 177
phantasy system of tower, in relinquishment of omnipotence in traumatised patient 125, *126*, 127, 128, 130–131
pharmaceuticals, and omnipotence 115–116, 120
pleasure principle 119, 174–175
Pontalis, J.-M. 93
populism 7; *see also* Trump, Donald, as destructive narcissistic populist
postmodernity and postmodernism 201–203
'Prelude, The' (Wordsworth) 178–180
primary narcissism 10, 13, 17
primitive humans 192–194
primitive omnipotence 9–10; *see also* survival function of primitive omnipotence
'Problem of Acceptance of Un-pleasure, The' (Ferenczi) 43
projective identification 15, 17, 87, 182, 186
propaganda, of Hitler and Nazis 218–219
Prospero (in *The Tempest*) 232
psychic retreats 123, 155
Psychic Retreats (Steiner) 17
psychoanalysis: obstacles in *see* receptive femininity, and obstacles in analysis; origins of 191; purpose and practice of 44; shift in emphasis from what patients think to the way they think 85, 104; treatment of omnipotence 230–231
psychoanalytic literature, citations of 'omnipotence' 7–18; Abraham, Karl 10; Balint, Michael 14; Bion, Wilfred 14–15; Britton, Ronald 17; Fairbairn, Ronald 13–14; Ferenczi, Sandor 9–10; Freud, Sigmund 8–9; Green, Andre 17; Isaacs, Susan 10–11; Klein, Melanie 10–12; Kohut, Heinz 14; Rosenfeld, Herbert 15–16; Sandler, Joseph 16; Segal, Hanna 17; Steiner, John 17–18; Winnicott, Donald 12–13
psychosis: and magical thinking 87; theory applied to Nazi phenomenon 7, 217–219
pubertal scene, adolescent omnipotence 53–54, 56, 57

Rat Man 87, 192
reality, distortion of 225
reality principle 119
receptive femininity, and obstacles in analysis 5–6, 159–173; antilife instinct expressed as envy 160; envy and repudiation of femininity 161–163; Freud's pessimism 159; intelligence and creative femininity 167–170; phallic phantasies and narcissistic idealisations 164, 171; phantasies of feminine mutilation 165–167; provoking envy 160–161; receptivity and thinking 167; redefining the creative link 163–164; relinquishment of omnipotence 164–165
reflective thought 195–198
relationship presentations 197
religious belief systems: dogmas in 135–136, 140; perfectionist demands in sects 140
relinquishment of omnipotence 5–6; and acceptance of receptive femininity 164–165; separation anxiety and manic reparation 181–187; unconscious guilt as difficulty 174–180
relinquishment of omnipotence in traumatised patient 5, 122–134; childhood history 124; collapse of pathological organisation 127–129; ending phase 129–131; pathological organisation of personality 122–123, 124–127; termination of analysis 131–133
repetitive compelling behaviour 54
Republican Party 227, 228n7
repudiation of femininity 159, 161–163, 170
Richard II (Shakespeare) 208
Riviere, Joan 1, 40, 122, 128, 201

Index

romanticism 201
Rosenfeld, Herbert xii, 15–16; mafia-like gangs and destructive narcissism 7, 122, 217, 222, 227; relinquishing omnipotence 185, 186
Roth, Priscilla 40

Sacks, Oliver 4, 115, 120
Sandler, Joseph 16
savages 193
schizoid personality 13–14
secondary narcissism 10–11
SEEKING system 116–120
Segal, Hanna 17; delusion and thinking 110, 112–113; omnipotent phantasy 35; relinquishing omnipotence 132–133, 175, 185, 186–187, 214
self-aggrandisement 145, 147, 149
self-esteem 147
Selfish Giant tale (Wilde) 231
self-made phantasy 69, 73
self-object 14
self-organisation, illusion of omnipotence as 147–148, 149–150, 151
self-recognition, and evolution 196, 203
sensory stimulus to hold self together 24–26
separation anxiety 181–183, 187
separation-distress cascade 118–119
sexual love 9
Shakespeare 166, 207–210, 215, 232
Simpson, David xii, 6, 174, 181, 187
Sodre, Ignes 113
Solms, Mark xii, 4–5, 115
Spitz, Rene 203
'Stages in the Development of the Sense of Reality' (Ferenczi) 43
state of unintegration in survival function 23, 25, 27, 30
Steiner, John xii–xiii, 17–18; appeal of omnipotence 109–110; Garden of Eden phantasies 33, 40; overcoming obstacles in analysis 5–6, 159; pathological organisations and relinquishment of omnipotence 122–123; relinquishing omnipotence 185, 215, 231
Steiner, Riccardo 231
Sterling, Gabriel 228n7
Steyn, Lesley xiii, 3, 31
stimulant drugs, and omnipotence 115–116, 120
Strenger, C. 202

suicidal mentation, and omnipotence in adolescence 54–55
Summers, Frank xiii, 5, 144
superego, as internal bully 137, 186
survival function of primitive omnipotence 3, 23–30; adult defences 25–27; baby's survival mechanisms 23–25, 27; child's survival mechanisms 27–28; state of unintegration 23, 25, 27, 30; youth's mockery 28–30
Symington, Joan xiii, 3, 23

Tamm, Carlos xiv, 5, 135
Tempest, The (Shakespeare) 232
termination of analysis, and relinquishment of omnipotence 129–133
Thalassa (Ferenczi) 43
thinking: and appeal of omnipotence 111–113; for oneself 182–183; and receptive femininity 167–169
thinking, three forms of 4, 85–107; definitions of 86; dream thinking 86, 92–95, 104–105; magical thinking 86, 87–92, 104; shift in psychoanalysis 85, 104; transformative thinking 86, 95–104, 105
Three Essays (Freud) 8, 116
thumb-in-the mouth phantasy 3, 31–42
timelessness in relinquishment of omnipotence 128–132
totalitarian psyche 44
Totem and Taboo (Freud) 8, 192, 193, 196, 197
transference-countertransference interaction 151
transference cure 181
transformative thinking 86, 95–104, 105
transgender adolescents 74–77
transitional phase, in childhood 146
trauma: body modification as adaptation to 77–79; *see also* relinquishment of omnipotence in traumatised patient
triangulation 224–225, 227
Trump, Donald, as destructive narcissistic populist 7, 220–229; omnipotent phantasies as driver 220–222; perversion of values 223, 224; perverted containing 220, 222–225, 227; real threats 225–226; and Republican Party 227–228
Trump, Donald, Grand Illusion of omnipotence 148–151
Twitter messages 221, 228n7

unintegration, state of, in survival function 23, 25, 27, 30
U.S. Capitol insurrection 150, 226, 227, 228

violence as defence, and adolescent omnipotence 61–66

We Are Who We Are (Guadagnino, TV drama) 74–77
Weiss, Heinz xiv, 5, 122
Welles, Orson 206, 211, 215
White, Kristin 196

'Why War?' (Freud) 228
Wilde, Oscar 231
Williams, Gianna 56
Winnicott, Donald 12–13; appeal of omnipotence 108, 109; childhood omnipotence 33, 43, 49; forms of thinking 85, 98; and illusion of omnipotence 146, 152
Wordsworth, William 178–180

Zienert-Eilts, Karin Johanna xiv, 7, 217, 220

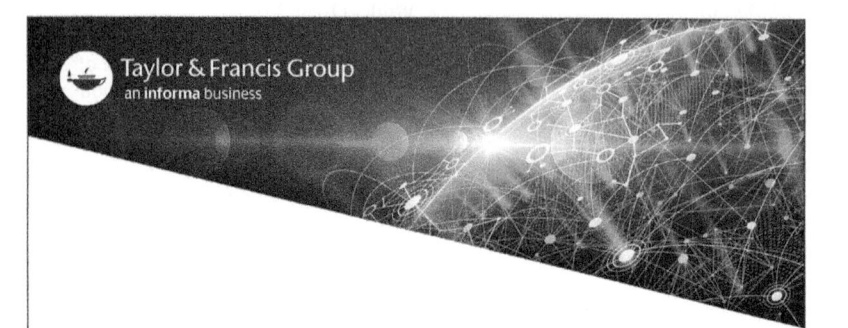